COMFORTING FOOD

Books by Judith Olney

COMFORTING FOOD

Judith Olney

ATHENEUM   New York   **1979**

Drawings by Lauren Jarrett

Library of Congress Cataloging in Publication Data

Olney, Judith.
    Comforting food.
    Includes index.
      1. Cookery, International.   I. Title.
TX725.A1043   641.5   79–63845
ISBN 0–689–11007–3

Published simultaneously in Canada by McClelland and Stewart Ltd.
Manufactured by American Book–Stratford Press,
Saddle Brook, New Jersey
Designed by Kathleen Carey
First Edition

For my Mother and Father

Ponder well on this point: the pleasant hours of our life are all connected by a more or less tangible link, with some memory of the table.

CHARLES MONSELET

Acknowledgments

I especially thank Beni Hargrove, Ruth Klingel, Susanne Naegele, Mary Putnam, Sheppy Vann, and my editor, Judith Kern.

Contents

COMFORTING FOOD

On Comforting Food

ASK ANY RANDOM hundred people that you meet, "What is the most comforting food you know?" and there will be a pause, a reflective searching back through memory and time, and then, almost invariably, an answer sprung from the farthest reaches of childhood: a certain dish, its aroma floating from a long-ago kitchen but still vital in the memory; something hot offered over and over and always after a day of wintry play; something bland that tasted rich after a week of eating nothing during illness; nursery foods; odd, peculiar little dishes in which one crumbled crackers in warm milk and seasoned them with butter; or probed bread fingers into a soft-boiled egg; or placed five lumps of sugar on a cereal and waited for them to dissolve just so; or a glass of milk and beaten egg over which Mother held a grater so that one might scrape some nutmeg on; and behind the simple bread, egg, milk (could we but admit the small, tasty thumb) there lies that nourishment of which we can have no individual memory but only a collective one speaking to us of a deep security and union which we remember or imagine as the state of infancy; the entire comfort and contentment of the child at the breast.

Ask the same hundred people what foods give them comfort now, and the answers are more mature, more diverse. Surely soups, they will say; something that stews a long time; hot cereals; and a listing of potato dishes, apple dishes, egg dishes, dishes "my grandmother used to make"; then there is a pause, and just as surely, a kind of defensiveness seems to arise, for the foods are more humble than prevailing style might dictate; they are old-fashioned; and—this may be the most damaging—in being unassuming they are often economical as well, which hinders our all too human desire to consume conspicuously. If there ever was an unjustifiable defensiveness, this must be it, for the gentle, simple foods that feed the body and the soul are those that have triumphed and endured from the past, that are with us still, and that will be when we are no more.

Comforting Food, then, as its title suggests, is about those diverse, mature, multi-rooted foods; those earnest, amiable, cozy foods that promote an extraordinary sense of well-being both in the cook for having provided them, and in the consumer for having eaten them. There is a certain characteristic flow to the dishes in this book, a recognized selectivity in their choice. (As I was in *Summer Food*, so I am here interested in a certain type and style of food, a certain psychology inherent in the dishes themselves that, when they are taken as a whole, bespeaks a small philosophy.)

There are, therefore, physical characteristics and visual appearances largely shared among all categories of food within this book (since they are foods that we are most likely to eat in winter when in most need of comfort). The sensuous aspects of comforting foods, if I can be forgiven for scrambling them together, revolve around creaminess, smoothness,

gold, amber, brown, dapples, speckles, lumps, chunks, round-
ness, plumpness, wholeness, juiciness, aroma, fullness, expan-
siveness, abundance, repletion. The foods will most likely be
hot or warm and in combination; and, echoing the season,
they will often be found blanketed under gratins, suffused
with sauces, their colors as muted and subdued as a winter
landscape's. It is thoughtful food, composed food, with none
of the easy insouciance of summer when bright raw ingredients are thrown together in carefree bouquet as effortlessly as
flowers.

And this seasonal, cyclical aspect is good and as it should
be. Summer extends outward, expands the line of life; winter
contracts that life, protectively drawing the line inward. And
so the psyche, ever following, wills its own descent, has its
winters as well as its summers, and needs both the movement
out into the world and the movement back to gather round
the hearth, around the central fire that must be used, protected, and sustained until the circle swings again to greening
spring.

Comforting foods inevitably have about them a repetitive,
old-fashioned sense of staples kept by generations in the dark
larders of the winter months: potatoes, turnips, carrots,
onions, apples, spices, flour, eggs, in a multitude of forms,
and above all bread appearing everywhere, in every guise.

If winter has its characteristic ingredients, so do these ingredients lead to certain types of dishes: soups, stews, ra-
gouts, complex dishes wherein many elements generously give
their substance in cooperative effort for the life of the whole;
noodles, dumplings, potato dishes, providing, if there is nothing else, farinaceous bulk, abundance so we may endure. And
these types in turn impart a certain look to the food. (Indeed,
often as I composed dishes for this book, I found myself starting with a final vision of how something should look to be of
comfort, and then thinking backward through the steps necessary to fulfill that vision.) There are a great many round fired-
gold dishes here—tarts, flans, gratins, galettes, both sweet and

savory, for nothing can be more heartening than to share from the cheerful, whole perfection of that shape. There are deep dishes, deeper, thicker than any of summer's offerings; dishes that must be plunged into, plundered of their buried warmth, and shared. And sharing itself should be the final goal of all comforting foods, sharing from the same source, partaking together of heat and sustenance, and so this book presents a series of participation dishes wherein each guest must break a piece from the whole or stir a final seasoning into his dish, and thereby involve himself, if only symbolically, in the task of preparation as well as the final act of eating. These small involvements lead us back to the crumbled crackers, the dissolving sugar lumps of childhood for the very reason that those most memorable of foods comforted by their very ritual involvement, and those involvements, repeated over and over, instilled certain moments, certain sensations intransient in the mind's core.

It is good that we should encourage that powerfully emotive strain within our cooking, that we should have seasonal dishes, ritual dishes that are looked forward to. Their very repetitive scheduling can play into a wise and thinking cook's hands. Like Proust's madeleine recalling the whole warp and woof of a society; like Henry Adams's baked apple, forever reminding him of life triumphant after illness; like the pale ceremonial biscuits that Graham Greene remembers synonymously with his mother ("If I could have tasted her, I am sure she would have tasted of wheaten biscuits"), these dishes remain memorable, comforting to the child and even more so to the child as a man.

On the Ritual Meal

IF, WHEN GROWN, a child is to remember the nurturing parent/
mother *cum* food kindly, then it is necessary to establish a
repetitive pattern in the course of the child's culinary development, a timed sequence of meals appearing in regular,
dependable order that settle a ritual aspect in his mind.

When life used to turn on seasons and revolve around the
getting and growing of food (and in some few places it still
does), ritual meals and feasts paced regularly through the
socio-economic year. But in these days of plenty, we have lost
that interdependent feel of feast-or-famine-together brother-
hood. There is no particular need to rejoice and celebrate the
fertility of land when spring brings an end to winter's want
of food. There is no communal sharing in autumnal harvest
or little imperative for the cooperative putting up of nature's
plenty to see us through the dark season. And so those times

and places of communal need and necessity, those occasions so often resulting in ritual feast and celebration, are largely lost to us.

If one has not had the good fortune to be born privy to an ethnic or cultural heritage rich in Hanukkahs or saints' days, then the most successful and memorable drilling of food, scene, circumstance into the childish mind probably occurs in our main food-allied holiday, Thanksgiving. Awakening in a small bed, the outer world still gray, the child snug in the warmth of his covers first realizes the penetrating odors of the turkey, and perhaps the most important sensory impact here is the olfactory, for he is deluged with the aroma for hours on end before he eats. The smell perfumes the time, the day, over a period of protracted waiting until the actual eating of the bird itself is almost anticlimactic. Then, too, he sometimes remembers other aspects of the occasion—the overeating, overextending restless surfeit of the day.

For a ritual to be set, however, the established holiday or the full feast proper is hardly necessary. One dish can do it— the *pot-au-feu,* the whole meal stew, the Lancashire hot pot, the New England boiled dinner, red beans and rice—any one dish where elements stew and intermingle into a powerful, cohesive whole suffices. Or a simpler soup that demands and provides the full, dominating focus of a meal and against which the accompanying food is mere ornament—a crouton or cracker, a light salad, a piece of cheese or small dessert. But it must be a soup or stew that appears and reappears with regularity, once a week in certain season and most often winter. And it will not be contrived cooking, but rather some old favorite or known, familiar dish, perfected through centuries and eaten by generations that pleases most and that, in turn, will speak to us most clearly down through the haze of time and culinary dross. It is, in the main, not our hit-or-miss attempts at culinary grandiosity or the dishes tried for effect, impressing one time but soon out of mind, that are remembered. And it is to such simple feasts that we should invite relatives and close or longed-for friends over and over again, not necessarily pushing on to greater gastronomic heights but inviting them to share in what is most comfortable, for comfortable foods, like comfortable old clothes and houses, are most contenting . . . fit best . . . become most.

This repetition is a small thing, a small even *easy* matter, a simple choosing of some dish (after children come to the maturity needed to accept such things) that all enjoy. A simple bean soup, a thick minestrone, a potato noodle soup, a boiled dinner with dumplings—anything that tastes pure, cleanly pure and of itself, so that the very purity of the bean, the onion, the potato, the plump dumpling fixes in the mind and remains there embedded. From such meals are familial archetypes made.

People say, speaking back the generations, "I remember how my grandmother used to fix spetzli. No one could make spetzli like my grandmother."

I ask, "Have you tried?"

And the answer is "No," or "Yes, but it was not the same . . ." and there a budding tradition/ritual falters, stops.

But we must gird up, allow for our own diminishing senses, allow for ever changing time and space and place, and attempt the re-creation for our children's sake. And it matters even more if there are cherished roots and origins. This, you say, was the dish your Irish grandfather liked best; this came from great-grandmother's Bavaria; that is what they ate in our African homeland; or even, this came with us from the North or South. And if there is no established tradition, no ritual to support and maintain, here and now start one. And if there can be some simple task involved, making noodles, cutting sippets of bread, setting table in some "special" way for this meal and this meal alone in which a child can involve himself, so much the better.

Again, there must be repetition. Memorable meals or dishes always involve repetitive ritual.

"When I was sick, Mother always fed me _____."

"For Sunday dinner we always had _____."

"Every Friday night Mother fixed _____."

If there is nothing from established family source, then turn to one of the many participatory dishes that holds fixed, near-mythic ritual within itself, like France's *garbure*, eaten every Sunday by countless families in the Béarn. *"Faire la goudale."* Eat the solid elements of the stew, then mix a glass of wine with the remaining broth and swallow it down with bonhomie and cheer. Or pick from among the dishes with almost religious auras which are put to stew in early morning or before the Sabbath, then eaten after church or mass or synagogue, so that a certain element of the mystical settles like a mantle on those who partake. Choose one such dish. Choose a ceremony. Support the nationalistic, ritualistic necessities of a Japanese or British tea; pour out a libation on the ground as a gift to and appeasement for your ancestors, as the Africans do; break bread together on your knees; share a loving cup.

And always the ritual meal demands that everyone is served from the same wellspring source, be it a sacramental, transubstantial body, stew or tea pot, a cauldron, or a pit. Or even more fundamentally, the meal is carved from the same animal —the whole lamb roasted for the North African *méchoui*, the entire pig barbecued and picked, the large turkey which serves us all and then some—and the ritual given further credence by the carver who, though he has not necessarily cooked, yet stands for a few moments as the primal source of nourishment, who doles out and provides and from whom comes our sustenance. (And the carver, whether consciously or not, often adds to the ritual—joking, performing knife maneuvers; demanding complete silence as he acts his task; holding and relishing the dramatic power to decide who shall receive choice morsels.)

And even in the simplest ritual meal there should be a moment of drama, planned for and acted upon . . . a transcendent moment.

Stop time and the day. Shorten the dining table, compacting and enfolding the participants together. Carry on the soup tureen, place it at the table's center, whisper something, and when people are hushed and bent to hear, with all eyes fixed, slowly remove the cover. Let the steam rise, the savory odors flood the room and drown those who await in heady delight. Flourish on the croutons. Make Chinese rice cakes and drop them into the soup at the last moment so they hiss and sizzle. If the dish has crusted surface, break it with dramatic gusto. Carry on the roasted joint to sputter and rest at table, rather than in the kitchen, before carving. Make everyone wait.

Use the best silver. Tuck snowy napkins under chins; tie on bibs. Let the family eat in bathrobes for this our family treat. Chant a special prayer. Listen to the same classic music. Allow the children a wine goblet filled with cold water and a spoon of wine "just this meal," then toast each other. Sing, joke, dance about the table—whatever it takes to shake the normal dinner time from its settled course of daily complacency.

Foster contentment and well-being. Use the time to heal and mend and nurture. Charm the eaters, willing the occasion well and fiercely into their very minds and being, and then repeat the glad ritual again and then again, for if one *would* establish confluence with the past, there is no better way to do it than to say, tonight we eat what I ate as a child, what my father's father ate, and his father before him, for in such a way are ancient bonds maintained and new links forged for future.

UTENSILS USED AND NEEDED

There is abundant use made, in this book, of a pasta machine, both for traditional pastas and noodles, and for crackers and a crisp dessert. Over and over again, recipes will call for a Mouli-julienne, that versatile five-bladed grater, and for a

12-inch pizza pan with sides. The tarts, breads, and galettes baked in this shape then need to be presented on large round flat platters or baskets.

A generously sized and rustic *daubière* or casserole with a glazed interior can serve double duty as either a container for stews or a soup tureen. A set of oval or round cocottes of ceramic, enameled iron or copper, each holding about 3 cups, can also be used frequently and to good advantage.

A NOTE ON INGREDIENTS

All butter used is meant to be unsalted. Choose butter with the words "sweet cream" on the carton. The butter should be pale in color. If there is a defined yellow to the stick, particularly an outer encrustation of yellow, the butter has been made from reprocessed cream and colored artificially.

I have consistently called for heavy cream throughout the book. The current market practice is to label some cream as "heavy," some as "whipping." Heavy cream contains about 8% more butterfat than whipping cream, and the latter is, to my experience, sometimes just on the edge of being whippable. If heavy cream is not available, however, by all means use whipping cream.

It is assumed that standard pastry doughs, tomato sauce, and fresh pasta recipes are either known, or so easily available in standard cookbooks that they are not given, yet again, here.

The firm white bread required in so many of the recipes is, ideally, that presented as *pain au levain* in the following section.

On Rustic Breads

---

*And I will fetch a morsel of bread,
and comfort ye your hearts. . . .*
Abraham to visiting angels in *Genesis*

IT IS NECESSARY that a book on comforting foods should begin with bread, that basic mortal (and divine) need, for bread historically and particularly in western cultures has been a mainstay for humanity, the very staff of daily life for the poor. The ritual offering of bread, whether as part of the Eucharist or to visiting strangers, has always symbolized oneness, confraternity, the desire for friendship, and above all, proffered bread suggests simple hospitality, the same thing meant when a West African offers a cola nut, a Moroccan some dates, or a Hawaiian a pineapple.

In my own life, it would be unthinkable to entertain without having baked a loaf of bread to offer guests. I want the bread there and obvious, whole, fresh, fragrant . . . waiting for people in the convivial kitchen. And I want the passing of a communal breadbasket at table, or even better, the passing of a communal loaf from which the diners can break a portion, each one taking as much or little as he needs.

Beyond the simple bounds of hospitality, bread functions in many ways as an integral part of other comforting foods. It builds crisp surfaces for gratins; it adds substantive binding to panades, meatloaves, stuffings; it soaks in soups, lending farinaceous body and expanding quantity in a frugal way. It melds into a bread sauce; shapes a sweetened pudding; forms an omelet. . . . All of these utilitarian services are best rendered from large, plump, sliceable loaves that offer more crumb than crust, that taste clearly of salt, yeast and grains, yet are not so strongly flavorful that they overshadow foods they compose or accompany in strength of character. These specifications, in turn, all suggest that handsome French bread, *pain au levain.*

Pain au levain is not, as its name might suggest, merely yeasted bread. The *levain* refers to a portion of soured dough which is saved from the basic batch at each baking session, then used to impart its flavor and leavening qualities to the subsequent batch of new dough. Visually, *pain au levain* is the quintessence of a comforting loaf for it is usually formed in large inviting rounds, its surface a compilation of flour-dusted furrows and razor-slit clefts. (The look-alike loaves in French *boulangeries* made with unsoured *levains* are called *pain de campagne,* "country bread.") Its ingredients are simple and few: water, salt, flours, a sourdough *levain* and, frequently, more yeast. It is by regulating the strength of the *levain* and choosing the flours and their mix that the best known of French bakers (such as M. Poilane in Paris) achieve the very personal loaves for which their bakeries are famous, and in the same way at home, one can determine texture, flavor, color of bread crumb through experimentation and in turn develop truly individual loaves that are a pleasure to eat as well as to look at.

The following formula for *pain au levain* is one that I've evolved over a long period of time and one which will probably change a bit in time to come, but it strikes me now as an almost perfect winter bread. First, a word on the flours in its composition and then some thoughts on *levains*.

ON FLAVORING BREAD

Though when in a hurry I frequently make bread with just flour, water, yeast, and salt as ingredients, I also like to take the time to season rustic loaves whenever possible. The best country breads of France are composed from specially milled, mixed, and blended-to-order flours that distinctively flavor the bread. One has only to look at certain of those loaves to know that more than plain flour is involved in their composition. Tiny specks of black float through the crumb, denoting buckwheat. Bits of coarse fiber roughen the crust, suggesting either unrefined flour or the addition of bran. The slices are off-white in color, with an almost pale beige tint, which can only mean whole wheat and rye flours. Yet, one would not say of the bread, taken as a whole, that it is anything but *white* bread meant to accompany the daily meal. In the following recipe, small amounts of various seasoning flours appear. The rye adds mainly color; the buckwheat gives color and a bit of stringent bitterness; the sesame provides the slightest hint of nut-like flavor; and the bran roughens the texture. None of these seasonings is so potent as to be recognizable, and if any were added in much larger quantity, the bread would darken, compact, and start to have about it a health-food-store quality, and by that I mean nothing derogatory. It is a simple matter of wishing bread to remain complementary to other foods rather than the bread demanding to be a heavy meal on its own. The last seasoning of malt adds a slight sweetness and "bloom" to the loaf, i.e., the loaf will color and, what is even more important, rise with greater avidity—a particular blessing in wintertime.

ON THE CARE AND KEEPING OF A LEVAIN

Pain au levain is dependent for its slightly soured flavor on a *levain* that also is soured, and to propagate this *levain* it is necessary to have a sourdough starter. The simplest way to come by a starter is either to be given two cups worth of sourdough (which is, in effect, already a *levain*) by someone, or to buy a dry sourdough starter mix at a specialty food shop. One should simply follow the package directions to activate the starter and wait the designated time for the culture to become sufficiently soured. On the night before bread is to be made, one builds a sponge (i.e., flour and water are added to the starter, it sits overnight, then half the mixture is bottled the next day as *levain* and refrigerated to await the next baking session). In a bakery, the formulating and dividing of the *levain* is a daily procedure, so the baker has a firm control over the actual degree to which his breads taste of sourness. In the home, however, where bread is baked less frequently, the *levain* can grow powerfully acerbic when left overlong and unused, but by no means should one feel a slave to a starter or the demand on its package that it be used every week. In the home, it is perhaps easiest to think of the *levain* merely as a flavoring element rather than as the active yeasting agent within the bread. The *levain* will become less of a tyrant, and with this thought in mind, one uses the *levain* plus additional yeast at every baking. Most bakeries follow the procedure of adding yeast plus *levain* because, though their very active *levains* may indeed raise the dough mass in time, they would take too long in so doing to be commercially practical.

I have done all of the following with my *levain* at various times with no ill effect on its *flavoring* properties:

1. Added beer to the sponge to increase the sourness of the *levain*.
2. Left it for three weeks. Poured off the pungent liquid floating on top after a three-week baking hiatus and replaced the amount with water, a bit of yeast, and a pinch of sugar.
3. Intensified flavor by adding malt and mixed grains.
4. Lifted off the top crust and thrown half of the *levain* away.
5. Loaned it to friends during my vacation time.

The point to all of this is that *levains* can be easier to keep and maintain than most of the packaged starter directions suggest *if* in home baking one views them primarily as flavor enhancers whose degree of sourness can be regulated, modified, intensified, or decreased.

PAIN AU LEVAIN

FOR THE SPONGE:

>   2 cups sourdough starter (or *levain*)
>   1 cup lukewarm water
>   1¼ cups unbleached flour (preferably Pillsbury's Bread
>   Flour)
>
>   1 package (¼ ounce) yeast
>   1½ cups warm water
>   2 tablespoons rye flour
>   1 tablespoon buckwheat flour
>   2 tablespoons toasted, ground sesame seeds
>   1 tablespoon bran
>   1 tablespoon malt (unflavored powdered malt
>   as in malted milk)
>   2 teaspoons salt
> About 5 to 5½ cups unbleached flour

To make the sponge, empty the starter or *levain* into a mixing bowl. Stir in the lukewarm water and then the flour. Cover the sponge with a towel, place in a warm spot (in pilot-lighted oven, near a heat register, etc.), and leave for 24 to 36 hours. At the end of this time, stir down the sponge and put half of it back into the container to act as *levain* for your next baking.

Note: when using a new starter, I add half water, half beer as liquid to increase sourness. I also stir in a bit of flavoring flours in place of regular unbleached flour.

To make bread, dissolve yeast in 1½ cups warm water. Stir the dissolved yeast into the sponge and add flavoring flours, seeds, bran, malt, and salt. Add enough unbleached flour to form a soft dough, then turn the mass out onto a floured countertop and start kneading. Knead hard and well, pressing the entire weight of the upper body to the task. Sprinkle

flour on the counter as needed and work the dough for a good
12 minutes until it feels firm and elastic to the touch. Add
only the minimum of flour necessary to reach this point, and
keep in mind that the dough should above all remain mal-
leable and soft enough to form easily. Don't bind it into a
difficult-to-work lump by using too much flour.

Place the dough in a clean, lightly oiled bowl, cover it
over with a kitchen towel, and let it rise until doubled in
bulk. (This step can be hastened by placing the bowl in a
slightly warmed oven for about 1 to 1½ hours. If, on the other
hand, time is not pressing, it is good to let the dough have a
leisurely rising period and more time to develop flavor. Let
the dough rise in a slightly cool room even, and give it 2 to 3
hours.) When the dough has risen enough, remove it from the
bowl, punch down all the air pockets, and shape. (See On
Forming Rustic Loaves, below.)

Let the formed loaf rise, towel-covered, in a warm place
until it has reached almost full size. (Again, this rising can
be slowed by placing the bread in a cooler spot and again it
is often desirable to do so, both because it allows the flavoring essences to develop more fully and because it permits one
a flexibility in time schedules.) In the case of full, bulky
loaves (such as the snail or round basket bread) and particularly in winter, it will take a good hour at the very least for
the bread to rise and expand enough, even in a warm place.
In a cooler location, a solid loaf could take from 2 to 3 hours.
The more open shapes, such as the heart, will take less time.

Bake the bread from 50 minutes, for open shapes, to an
hour for more solid loaves. Test doneness by turning the
baked loaf over and knocking on the bottom with a fist. If
the sound is hollow, the bread is finished. If possible, and if
the bread is the only item baking, the baking process should
take place on a falling heat. Start the loaves at 375° to 400°
(your oven's strength must be taken into account here); let
it bake for 15 minutes, then lower heat to 350° for 20 minutes,
and then lower again to 325° until the bread is done. (This

lessening heat progression attempts to duplicate the falling heat in a wood-fired baker's oven.)

Remove bread from oven and let it cool propped at a tilt or on a cake rack so the bottom crust does not become moist and soft. *Pain au levain* should have a good crisp crust, but if your loaves seem too heavily encased, look to these causes:

If bread forms too heavy a crust, either one or both of the following has happened.

1. The atmosphere in which the bread rises is too dry (a common occurrence in artificially heated winter kitchens) or too warm (too thick a surface crust forms before baking).

Remedy: Spray the bread with water from a plant mister several times as it rises so that the surface stays moist. (Leave the towel covering off and brush with egg or sprinkle with decorative flour just before baking.) Place a pan of water in the warming oven. Try a piece of plastic wrap placed lightly over the rising loaf.

2. The oven in which the bread bakes is particularly small and allows for little air circulation around the large baking pan. The heat in small ovens becomes overintense, the bread's top crusts over before the center has a chance to expand fully and this crust keeps baking thicker and heavier.

Remedy:

• Place a pan of water on a lower shelf of the oven during baking.

• Open the oven door and mist the loaf several times during the first 20 minutes of baking.

• Make sure the razor cuts on the loaf are sufficiently large; make more slashes than usual.

• Lower the initial baking temperature.

• Try baking solid loaves on a Greatful Bread Plate (manufactured by the Carmel Kiln Company, P.O. Box 6433, Carmel, CA 93921). Its preheated baking surface helps give bread an extra rising thrust when it first enters the oven. Use the plate in the lower third of your oven's space. Particularly practical in small ovens.

• If, when the bread comes from the oven, the crust still seems too evidently heavy, wrap the loaf in a towel and leave it to cool trapped in its own escaping moisture, which will soften the crust.

ON FORMING RUSTIC LOAVES

Rustic loaves are molded in two ways, either by hand or in basket forms.

HAND-SHAPED BREADS

Four configurations I particularly like are shaped by hand as follows:

THE SNAIL On a work counter or table, roll the punched-down dough back and forth under the palms of the hands until it stretches to a 24-inch length. Lightly oil a large pizza pan or baking sheet and coil the roll into a snail-like circle, with one end of the roll propped slightly up in the center. Using scissors, outline the center circle with small cuts. Sprinkle the loaf generously with flour and let rise. Immediately before putting the bread in the oven, use scissors to take three big snips where the dotted lines in the drawing indicate. This bread should bake for 1 hour.

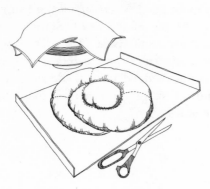

THE TWIST On a long counter, spread and roll **the** dough back and forth under the palms of the hands. Keep the central portion of the mass thick, but work the two ends of the dough into progressively thinner points. When the roll reaches 40 inches in length, bend the dough on the baking sheet into a fat knuckled knob at the thickest portion and twist the lengths loosely together from thicker to thinner. Moisten the two ends with a touch of water and press them into a neat ball. Let rise. The twist may be sprinkled with flour or brushed with an egg yolk beaten with a teaspoon of water for a glazed surface. Let bake for about 50 to 55 minutes. (The more rugged this loaf looks, the better. Twist and tear the dough as the rope is being formed for the most handsome look.)

THE HEART On a long counter, extend the dough to a 45-inch-long roll. Lightly oil a baking sheet and form the dough into a great heart, overlapping the two ends as neatly as possible at the top of the heart. Sprinkle with flour and cover with a towel until risen. (Do a little gentle cosmetic tucking if necessary from time to time.) Immediately before baking, use a single-edged razor blade to make a long light cut all around the shape an inch from the outer edge. Bake for 45 to 50 minutes.

THE TWINS In order to have two small loaves at once, perhaps one to eat and one to freeze, make *les gémeaux,* the twin loaves for sale by half or whole in most French bakeries. Flatten the dough into a long oval. Slit the dough through the middle, leaving only a small, 1-inch attachment between the two portions. Twist each section away and to the side. (This fragile link where the two breads will touch and remain white is known as *la baisure* or "kissing crust." Sprinkle breads with flour and let rise. Immediately before placing in oven, use a single-edged razor blade to slit two Vs in the ends. Bake for about 1 hour.

BASKET BREADS

Pain au levain is usually found in two basic shapes, both formed in canvas-lined baskets. It is little bother to find baskets of appropriate size and to sew canvas to their interiors. The canvas, which is heavily floured, becomes inpregnated in time with its own molds, which in turn add to the bread's flavor (indeed, Poilaine's famous bread is claimed to be highly affected by the natural molds found in that firm's ancient shaping baskets). The baskets are never cleaned in any way— just given a good tap on a table edge from time to time.

SOLID ROUND LOAVES Buy a basket about 3 inches tall and about 12 inches in diameter at the top, with gently sloping sides. Buy a yard of medium-weight, natural bleached canvas at any fabric store. Cut a round and shape it to the inner curve of the basket. (It will be necessary to make three or four darts in the canvas and to cut away the extra material where it bunches behind the darts.) Using a heavy needle and thread, attach canvas to basket around the top by either whip-stitching over the rim or weaving stitches in and out around the top of the basket.

To make bread in the basket, dust the canvas thickly with flour. Place in the punched-down dough and let it rise a second time (for at least 1 hour) covered lightly with a towel. Flour a counter and gently turn out the loaf on the flour. Let it rise another 15 minutes *uncovered*. At this point, you deliberately *want* the bread to develop a crust. Now gently lift the dough onto an oiled pan and as you do so, make sure the surface bends in slightly. This will form that lovely network of cracked and creviced flour that is the most distinctive look of traditional *pain au levain*. Use a single-edged razor blade to

make either three slanted cuts (*coups de lame*) or two cross-cuts just through the thin top crust. Put the bread to bake immediately for 1 hour.

Note: both the bending and cutting of the dough must be done almost as unthinking reflexes. Too much thought and time given to the bending and one can start punching down and deflating the dough. Too much thought given to razor cuts and the blade will start tearing the dough rather than just skimming the surface.

C O U R O N N E S A *couronne* is a large, circular "wreath" of bread with a hole in the middle, much like an overgrown bagel. This form is always shaped in baskets in a professional bakery. Buy a somewhat loosely woven basket with a 10- or 11-inch diameter measured across the bottom. It should have slanting sides 3 to 4 inches tall. Cut a round of canvas to fit the basket, make the darts to shape the canvas, and cut a 4-inch hole precisely in the material's center.

With a pair of wire cutters, trim a 4-inch-diameter coffee can down to a height of 5 inches. Make a snug canvas jacket to fit one end of the can and its sides. (None of this has to be the finest sewing in the world, just *sturdy* sewing.) Sew the jacket to the edge of the center hole, keeping all seams on the inside.

Punch a few holes around the cut rim of the can (use an awl or simply hold the can against an old board and hammer a nail through). Using a heavy needle and some twine, tie the can to the basket. Fit the canvas covering over all and sew the top of the material to the rim of the basket.

To make bread, flour the basket well and rub it into the canvas. Take once-risen dough and form it into a neat ball. Make a hole in the center by plunging the index and middle fingers of the right hand down through the center. Lift the dough and press the same two fingers of the left hand through the hole from the other side. Start twirling the dough around the fingers and it will soon spread the center opening to a width of 4 inches. Fit the dough into the basket, cover with a towel, and let rise. Sprinkle the surface with flour and turn the dough directly out onto a lightly oiled baking pan. Let rise again briefly, then slit around the top surface with a razor blade and put to bake immediately for close to an hour.

PULLED BREAD

This old-fashioned concept must be included here for it is a handsome and delightful addition to a stew-like meal, and it can occasionally serve in place of potatoes as a farinaceous attendant. To make pulled bread, sacrifice a loaf of fresh bread (ideally an hour from the oven but day-old will also work) by slicing off a side crust and literally pulling out large (2- to 3-inch) portions of crumb from the center. (Eat the crust separately if you are a crust lover or turn it to crumbs.) Melt a quantity of unsalted butter—flavoring it, if you please, with the essence of garlic or herbs—dip the pulled bread in the butter, then place the chunks on a baking sheet and bake them in a 350° oven until they just tinge a light brown. Serve massed in a bowl or basket.

DRIED BREAD

In this book there are a multitude of recipes calling for dried bread or crumbs. If you see that an overabundance of bread is going to remain uneaten, turn it into one of the following categories. (I keep large jars of each of these close to my work table, particularly throughout the winter months.)

Soup rounds—Cut the bread into generous ½-inch-thick slices. Trim the slices to 3-inch squares or stamp out perfect rounds with a cookie cutter. Leave these to dry completely in the open air or in a warm oven. Keep them in an airtight storage jar. These rounds will be used, as the French say, to *"tremper la soupe"*—a strange little expression that translates literally to mean "soak the soup" but in actuality means to pour soup over bread and, in so doing, to soak the bread.

Fine crumbs and coarse crumbs—grind dried or drying bread into crumbs. Use a food processor, a Mouli-julienne, a grater, whatever. Place the crumbs in a sieve and shake out all the very fine particles. Store the fine crumbs in one jar, the coarse crumbs in another. The coarse will be used for rough gratins, the fine for breading things and thickening sauces.

Here are some other shapes and forms, all made, with a few variations, from the same dough.

A SHEAF OF WHEATEN BREADSTICKS A half batch of dough makes a great many breadsticks. Use the other half for a small loaf if so desired. Give the dough its initial, fully developed rise, then punch down well. Roll out small portions of dough into thin sticks ranging in length from 8 to 12 inches. Leave the top half of the lengths plumper than the bottom and flatten them out slightly. (This is all best done directly on a lightly oiled baking sheet.) Using small scissors, clip small portions of dough from the flattened tops, so that the tops resemble heads of wheat. Spread and lift the dough out as much as possible to give the heads an appearance of fullness.

Curve some of the stalks slightly, a few to the right, a few to the left. Place the breads at once into a 350° oven (they should *not* be given a second rising). In approximately 10 minutes, the breads should have set enough that a light glaze of egg yolk and water can be brushed over their tops without disturbing the design. Bake the wheat stalks for about 25 minutes in all, and turn them over once toward the end of this time. The breads should remain soft and chewy on the inside—do not overbake.

Cool the wheat sticks, then serve them congregated and upright in a small basket, or tie them up with a hempen rope.

POPPY SEED GRIDS This design will take a scant half of our bread recipe. From a batch of once-risen and well-punched-down dough, form eight long fat breadsticks. Brush their tops with beaten egg yolk and water and dip the glazed side into a plate of poppy seeds. Arrange four of the sticks, poppy seeds up, diagonally across the bottom of a large pizza pan, then lay the other four sticks at angles across the top so a fretwork of open diamonds is formed. Make a very long breadstick (long enough to encircle the edge of the grid), glaze and poppy-seed it, then place it around the grid's outer edge. Trim off any protruding breadstick ends and place the grid immediately into the oven. Bake for about 25 to 30 minutes. A nice loaf to pass around at table . . . and other patterns are possible.

PITA BREAD HORS D'OEUVRES AND CRACKERS

FOR THE DOUGH:

> ½ batch *Pain au Levain* (see page 18), seasoning
> elements can be omitted if so desired.

Make the dough as directed and let it rise once. Punch the
dough down well and divide it into approximately 9 small,
fistful-sized portions. On a lightly floured board, roll out each
piece into a thin rough circle about 5 inches in diameter
(don't strive for uniformity of size). Transfer the rounds immediately to a lightly oiled baking sheet and place in a 350°
oven for approximately 12 to 15 minutes. The breads should
puff into fat pillows and develop a light tinge of brown. The
point is to catch them while they are still rather soft and flexible and before they turn crisply brittle and lose their pliancy.
MAKES 8 TO 10 PITAS

MELTED CHEESE PITAS

Push a knife into a finished pita bread and slit it one third
open. Dribble in a tablespoon of melted butter and stuff the

opening with a large handful of grated Gruyère cheese (also include bits of ham or sausage if desired). Place the bread in a 325° oven for 5 minutes so that the cheese can melt. One of these per person, used as an hors d'oeuvre, is sufficient. (The dough used for these pitas can be brushed over with an egg yolk mixed with a tablespoon of water before they are first baked for a more decorative shiny surface.)

SESAME CRACKERS

Split the pita breads open by running a knife around the edges. Cut the thin halves into quarters. Dip the pieces in melted, unsalted butter, sprinkle them with sesame seeds, and place the crackers on a baking tray. Bake briefly at 350° until the morsels are crisp and golden but do not overbrown. Heap them into a bowl and serve with soups.

PASTA MACHINE CRACKERS

¼ teaspoon baking soda
1 tablespoon powdered malt
1 teaspoon yeast
4 tablespoons melted, unsalted butter
1 teaspoon salt
Large pinch of sugar
1⅔ cups flour

FOR THE GLAZE:

1 egg yolk beaten with 2 tablespoons milk and
½ teaspoon salt

Place ½ cup hot water in a small bowl and add the baking soda. Stir, then add the malt. When the malt has dissolved and the water cooled to just warm, stir in the yeast and let it dissolve. Add 3 tablespoons melted butter, the salt, sugar, and flour. Knead the dough until it is very smooth, then put it to rest and rise in a lightly greased, towel-covered bowl for 1 hour.

Divide the dough into two portions. Run each through the three largest openings of the pasta machine's kneading blade. Brush the dough strips with melted butter, leaving a ½-inch border free. Fold each strip over double, then run them through the largest kneading opening. Continue working the strips down four more notches (three will remain unused). Cut the dough strips into 5-inch circles. (I use one of the metal blades from my Mouli-julienne for this as it leaves a small decorative hole in the middle.) The scraps may be gathered into a ball and worked through the machine again.

Brush a baking sheet with the remaining tablespoon of butter and place the crackers on the sheet. Prick a pattern over the rounds, brush them with egg yolk glaze, and leave to rise for 20 minutes. Bake in a 350° oven for about 10 minutes and turn once during the baking period. Cool, then store in an airtight box. These crackers are best eaten when fresh. I like to string them onto a hemp rope necklace and serve them with a rustic soup. Each diner then breaks off his own crackers.

MAKES ABOUT 12 CRACKERS

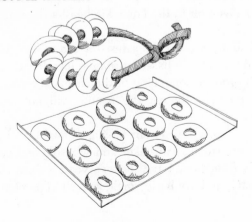

SOFT PRETZELS

This recipe is an amusing one for children to execute, for the whole process of making dough, letting it rise, and shaping the pretzels is a busy time and does not take very long. Basically, soft pretzels are made with strong bread dough that is highly yeasted and flavored with barley malt. During the rising and forming periods, the dough should be covered, always with a sheet of heavy plastic (simply cut open, say, a large garbage bag), so that no air is allowed to reach the dough and crust its surface.

There are a variety of chemical ways in which bakers aerate and glaze their pretzels. The most professional way is to dip the pretzels rapidly in a brine of lye, but this dangerous acid is hardly suitable for home use. Other bakers use a solution of ammonium carbonate, or VOL as it is sometimes known. A quick dip in these briny waters produces those small tight bubbles of dioxide and ammonia gases which permeate pretzels and remain trapped in the interior. (This same carbonate is also frequently used by commercial bakers to produce wretched eclairs. Instead of using more expensive eggs to raise the dough, a floury dough is dipped in brine and chemically forced to aerate.) Though the objectionable taint of ammonia removes itself for the most part in baking, still the fumes given off in the home kitchen hardly warrant using the substance.

A final solution (and the safest for use where children are concerned), is a brine based on simple bicarbonate of soda. It alone will produce something of the chemical reaction needed to make pretzels, though the results will not be quite as authentic.

If one is involved in serious baking, it might be a good idea to cultivate a small local baker and wheedle and cajole what one needs from him. I buy baker's yeast (always fresh and very potent), and dry barley malt, as well as parchment paper triangles for pastry work, baker's doilies, and other assorted items from a friendly baker from time to time. It took rather a long time for him to decide to sell to me however, for, as he confided sometime later, living in the South as we both do, he first assumed I was out to make moonshine.

> 1 batch *Pain au Levain* (see page 18)
> (Use 2½ times the amount of yeast; omit all flavoring elements except malt, which should be increased to ¼ cup. Purchase dry barley malt from a baker; or use plain "malted milk" malt. Use 1 cup gluten flour in the dough, if possible.)

FOR THE BRINE:

> 2 quarts water
> ¼ cup bicarbonate of soda
> ¼ cup salt

FOR THE GLAZE:

> 1 egg yolk beaten with 3 tablespoons of water
> Cornmeal
> Coarse sea salt
> Heavy plastic wrap
> A single-edged razor blade

Make the bread dough as in the basic recipe. Knead the dough well, then leave it to rise in a warm place for one hour. Keep the dough covered with heavy plastic.

Press the dough out into a flattened circle and, using a knife, cut the dough into portions each the size of a medium lemon and weighing about 2 ounces. Place these portions on a counter (do not let them touch) and cover again with plastic. Let rise for 20 minutes.

The next step can be greatly facilitated by using a pasta machine if you have one. Tighten the kneading blade to 3 or

4 stops from the beginning. Run each ball of dough through the blades so that it stretches to a flat, thin mat about 6 inches long. Immediately roll each portion up so that it resembles a stubby cigar. (If you do not possess a pasta machine, thin out each portion with a rolling pin.) Place the "cigars" under plastic wrap as they are finished. Again, do not let them touch, and always protect them from air as much as possible. Let the dough rise for 30 minutes.

Scatter corn meal on 2 or 3 baking sheets.

Form the dough into pretzels. With the flat of the hands, and leaving the center of the dough as full and untouched as possible, start rolling the ends of each portion out, back and forth, pressing very hard with the fingers. Roll out on an unfloured surface until the dough stretches to a length of about 17 inches. Keep the bulk of the dough in the plump center, and stretch the last 5 inches of each end to a very thin ⅓-inch width.

Holding an end in each hand, shape the dough into an upside down "U." Cross the left end over the right (the wrists will cross each other). With the pointer finger of the left hand, flip the left edge of the dough circle over, so that the pretzel twist is formed. Then simply raise the two ends and lay them on top of the pretzel sides. Place each pretzel on a baking tray as it is formed, and keep the trays covered with plastic wrap. Let the pretzels rise for 30 minutes.

Boil the brine ingredients for 3 minutes. Turn off the heat. Preheat the oven to 375° to 400°.

Dip each pretzel for 5 seconds into the brine. Lift out with a wire strainer and place on a clean baking sheet. Brush the pretzels rapidly with the egg yolk glaze. Make a shallow, 2-inch slit in the fat top of each pretzel, and place a large pinch of coarse salt on the plump upper portion only. Put the pretzels to bake for about 20 to 25 minutes.

To eat when fresh, slit the warm pretzels open at their thickest point and place a pat of unsalted butter inside.

MAKES ABOUT 20 PRETZELS

TWO HEARTH BREADS

The following two breads can be made either on top of the stove or, more romantically, in a fireplace on a braise of hot cinders. Children find the latter method most enchanting.

FLANNEL CRUMPETS

1 teaspoon yeast
2 cups flour
½ teaspoon salt
1 egg, beaten
½ cup warm milk
A lump of butter

Dissolve the yeast in 3 tablespoons of warm water. Mix flour and salt in a bowl, then add egg, yeast, and milk, mixing slowly and smoothly all the time with a wooden spoon. When well blended, cover the bowl, first with a piece of plastic wrap and then with a kitchen towel. Leave to rise in a warm place for a good hour.

Butter a skillet lightly and heat it: either over a medium-hot burner, or on the swept-clean hearth of a fireplace that has had a fire burning on it for an hour, or directly on some hot cinders. Divide the dough into 8 pieces and, on a lightly floured surface, roll each piece into a 3½-inch circle. (I prefer a homespun look to the perfection of crumpet molds, though they can, of course, be used.) Place some crumpets on the skillet and cook them until brown on one side. Turn them over and let them brown on the other side—a matter of 8 to 10 minutes' time in all at the correct, moderate heat. Serve with unsalted butter and jam.

MAKES 8 CRUMPETS

SPICED ASH CAKES

> 1 teaspoon yeast
> 1 tablespoon cognac
> ¼ teaspoon powdered saffron
> Pinch of allspice
> Pinch of ground cumin
> 1 teaspoon salt
> Pepper
> 1 egg plus 1 egg yolk
> About 2 cups unbleached flour

Dissolve the yeast in ½ cup of warm water. Add cognac, saffron, allspice, cumin, salt, and pepper. Stir in the egg and the extra yolk. Add the flour and knead the dough until it is smooth and elastic. Place the ball of dough in a lightly greased bowl, cover with a towel, and let rise for 1 hour.

Divide the dough into 6 or 7 portions and roll each out into a very thin 6-inch circle. Let the cakes rise for 15 minutes (covered and in a warm place), then cook them in a lightly greased skillet on top of the stove or on baking sheets in a 350° oven until browned (about 10 to 15 minutes). *Or,* some or all of the cakes may be baked on a hot, swept-clean hearth. Put the cakes to bake directly on the hearth; cover them with an iron skillet, and heap hot cinders on top of the pan. A bit of grit enhances the authenticity of this one.

MAKES 6 OR 7 CAKES

Hors d'oeuvres, Eggs, Abat-faims

THE FOOD IN THIS chapter is definitely of a type. Starting with the bread-based toasts and ranging through a series of pancakes, porridges, crusted tarts, and egg dishes, the recipes for the most part (though there are some few exceptions) present simple and rustic examples of how a variety of peoples expand upon common, inexpensive ingredients in everyday ways to gratify their hunger. (These are the kinds of dishes that would be termed *abat-faims* in France—inexpensive, filling "hunger appeasers" meant to oppose the cold and to stoke internal fires.) Especially those dishes given their foreign titles are dependent, over and over again, on bread, the primal egg, flour, potatoes, meal, greens, onions, a bit of pork —the common goods of a peasant's larder; and on milk, cream, butter, and cheese from the peasant's cow. Though our dairy products are neither as rich nor as cheap as a peasant farmer's, yet even in these times the dishes they help compose are still most economical.

What is of interest here, and what should be noted, is the spirit behind the food. There is an earnestness about that spirit, a thoughtfulness that takes a humble little and turns it to a noble lot. There is ingenuity. Meager amounts of cheese or leeks encapsulated between thin golden crusts yield a *flamiche* tart that stretches to feed twelve people. Flour and eggs combined into farinaceously filling *noukles* are poached in salted water, then snipped into small grains and eaten with cream and cheese; flour and eggs again make pancakes and, with a touch of added yeast, they turn into *matefaims,* the essence of bread expanding the pancake until it literally "displaces hunger." Eggs are baked with only a lump of butter, but the butter is blackened first so that even that lone seasoning is pitched to its most flavorful intensity. (A variation on this burning theme is often carried to its extreme in poor cultures. In West Africa, "soup" is the daily mainstay. A pot of "too much" rice is boiled; another pot of greens and sometimes meat stews on the side. The greens are poured over the rice to make "soup," but then the more important diners eat all the good parts. The kitchen help, which will have only the "too much" rice for its dinner, is left with the remains which they have quite deliberately burned in cooking . . . that crusted rice, its scorch providing the only seasoning, makes their meal. And I've seen the same occurrence in Morocco, with the men consuming all the choice morsels from the couscous, and the women and children, who are left with the remaining unseasoned grain and the dishes to do, placing the grain back over the fire to scorch. And even in more affluent circumstances this is a tasty trick. A famous Chinese cook once offered me a most delicious bowl of fresh noodles which she had seasoned with soy sauce, then allowed to scorch in the wok.)

In this chapter also are a great many foods that can serve

for breakfast or a light supper and that lend themselves to being cooked in individual serving dishes. I like the individual portion when it is not too much trouble to prepare because its psychological impression is so pleasing. There is a certain coziness in receiving your own small dish with its preordained amount of food and its own unique appearance, and there is a certain (though perhaps childish) comfort in the assurance that "this is my portion and no one else can have it."

THREE LITTLE TOASTS

GARLIC TOASTS

> 2 heads of garlic
> 6 to 8 slices firm crustless white bread,
>   preferably homemade
> Fine dry bread crumbs
> Olive or walnut oil

Make a purée with the garlic: either wrap the heads in aluminum foil, put them to bake when another dish is roasting for an hour, and squeeze out the cooked garlic, or peel the cloves and boil them until tender. In either case, pass the softened garlic through a sieve.

Lightly toast one side of the bread slices under the broiler. Spread the unbrowned side with garlic purée, then scatter a thin layer of fine bread crumbs on top and drizzle a bit of oil over the crumbs. Toast, garlic side up, under the broiler until golden. Cut the slices into halves or quarters.

SERVES 6 TO 8

MARROW TOASTS

> Beef marrow or several slices of beef shank bone
>   (you need 3 inches of marrow per slice of toast)
> Salt
> Softened, unsalted butter
> Thin, homemade bread slices, trimmed of crust
> Parsley, minced fine

In large cities it is possible to buy beef marrow already pried from the bone. In some places butchers still give away shank bones free. Ask them to slice the bones across in 2-inch sections; then you can push out the central marrow with your thumb. (Take as many bones as possible, for the emptied marrow freezes and holds well.)

Bring a small pot of salted water to the boil and regulate to a low simmer. Cut the marrow into slices ½ inch thick, then poach the slices until they turn a pale pinkish gray. (A certain amount of their bulk will melt away.) Drain and mash the poached marrow to a paste.

Spread one side of some bread slices with butter, then toast both sides lightly under a broiler. Spread the buttered sides with a thin coating of marrow, place the toasts back under the broiler so that the marrow can be gilded slightly, and sprinkle with parsley. Marrow toast, taken with tea, was a great favorite of Queen Victoria.

CHEESE TOASTS

> 1½ cups fresh-grated, mixed Parmesan and
>   Gruyère cheeses
> 2 tablespoons fine-minced onion
> Mayonnaise
> 8 slices crustless bread
> Unsalted butter, softened

Mix the cheese and onion. Stir in mayonnaise until a paste forms that is the consistency of peanut butter.

Cut the bread diagonally into halves and place the halves on a baking sheet. Toast one side of the bread slices under a broiler. Lightly butter the untoasted side, and spread on a thick layer of cheese. Place briefly beneath the broiler until the tops are lightly browned and bubbling.

SERVES 8

MELTED CHEESE AND ONIONS

    1 large onion, sliced thin
    3 tablespoons olive oil
    1 medium red or green pepper, seeded and sliced thin
    1 teaspoon minced parsley
    ½ teaspoon mixed dried oregano and thyme
    Salt and pepper
    2 cups grated Bel Paese cheese
    4 slices hot toast, dribbled over with olive oil

Sauté the onion in the oil over medium heat. When tender, add the pepper, parsley, and herbs. Turn down the heat and as soon as the pepper is *al dente,* season well, then sprinkle the cheese over the vegetables. Muddle the mixture around and when the cheese is melted and very hot, place a slice of toast on each of four heated plates and divide the cheese over the toasts.

SERVES 4

FRIED BREAD FRITTERS—SAVORY OR SWEET

4 cups (6 slices) 1-inch-square bread cubes, cut from
  fresh *or* stale (but not dry) bread
1 cup milk *or* water
2 eggs
Salt and pepper
Olive oil *or* a mixture of butter and peanut oil

To make Savory Bread Fritters, soak the bread in water for
10 minutes. Squeeze the bread dry, then crumble it into a
bowl and stir in the eggs, salt, and pepper. Heat some olive
oil in a frying pan, drop in the batter by tablespoons, and fry
the pillows, a few at a time, until golden brown. Drain them
on paper towels. Serve the fritters, three to a person, covered
with a thick "sauce" of sliced onions (stewed a long time in
butter) or a tomato sauce. Place a piece of Parmesan cheese
on table and let people grate on cheese to taste.

To make Sweet Bread Fritters, soak the bread in milk for
10 minutes. Squeeze the bread dry, then crumble it into a
bowl and stir in the eggs and a small pinch of salt. Fry in a
mixture of butter and vegetable oil. Sprinkle the fritters with
powdered sugar and cinnamon and serve accompanied by
sweet butter and syrups of choice.

SERVES 4

GRAN CROSTINI ST. LUC

One of the most succulent morsels I know, this dish is
served at the Santa Croce restaurant in Florence. Crostini,
which are usually grilled slices of bread with thin and simple
spreads of cheese or other savory items, become, at this

restaurant, very grand indeed, with four elements composed into one largely filling first course.

> 1 stick unsalted butter
> 2 tablespoons flour
> 2 cups milk
> Salt and pepper
> 1 small onion
> ½ pound chicken livers, trimmed of fat and any green portions
> 1 cup very thick homemade tomato sauce
> 4 thick slices white bread, crusts removed, cut into rounds
> 1 medium garlic clove, peeled
> Parmesan cheese, grated

Make a white sauce: melt 2 tablespoons of butter in a small saucepan. Stir in the flour, and let this roux cook over low heat for 3 or 4 minutes (do not let it brown). Gradually whisk in the milk. Season with salt and pepper and let the sauce cook at a slight simmer for 30 minutes over low heat. Halfway through the cooking (and once again at the end), carefully pull to one side and lift off the skin that forms over the surface.

Melt 2 tablespoons of butter and cook the onion until soft. Add the chicken livers and salt and pepper and cook over brisk heat until the outsides are gray but the interiors remain a pale pink. Spoon the livers into a sieve and press off excess juices. Purée livers in a food processor or blender.

Heat the tomato sauce. It should be so thick that it does not run. Reduce the sauce if necessary.

Melt 4 tablespoons of butter and fry the bread circles until crisp and brown on both sides. Rub the croutons with the garlic clove, wearing the clove away in the process. Keep the croutons warm.

To compose the crostini, preheat a broiler. Place each crouton on its serving plate. Spread them first with the chicken liver paste and then with the tomato sauce. Spoon the white sauce over the tomato (it should be of medium-thick coating consistency—thin with a bit of cream if necessary), and sprinkle liberally with grated Parmesan cheese. Place the crostini briefly under a broiler until bubbling and speckled with brown; serve very hot.

SERVES 4

MIQUES

I include *miques*, the fat cornmeal "breads" from Périgord, in the *abat-faim* category, for though they more often accompany foods such as Garbure (page 116), Little Stuffed Lettuces (page 172), or Périgord Soup (page 98), they also serve as entire breakfasts when sliced and refried in lard or butter or as light suppers when dipped in broth or hot milk.

> 1¾ cups all-purpose flour
> ⅔ cup fine yellow cornmeal
> 1 tablespoon fine dry bread crumbs
> 1 heaped tablespoon fine-diced lean salt pork
> 1 garlic clove, pressed
> A pinch of salt
> Pepper
> 2 eggs
> Stock (optional)

Mix the flour, cornmeal, bread crumbs, salt pork, garlic, and seasoning in a bowl and make a well in the center. Beat together 1 egg plus 1 egg yolk and stir into the dry meal. Beat the remaining white until mounded and firm, then fold it into the batter.

With lightly oiled hands, shape the batter into round,

slightly flattened balls about 1½ inches in diameter. Bring some stock or salted water to a boil in a pan with a lid. Lower the heat to a simmer, then drop in the *miques*. (Turn them over once during this time.) Lift them out with a strainer and let them drain on paper towels. Hold in a warming oven until all are cooked. Serve warm.

MAKES ABOUT 10 *miques*

LE POUNTI

Le pounti is a rustic Burgundian "cake" that is cooked first, then reheated later in butter or lard. This refrying process occurs often in humble French and Italian "filler" dishes. One has only to think of *miques, polenta* (the cornmeal porridge baked as a cake), and *socca* (that starchy pancake made from chickpea flour) to be reminded of inexpensive staple dishes that are prepared ahead, then sliced and reheated for a later meal. *Le pounti* is composed of a flour and egg batter containing a hash of salt pork and greens. To be authentic, one should use a mixture of chard and sorrel, but failing these, beet greens will offer the same rough quality.

> ⅓ cup flour
> ⅓ cup milk
> 2 eggs
> ¾ cup salt pork, rinsed of salt, dried and chopped
> ¾ cup sausage *or* leftover meat, chopped
> 2 tablespoons minced parsley
> 1 cup raw greens (beet, chard, sorrel or
>   a mixture of these, shredded fine)
> 2 shallots, minced
> 1 garlic clove, minced
> Salt and pepper
> Butter for frying

Stir the flour and milk together to a smooth paste. Add the eggs.

Combine the salt pork, sausage, parsley, greens, shallots, and garlic, and chop the mixture to a fine hash by hand, or place it briefly in a food processor. Stir the hash into the eggs and season well. The *pounti* can either be fried (covered and over low heat) in an oiled pan for about 20 minutes on each side, or it can be baked, covered with aluminum foil, in a small, greased tin for about 1 hour at 325°. Let the cake cool.

At mealtime, cut the cake into strips and fry them in butter until lightly browned.

SERVES 3 OR 4

MATEFAIMS WITH SAVORY BUTTER

The *matefaim,* its very name translating as "hunger sub-duer," is a large, thick pancake popular in the mountainous Savoy region of France. With tasty (but inauthentic) additions of scallions and sausage, the concept becomes quite palatable, and with the further refinement of a sophisticated compound butter to spread and melt over the pancake, the dish becomes a most delicious breakfast or brunch, indeed.

FOR THE MATEFAIM:

    1 teaspoon dried yeast
    ¾ cup milk, scalded then cooled
    2 eggs
    1⅓ cups all-purpose flour
    ½ teaspoon salt
    3 tablespoons melted butter
    ¼ cup thin-sliced scallions (whites and tender greens)
    2 slices bacon (fried and crumbled) *or* 2 tablespoons minced hard sausage of choice
    Butter for frying

Dissolve the yeast in ¼ cup warm water. Add milk and eggs and blend well.

Place the flour and salt in a mixing bowl and make a well in the middle. Slowly whisk in the liquid and then the melted butter. Stir in the scallions and bacon or sausage, then cover the bowl with a towel and place in a warm spot for 1 hour.

Lightly butter a 9-inch frying pan or griddle. Stir the batter down. When the griddle is hot, pour ¼ of the batter onto the surface and spread the thick mixture out gently with a spatula. Let the pancake puff and brown on one side, then turn it over to brown on the reverse side. The cooking should take about 5 minutes in all per pancake. Place each *matefaim* on a tray in a warming oven until all 4 are finished.

SERVES 4

FOR THE SAVORY BUTTER:

> 2 tablespoons sliced shallots
> 1 tablespoon minced parsley
> 1 tablespoon minced scallions or chives
> 1 anchovy filet *or* 1 small garlic clove,
>   depending on taste
> 1 stick unsalted butter, slightly softened
> Salt and pepper

Bring a small pan of salted water to the boil. Add the shallots, parsley, and scallions and let them blanch for 2 minutes. Drain, refresh under cold water, and blot very dry. In a mortar pound the blanched greens and either the anchovy filet or the garlic clove to a smooth paste. Work in the butter, bit by bit, and when the butter is smooth, season to taste. Divide into 4 little snail pots and chill.

FILIGREED CRÊPES

Two crêpes, one solid, one lacy, set off this pretty and lighter-than-blini presentation for sour cream and caviar. Try rethinking the concept in dessert terms, also, with a crimson jam as filling.

FOR THE CRÊPES:

2 tablespoons flour
Pinch of salt
1 large egg
1 tablespoon melted unsalted butter
About ½ cup lukewarm milk

6 to 8 ounces sour cream or to taste
Fresh minced dill *or* dried dillweed
4 ounces black caviar or lumpfish roe
4 slices of lemon
Fresh dill or parsley, for decoration

Put the flour and salt in a small mixing bowl and make a well in the middle. Gently whisk in the egg and melted butter. Add milk until the mixture is the consistency of whipping cream. Crêpe batter does not have to sit before it is used.

To make crêpes, heat a well-seasoned crêpe pan until hot. Add a drop of batter. If the batter sizzles and rapidly turns a light brown, the surface is ready. Have the bowl of batter next to the stove. Holding the crêpe pan over the bowl and using a small ladle, spoon a generous amount of batter into the pan. Immediately swirl the pan so that the batter can completely cover the hot surface and, at the same time, tip the pan so any extra batter can fall back into the bowl. In such a way are the very thinnest of crêpes formed. Cut off the uneven edge with a spatula.

Make 4 plain crêpes, cooking each on both sides until it is nicely browned. Place the remaining batter in a small pitcher with a neat pouring lip. Pour out a thin stream of batter onto the crêpe pan and in the process, move and twirl the pitcher so the mixture traces thin, lacy loops in a sort of daisy petal pattern. Move rapidly so the batter has no chance to spread into large blots. When the pan side is thoroughly cooked and brown, gingerly turn the delicate crêpe over and let it brown on the other side. Make 4 filigreed crêpes.

Mix the sour cream with fresh minced dill or dried dillweed to taste. Place each plain crêpe on a serving plate and spread with a layer of cream, then top the cream with a thin but dense covering of caviar. Place a filigreed crêpe on top. The caviar should show as solid black through the open fretwork. Cut the lemon slices ⅔ of the way through and twist them. Decorate each crêpe with a lemon twist and a sprig or two of fresh dill or parsley.

SERVES 4

BRETON BUCKWHEAT CRÊPES

⅔ cup buckwheat flour
¼ teaspoon salt
2 tablespoons melted butter
1 tablespoon cognac
1 cup buttermilk
2 eggs
Butter for frying

Stir together the flour and salt in a mixing bowl. Make a well in the center and add the butter, cognac, buttermilk, and eggs, slowly whisking all the while until the batter grows very smooth. Add water until the mixture is the consistency of heavy cream. Stir frequently during use as the flour tends to settle.

Grease a frying pan lightly and fry small, medium, or large pancakes. Give the crêpes a long cook on both sides, so that they brown and crisp—even try one slightly scorched.

Breton Crêpes, made with batter as in this recipe, are often sold in the streets of France. They are cooked in 12-inch pans, then spread with butter, whipped cream, or jam and folded into quarters.

SERVES 4 TO 6

GAUDES

For a filling treat, my mother often made us crêpes in a big skillet, with homemade plum or quince jam. But more often we had *Gaudes,* a kind of cornmeal porridge. I come from Bourg-en-Bresse in Burgundy, and the people from my area are often called *"Les Ventres Jaunes"* or "yellow-bellies" because we eat cornmeal. My mother would cook the Gaudes, stirring it a long time, then she would serve it in soup plates. The porridge would be left briefly until a crust formed, then we would consume it, breaking the crust and adding spoons of cold milk as we ate along.   JACQUES PÉPIN

> 1 cup fine yellow cornmeal
> 4 cups lightly salted water
> 2 tablespoons unsalted butter

Stir a small amount of cold water into the cornmeal, just enough so that it mixes to a smooth paste. Bring water to a rolling boil and add the cornmeal, stirring all the while with a wooden spoon. Continue cooking and stirring over low heat for about 30 minutes or until the porridge is very thick, then stir in the lump of butter.

SERVES 4

OAT PORRIDGE

During the week we did not bother much about knives and forks and tablecloths. A big plate of herring or other fish was set in the middle of the table, along with a dish of potatoes, and we simply stretched out our hands.

. . . our supper was porridge. The porridge-pot was set down in the middle of the floor, and we all sat round it with great bowls of milk and ladled the porridge into the milk. . . .   EDWIN MUIR, *An Autobiography*

True Scottish porridge must be made of Scotch or steel-cut oats (available at health food stores among other places). Use none of that instant or short-cooking stuff that passes itself off as oatmeal. The porridge must have a long cook, and the final consistency should have a distinctly grained, chewably nutty texture, with no hint of feeble infant gruel about it.

    3 cups boiling water with a pinch of added salt
    1 cup steel-cut oats

When the water is boiling at a good clip, throw in the oats and stir briefly. Bring back to the boil, then regulate the heat to a simmer and cover the pan. Cook, stirring frequently, for 30 minutes. Be particularly mindful not to scorch the porridge toward the end of the cooking time. Serve with butter or thick cream, sugar (white or brown), and cinnamon. People who cannot be persuaded to like common oatmeal may grow to quite appreciate the real thing.

SERVES 2 TO 3

The oriental equivalent of porridge, called *okayu* in Japan and *congee* in China, is a loose, soup-like mixture of starchy rice cooked in salted water. With an addition of chicken, it also serves as a health-promoting analeptic.

After many banquets, then you have comforting *congee* with salty pickles—one mouthful of plain *congee*, one little mouthful of salt pickle, just like tea and toast to you. If there is sickness, some chicken goes in, but there should be no fat in comforting food because it sits badly on the stomach.   FLORENCE LIN

To make *congee*, bring three cups of salted water to the boil and stir in ½ cup of rinsed rice. Regulate the heat down to a simmer, cover the pan, and cook very slowly for one hour. This dish is, perhaps, an acquired taste.

SERVES 2

KNEPPES

Kneppes, an ancient Alsatian/German dish, are the very model of an *abat-faim.* Composed from flour, egg, milk, and salt, these small dumplings are put to stew briefly in cream, then seasoned with the browned-butter flavor of croutons. They are served in soup plates and each diner has the pleasure of seasoning his bowl to taste with grated cheese and pepper. My German grandmother often made another version of *kneppes* for Sunday dinner; hers, flavored only with nutbrown butter, accompanied to perfection a roasted chicken. Creamed *kneppes,* however, are meant to serve as a poor man's satiating lunch or supper.

> 1 generous cup flour
> ¼ teaspoon salt
> A good pinch of nutmeg
> 1 large egg
> About ¼ cup milk
> 4 slices homemade white bread, crust removed
> 4 tablespoons unsalted butter
> 1 cup heavy cream
> A large wedge of Parmesan cheese for grating at table

Put the flour in a mixing bowl and stir in the salt and nutmeg. Make a well in the center, break in the egg, start adding milk, and slowly stir the ingredients to a smooth, quite thick batter. Cover the bowl with a doubled kitchen towel and let rest for 2 to 4 hours.

Bring a large pot of salted water to the boil and drop in teaspoon-size portions of batter (wet spoon and fingers to facilitate the process). Allow the water to remain just at a boil throughout, and let the *kneppes* cook for about 12 minutes. (The batter will have to be cooked in two portions as the pot should not be overcrowded.) The *kneppes* will sink to the bottom of the pan at first, then rise to the surface. Half-way through the cooking, stir the bottom carefully with a wooden spoon to loosen any recalcitrant dumplings. When the first batch has cooked, strain them out with a slotted spoon and put the other half to boil. With a knife or a pair of scissors, snip any oversize dumplings into noodle-thin strips.

Cut the bread into cubes and fry the croutons in butter, shaking and flipping the pan frequently so the squares brown on all sides.

Place the *kneppes* in a not overlarge sauté pan or metal gratin that can also be presented at table, add the cream, and let the dumplings heat and the cream cook and thicken to a light sauce. Sprinkle on the croutons and serve the boiling hot *kneppes* out into heated soup bowls. Let each diner season with pepper, a lump of butter, and gratings of cheese to taste. SERVES 4

POTATO GNOCCHI WITH POPPY SEEDS

The secret of successful potato gnocchi is to work the dough as little and as rapidly as possible. Do not allow the potatoes any opportunity to develop their starchy content, or the finished gnocchi will have a rubbery consistency.

> 6 tablespoons unsalted butter
> 4 sage leaves
> 1 pound all-purpose potatoes, all of a size
> 1 egg plus 1 egg yolk
> Salt, pepper, nutmeg
> ⅓ cup flour plus flour for shaping
> ¼ cup grated Parmesan cheese
> 2 tablespoons poppy seeds

Heat 4 tablespoons of butter. Add the sage leaves, mash down on the leaves with a pestle, and let the leaves steep until the butter is needed.

Cook the whole and unpeeled potatoes in boiling, salted water until tender. The retained skins keep the potatoes dry so try not to poke any more testing holes than necessary to establish doneness—too many holes and the potatoes will become water-logged.

When the potatoes are cooked, drain them well, then spear a potato on a fork and immediately begin peeling. Place the peeled potatoes in a sieve and press down on them with a large pestle. Do not rub at them (and thereby intensify their starchy development). Instead, simply press straight down or, in effect, rice the potatoes into a bowl.

Add 2 tablespoons butter and the eggs. Season and scatter the ⅓ cup of flour over the mass. Work the mixture lightly with the fingers until the dough is more or less blended. Scatter some flour onto a work surface (using a minimum of flour in the actual dough allows one to use it more liberally when the gnocchi are formed). Place the dough on the surface and divide into four parts. With lightly oiled or moistened fingers, roll each portion on the floured surface into an inch-thick cylinder. Cut the lengths into ½-inch rounds and flatten each round slightly with the back of a fork.

Have a large pot of salted water just at the boiling point. Let the gnocchi cook in two batches. They will sink to the bottom, then rise to the surface. Keep a kitchen-towel-covered platter at hand, and when the gnocchi have risen, lift them out with a strainer and let them blot on the towel.

Lightly butter a gratin dish and place the gnocchi in it. Scatter the cheese over the gnocchi, then remove the sage leaves from the melted butter and dribble the butter over the top. Sprinkle with poppy seeds and put the gnocchi under a hot broiler until the surface has browned and the butter is bubbling.

SERVES 4

NOUKLES

An Austrian specialty, these tasty, farinaceous mock quenelles make an inexpensive first course or a pleasant accompaniment to simple chops or plain roasts of meat and chicken.

> 2 cups defatted chicken stock
> 8 tablespoons unsalted butter
> ¼ teaspoon salt
> Pepper
> 1 scant cup all-purpose flour
> 2 large eggs
> ⅔ cup grated Parmesan or Gruyère cheese or
>   a mixture of the two
> 1 cup heavy cream

Noukles are composed from a *pâté à choux*-like paste. In a
small saucepan, over medium-high heat, place ⅔ cup chicken
stock, 3 ounces butter, salt, and pepper. When the butter has
melted and the liquid is at a full, rolling boil, throw in the
flour all at once. Stir hard and fast until the mixture adheres
in a firm ball. Keep working the ball over heat with the back
of a spoon. Spread the ball out, draw it together, stir at it until
a film of dried paste covers the pan's bottom. Remove pan
from heat, let cool a minute, then stir in 1 egg. When the egg
is perfectly absorbed and the paste is again smooth, add the
other egg, half the cheese, and 4 tablespoons of cream. Beat
until smooth.

Half fill a large pot with salted water and bring to a boil.
Regulate heat until the water is at a bare simmer. Form the
noukles by spooning up quantities of paste about the size of
a large English walnut. Roll the paste between the palms of
the hands, and use fingers to shape dough into small cylin-
ders about 2½ inches long. When the water is nearly calm,
add half the *noukles,* cover the pot, and let them poach for

8 minutes. Butter a large gratin or quiche dish. Lift out the *noukles* with a slotted spoon and place them in the buttered dish. Poach the other half and add them, also, to the gratin dish.

Pour the remaining chicken stock and cream over the "quenelles," and sprinkle on the rest of the cheese. Cut the last ounce of butter into thin shavings and strew them over the cheese. Put the dish to bake in a preheated, 350° oven for about 45 minutes, or until the *noukles* are crusted a light gold and the cream has thickened into a sauce. Turn on the broiler and glaze the dish briefly so that the entire surface becomes speckled with brown.

SERVES 4 OR 5

FLAMICHES

Flamiche is a thin, many-versioned galette/tart that has varied in ingredients and useful intent from age to age and province to province in France. The earliest versions from Flanders and Artois, composed of thin, lightly yeasted dough and cheese, were meant to be eaten as hot-from-the-oven *abat-faims*. In more recent times, the word *flamiche* has come to mean a tart (either open or closed) filled with leeks (bound either with eggs or a thick white sauce). Both versions are delicious. The first lends itself most comfortably to the realm of hors d'oeuvres, and several of these rich pastries might be set out alone and with no other competition at a tasting where one wished to show serious red wines to their best advantage. The leek tart should stand as a first course in a rustic dinner, or it might mingle pleasantly with the juices of roasted beef or lamb. There is a slight sweetness to the leeks which must be reckoned with in menu planning, however.

FLAMICHE IN THE ANCIENT MANNER

FOR THE PASTRY:

>   1⅔ cups sifted flour
>   1 teaspoon salt
>   2 eggs
>   1 teaspoon yeast dissolved in
>   2 tablespoons warm water
>   ½ cup warm milk
>   2 tablespoons butter, cut into small pieces
>
>   1 egg
>   ⅓ cup whipping cream
>   ⅓ cup *each* fresh-grated Parmesan and
>   Gruyère cheese mixed together
>   Walnut oil (or melted butter)

Mix the flour and salt together in a bowl and make a well in the middle. Break the eggs into the center, add yeast, and half of the milk. Gradually incorporate the flour into the egg, adding the remaining milk as necessary. When the paste is smooth, stir in the butter. Cover the bowl with a towel and leave in a moderately warm place for 4 or 5 hours.

Lightly butter a deep-sided, 12-inch pizza pan and pour in the dough. Dip a spoon in water and use it to smooth the paste evenly over the pan bottom. Mix the egg, cream, and half the cheese together and spoon over the surface. Sprinkle the remaining cheese on top, drizzle lightly with walnut oil, and put the galette to bake in a hot (375° to 400°) oven for about 25 minutes. Serve the *flamiche* immediately and place a crock of unsalted butter nearby so that people may butter their slices. (Omit butter at a wine tasting.) This tart is easy to eat and it might serve 8 people, or then again, only 4.

MAKES 4 TO 8 PORTIONS

LEEK FLAMICHE

> 10 medium large leeks
> 3 tablespoons unsalted butter
> 1 tablespoon flour
> 1 cup heavy cream
> Salt, pepper, nutmeg
>
> Plain pie pastry
> 1 egg yolk for glaze

Clean the leeks by trimming off any wilted outer leaf layers. Cut off and discard all but 2 inches of the upper green. Slit each leek down the center, spreading back its leaves, and wash under cold water to dislodge any adhering dirt. Cut leeks across in 1-inch slices and put to cook until very tender in boiling, salted water. Drain well and squeeze the mass dry.

Make a roux by melting 1 tablespoon butter in a small saucepan. Stir in flour and cook over gentle heat, whisking constantly so the roux does not brown. After 3 or 4 minutes, whisk in the cream and let this thick sauce simmer for 5 minutes. Stir in the remaining 2 tablespoons of butter, the seasonings, and the cooked leeks.

Roll out two thin 12-inch circles of pastry. Place one circle on a baking pan and spread the leeks evenly over it, leaving

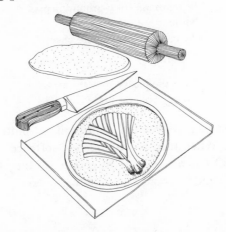

a 2-inch border free. Moisten this border lightly with water. Place the other dough circle over the top, and roll the two borders together. This will both seal in the filling and provide the look of a corded edging. Pierce a small hole in the middle of the upper crust to allow steam to escape. Mix the egg yolk with a little water and brush over the top. Any dough remainders could be cut into decorative leaves and tendrils and radiated from the central hole if so desired.

Bake for about 45 minutes and serve hot.

MAKES 6 TO 8 PORTIONS

FLAMMENKUCHEN (FLAMING CAKE)

Flammenkuchen (literally, "flaming cake") is an Alsatian specialty that is traditionally made with *fromage blanc*, the fresh, loose cheese of whole cow's milk quickly curdled with rennet. Cottage cheese is the acceptable substitute.

> 2 large onions, sliced thin
> 1 large garlic clove, minced
> 3 tablespoons butter
> 5 slices lean bacon
> 10 ounces cottage cheese
> ½ teaspoon salt
> ½ teaspoon fresh-ground pepper
> Nutmeg
> ⅓ cup grated Gruyère cheese
> 1 egg
>
> Plain pie pastry
> 1 egg yolk for glaze

In a covered pan, cook onions and garlic in butter over very gentle heat. When they are completely softened, remove the cover and let onions continue to cook until they turn a light gold. This should be about a 45-minute process.

Blanch the bacon in boiling water for 2 minutes. Drain and blot dry. Fry bacon until crisp and break into dime-sized pieces.

In blender or food processor, purée the cottage cheese until it is perfectly smooth.

Stir cottage cheese, seasonings, Gruyère, egg, onions, and bacon together.

Roll and trim the dough into a thin, 13-inch-diameter circle and place on a round baking sheet. Smooth the cheese mixture over the dough, leaving a 1-inch border free at the edge. Turn the border up and over the filling to provide a rustic shell. Beat the egg yolk with a tablespoon of water and brush glaze over the pastry's edge. Bake at 350° for about 45 minutes or until the top of the tart is covered with a multitude of golden "flaming" speckles. Serve very hot.

SERVES 6 TO 8

For decorative effect: cut some ½-inch-wide strips of pastry about 5 inches long. Attach them in lazy scallops to the edge.

CRUSTED CHEESE PIE

It is difficult to know precisely what to call the following dish. It consists of a thick batter laden with cheese that, when baked, puffs and portions itself into a bready lower casing, a quiche-like center, and a crisp upper crust. The creature also smacks somewhat of both a soufflé and a pudding.

    10 eggs
     1 cup milk
    ¾ cup flour
    ¼ teaspoon salt
    ¼ teaspoon pepper
     2 tablespoons grated onion
     8 ounces grated cheese (a mixture of Cheddar,
       Parmesan, and Gruyère, measuring about 2 cups)

Stir the eggs with ½ cup milk until smooth. Place the flour and salt in a mixing bowl, make a well in the middle, and gradually whisk the remaining ½ cup of milk into the flour. Then whisk in the eggs. Beat the batter until it is smooth. Add pepper. Cover the mixing bowl with a towel and let the batter stand all day (or for at least 6 hours) at room temperature.

Preheat the oven to 350°. Stir the grated onion and half the cheese into the batter. Butter or oil a 9- or 10-inch spring-form pan and place the pan on a baking sheet. Pour in the batter and bake for 20 minutes. At the end of that time, remove pie from the oven only long enough to sprinkle the remaining cheese on top. Replace in the oven for another 25 to 30 minutes or until the top is brown and firmly crusted.

The pie will, like a soufflé, expand greatly. Allow it to settle down for 10 minutes, then run a knife around the edge and open the pan at the side. Run a spatula under the pie and transfer it to a round platter. Surround with watercress and serve, slightly warm, as an hors d'oeuvre (let people cut their own thin wedges) or as a first course. Reheats not too badly.
SERVES 6 TO 8 AS A FIRST COURSE,
MANY MORE AS AN HORS D'OEUVRE

TURTLE TART

Turtle Tart is, in effect, nothing but a double-crusted quiche in the shape of a stolid turtle. The "shell" is formed over a rounded bowl, and when it has firmed in baking the shell becomes a baking dish which holds the quiche mixture. The following recipe is for a plain cheese-flavored quiche, but it could be seasoned with ½ cup of crisp, crumbled bacon or sautéed onions if so desired. A 1½-quart, 8-inch-diameter stainless steel bowl is needed as a baking form.

1½ pounds puff pastry *or* plain pastry given three turns,
     chilled
Oil
  1 egg yolk beaten with 1 teaspoon water for glaze
  5 eggs
1¼ cups heavy cream
  ½ cup grated Gruyère cheese
  1 tablespoon mixed fine-minced parsley and chives
Salt, pepper, nutmeg
Lettuce, savoy cabbage, or watercress leaves, for garnish

Roll out the pastry on a lightly floured surface. Place the 1½-quart bowl on the pastry and, using it as a basic round guide, cut a freeform turtle, outlining the head, four feet, and a tail. Transfer the flat turtle shape to a baking sheet.

Cover the bowl's exterior with aluminum foil and place it upside down on the baking sheet. Oil the foil lightly. Reroll the unused dough and place a sturdy layer of pastry over the foil. Trim the round edge. Preheat the oven to 350°. Let both shapes rest 15 minutes, then bake for 10 minutes. (Do not prick dough before baking.) Remove the flat turtle shape from oven, but continue baking the "shell" for another 10 minutes, then remove the bowl and foil from the pastry shell. Brush the top with egg yolk and water glaze. Place the "shell" hollow side up on a baking sheet.

Beat eggs, cream, cheese, herbs, and seasonings together and pour into the shell/bowl. Wet the rim of both pastry pieces with a little of the egg yolk mixture and place the flat turtle shape on top of the bowl. The turtle should now be completely formed and resting upside down on the baking sheet. Place in a 350° oven for about 50 minutes. Halfway through the baking, protect the turtle's feet and tail from excessive browning with aluminum foil. The eggs will eventually expand and glue shell to body.

Remove turtle from oven. There will be some small openings around the rim through which you can see if the egg is completely set. Tip the turtle slightly, and if no liquid egg appears, the turtle is cooked. (Replace in oven for another 10 minutes if any liquid shows.) Turn turtle right side up and place it on a serving dish covered with a bed of greenery. Cut in pie wedges to serve.

MAKES 8 TO 10 PORTIONS

GOUGÈRE

Gougère, the Burgundian pastry that complements so well the wines of that region, is made essentially of a *pâté à choux* (from which also come cream puffs and eclairs). *Gougère* paste should have a slightly higher percentage of flour, however, so that the resulting cake is crisp and nutty, with no hint of flab about it.

> 1 stick unsalted butter, cut in chunks
> 1 teaspoon salt
> 1½ cups all-purpose flour
> 5 large or 6 medium eggs
> 1 cup grated Gruyère cheese, plus 24 thin strips
>   cut into 2½-inch lengths

Pepper
Flour and butter for baking sheet
  1 egg yolk for glaze

Place 1 cup water, the butter, and the salt in a medium-sized saucepan and bring to the boil. Take the pan off the heat and add the flour all at once, stirring furiously with a wooden spoon all the while. Return the pan to heat and beat the paste into a firm ball. Continually spread the dough against the pan's bottom, then stir it up again until the paste is dry and steaming (there will eventually appear a film of dried flour over the pan's surface—a signal that the paste is truly dry).

Let the paste cool briefly, then start stirring in eggs, one at a time. Each egg addition will break the mass apart, but continued beating will reincorporate it into a solid dough. When all the eggs are added, stir in the grated cheese and the pepper.

Lightly butter a large baking sheet. Sprinkle a small scoop of flour along one rim of the pan. Tilt the baking sheet up and the flour will slide smoothly over the surface, leaving a uniform coating. Tap the sheet to remove any excess flour. Turn an 8- or 9-inch round pan upside down on one end of the baking sheet, using the rim of the pan to leave a neat, circular tracing in the flour. Mark off another circle at the other end of the sheet. Set aside.

Preheat the oven to 350°. Scoop the paste into a pastry bag with a large, plain round nozzle. Using the circles traced on the baking sheet as a guide, pipe the paste out into two open rounds (each will have triple encirclings of dough and the unbaked pastry will resemble a thin donut). Mix the egg yolk with a tablespoon of water and brush it over the *gougère*. Crisscross the long strips of cheese around the top and put to bake for 30 minutes. Take the *gougère* from the oven only long enough to puncture the bottoms with a few pricks of a knife point to release any interior moisture and help the pastry crisp. Let bake for another 10 to 15 minutes, or until the *gougère* is firm, crisp, and nicely browned. Set out in a pretty cheese basket or on a wooden board. Let people break off their own portions.

SERVES 12 TO 15 AS AN HORS D'OEUVRE

OPEN OMELETS

There is nothing more comforting and pleasing to the sight than the arrival at table of a large open omelet, its top a pretty glaze of golden cheese and cream and its interior replete with crisp and savory morsels of bread, potatoes, vegetables, sausage, whatever. Though the following two omelets can be made in smaller quantity, I give ingredient amounts commensurate with filling a 12- to 15-inch paella pan (and it is good to put that pan to more than the obvious use). Both the Savoy and Italian omelets, with their full gamut of nutritional elements, can provide a complete though light supper or lunch.

OPEN SAVOY OMELET

2 medium onions, chopped
2 garlic cloves, minced
1 stick plus 3 tablespoons unsalted butter
3 large all-purpose potatoes
½ cup green peas (preferably fresh but frozen will do)
⅔ cup diced sausage (chipolata, kielbasa, pepperoni, etc.)
3 slices firm bread, crusts removed
1 dozen eggs
Salt and pepper

Chopped parsley
½ cup grated Gruyère cheese
⅓ cup heavy cream

Over medium heat, fry the onions and garlic in 1 tablespoon of butter until soft and just beginning to brown. Place the onions in a large mixing bowl.

Peel and dice the potatoes into ½-inch cubes. Melt 3 tablespoons of butter in the same frying pan and raw-fry the potatoes, shaking and stirring the pan frequently until the cubes are nicely browned on all sides. Add potatoes to onions.

Cook the peas in boiling salted water until just tender. Drain well and add the peas, and then the diced sausage, to the onions.

Cut the bread into croutons (there should be a uniformity of size among potatoes, peas, sausage, and bread) and fry them to a very crisped brown in 3 tablespoons of butter.

Beat the eggs, generous seasoning, and 2 tablespoons chopped parsley until well blended. Pour the eggs over the potato/vegetable ensemble and carefully combine the mixtures.

Preheat the broiler. Melt 4 tablespoons butter in a large paella pan. When the butter has foamed and is just beginning to turn a light brown, pour in the omelet. Shake the pan over heat and spread the ingredients out evenly with a fork. Continue shaking the pan and gently pulling in the cooked egg at the sides while allowing the uncooked egg to run to the edge. Sprinkle the croutons and cheese over the top. When the bottom and edges of the omelet have set (the top center should remain liquid), dribble the cream over the cheese and transfer the pan briefly under the broiler until the surface has just set and lightly browned. (Keep the cooking time on top of the stove particularly short—the omelet should remain succulently moist and never dry.) Garnish with a sprinkle of parsley.

SERVES 4 AS A FULL MEAL, 10 AS A SLICED HORS D'OEUVRE

OPEN ITALIAN OMELET

> 2 medium onions, sliced
> 2 garlic cloves, minced
> ½ cup olive oil
> 1 large red or green sweet pepper
> 8 medium canned or home-preserved tomatoes, drained of their juices
> 1 teaspoon mixed dried oregano and thyme
> 2 tablespoons chopped parsley
> 1 dozen eggs
> Salt and pepper
> 2 cups cooked small pasta or spaghetti
> ½ cup grated mozzarella cheese
> 10 anchovy filets (blotted dry and cut in two lengthwise)
> A handful of small Niçoise olives
> Parsley sprigs, for garnish

Sauté the onions and garlic in 2 tablespoons of olive oil until tender but not browned. Add the pepper (cut into thin long slivers), the tomatoes (cut roughly into strips), and the herbs. Simmer until the mixture appears dry.

Preheat the broiler. Blend the eggs and seasoning together and stir in the tomatoes and pasta (if using spaghetti, cut it into 2-inch lengths). Heat ⅓ cup oil in the paella pan and, when quite hot, pour in the eggs. Shake the pan, arrange the ingredients, let the bottom set, and while this is happening, sprinkle the top with cheese and distribute the strips of anchovy in a crisscross pattern on the surface. Scatter on the olives, dribble the remaining oil over the cheese, and transfer the pan to the broiler for a quick, finishing glaze.

SERVES 4 TO 10

Note: even those who are not particularly fond of anchovies don't seem to mind them in this omelet's slightly crisped form.

EGGPLANT MAAKOUDE

The *maakoude* is a thick Tunisian omelet that can be adaptably used to hold leftover bits of fish, chicken, and meat; or it can involve itself exclusively with a specific vegetable, for example, carrots, zucchini, or mushrooms. The addition of typical North African spices makes the *maakoude* exotic fare—their simple omission allows the omelet to regain a Western bearing. Notice again the presence of bread expanding quantity and lending body.

> 1 eggplant, about one pound
> Salt
> 6 tablespoons olive oil
> ½ cup fresh or dry bread crumbs
> 10 eggs
> 1 large garlic clove, pressed
> 2 tablespoons minced parsley
> 2 teaspoons lemon juice
> Pinch each of cinnamon, powdered saffron, and
>   pulverized cumin seeds
> Salt and pepper
> ½ cup chicken stock
> Pimento strips and chopped parsley, for garnish

Cut the eggplant lengthwise into inch-thick slices. Score the flesh of each slice with a crisscross veneer of thin cuts and sprinkle salt over the slices. Leave to drain for 30 minutes. Preheat the broiler. Squeeze the pieces carefully to rid them of their water, then brush each section lightly with olive oil. Place the eggplant under the broiler. Turning the slices once, grill until tender. Scrape the flesh from the skins and mash it with a fork until relatively smooth. Put the skins aside for later use as garnish.

Soak the bread crumbs in water, then press the mass dry.

Mix bread crumbs, eggplant, eggs, garlic, parsley, lemon juice, spices, and seasoning and blend well.

Heat 5 tablespoons of olive oil in a straight-sided pan 7 or 8 inches in diameter (use preferably a heavy cake tin; failing that, an enameled iron casserole). Swirl the pan to coat the sides with oil, and pour in the eggs. Turn the heat to low and cover the pan tightly. In about 8 to 10 minutes, the egg will set at the edges. Run a knife around the omelet to loosen the edge. Re-cover and cook until the top is just firm. Place a plate over the cooking dish and reverse the omelet onto it. Pour a bit more oil into the mold, then slide the eggs back in to brown lightly on the other side, about 6 to 8 minutes.

Off the heat, pour the stock over the omelet, cover the dish, and let it rest for 5 minutes. Turn out onto a serving platter and garnish with chopped parsley, pimento strips, and petal-like strips of eggplant skin. Serve warm or cold.

SERVES 6 TO 8

WAKING TO SMELL BACON, ETC.

Waking just in time to smell coffee and bacon and eggs. And how rarely it happens! If there should be coffee and bacon and eggs (not all your eggs, of course) to smell, then it is long odds against our waking—or at least against *my* waking—just in time to smell them. If we should happen to waken bang on breakfast, the nit is probably fifty to one against there being bacon *and* eggs *and* coffee all hot and suitably odorous. We live in a world of fantastic events and staggering coincidences. The papers are full of them. After listening to an hour of our talk these days, Sinbad the Sailor would roll out in disgust, calling us a pack of liars. Few of us ask to be immersed day after day in all this far-fetchedness. Most of us could do with a smaller, plainer but more companionable world. We plan, we toil, we suffer—in the hope of what? A camel-load of idols' eyes? The title deeds of Radio City? The Empire of Asia? A trip to the moon? No, no, no, no. Simply to wake just in time to smell coffee and bacon and eggs. And, again I cry, how rarely it happens! But when it does happen—then what a moment, what a morning, what delight!

J. B. PRIESTLEY, *Delight* (Harper and Brothers, 1949)

BACON AND EGGS IN A MUG

> 4 tablespoons unsalted butter, softened
> ½ cup grated Gruyère cheese
> 8 eggs
> Salt and pepper
> ½ cup crumbled, crisp bacon
> 1 tablespoon minced parsley
> ½ cup cooked, chopped mushrooms
> 4 tablespoons heavy cream

Use 2 tablespoons of butter to grease the interiors of 4 medium-sized coffee mugs, and sprinkle the bottoms and sides of the mugs with some of the grated cheese. Break 4 eggs, season them with salt and pepper, and whisk them until well blended. Divide the eggs among the cups.

Mix the bacon, parsley, and chopped mushrooms together and spoon in a neat layer over the eggs.

Break an egg into each cup, season it, and pour a tablespoon of heavy cream over the yolk. Cover each egg with grated cheese and place a morsel of butter on top.

Put the cups in a pan containing 1½ inches of hot water and cook the eggs, loosely covered with aluminum foil, either on top of a burner or in a slow oven for about 10 to 12 minutes, or until the white of the top egg is set (though the yolk should remain soft). At no time should the water boil. Place the cups under a broiler for a brief moment so the cheese can begin to brown.

SERVES 4

SOFT-BOILED EGGS EATEN FROM THE SHELL

16 bread fingers (4-inch-long strips of bread cut from a firm whole loaf; they should be ½ inch thick and crustless)
4 tablespoons unsalted butter, melted
2 tablespoons salt (preferably coarse sea salt)
Whole peppercorns
2 allspice berries
8 jumbo eggs

Cut the bread fingers and dip each one in melted butter. Lay the strips on a baking sheet and bake in a 325° oven until crisp and lightly browned. Keep warm.

Place the salt and some peppercorns and the allspice in a mortar and grind together to a fine, pulverized powder. Divide the mixture among 4 little snail pots or saucers.

Bring a pot of water to the boil and carefully place in the eggs. Cook at a boil for 5 minutes, then remove the eggs and place them in egg cups or on plates.

Serve each person 2 eggs, 4 bread fingers, and a portion of seasoned salt. Each diner taps a hole in the side of his egg with a sharp knife point. The bread fingers are then dipped into the egg, a pinch of salt is added to the egg, and the eggs are eaten, bite by bite, and along with the bread, directly from the shell. See the jacket of this book for further presentation suggestions.

SERVES 4

EGGS BAKED IN BLACK BUTTER

These eggs are most successfully baked two to a serving in small ovenproof cocottes, but they could also be cooked en masse in a gratin dish if one does not mind hazarding a broken yolk in service.

> 1 stick unsalted butter
> 8 eggs
> Salt and pepper
> 2 tablespoons red wine vinegar
> 2 teaspoons capers
> 1 tablespoon minced parsley *or* chives *or*
>   a mixture of the two

Melt the butter in a small saucepan and let it continue cooking over medium heat until it turns a dark nut-brown. Pour half the butter into a gratin dish or divide it among individual cocottes. Carefully crack the eggs into the dish (or dishes) so as not to break the yolks. Season with salt and pepper.

Place the baking dish in a low (325°) oven, cover loosely with aluminum foil, and let the eggs bake for 15 to 20 minutes, depending on their size. Baste the eggs with the remaining hot butter after 10 minutes. The eggs are cooked when the whites are set and the yolks have a glossy film over them. Heat the vinegar, capers, and parsley in the butter pan until sizzling, then pour over the eggs.

SERVES 4

BAKED EGGS IN A CRUST WITH WATERCRESS

   1 loaf homemade bread *or* 1 uncut loaf bread,
      with crust removed
1½ sticks unsalted butter
   2 large bunches watercress, washed and trimmed
   3 large scallions, sliced thin
   2 level tablespoons flour
1½ cups milk
Salt, pepper, nutmeg
   4 large eggs

Cut the bread into four 2-inch-thick sections, then round each section slightly. Cut a circle from the center of each section but be careful not to cut all the way through. Dig out crumbs until there remain four neat cases of bread with ½-inch-thick sides and bottom. Melt 4 tablespoons of butter and, using a pastry brush, coat the breads inside and out with butter. Place the cases on a baking sheet and bake for 10 minutes in a 350° oven.

Bring a small pot of salted water to the boil. Select 16 handsome watercress sprigs and set them aside for garnish. Throw the remaining watercress and the scallions into the water and blanch for 1 minute. Drain and refresh under cold water. Wrap the greens in an old kitchen towel and squeeze them very hard until they are dry. Purée in a food processor or blender and set aside.

Melt 2 tablespoons of butter in a small saucepan. Stir in the flour and whisk over low heat for 4 minutes. Slowly stir in 1 cup of milk, season, then let this white sauce cook over low heat for 15 minutes. Stir frequently. At the end of this time, add the watercress purée and let the sauce simmer another 10 minutes. (It should be very thick.) Use ⅔ of this sauce to coat the interiors of the crisp bread crust cases. Break an egg into each hollow and return the crusts to the 350° oven for another 10 to 12 minutes. (The whites of the eggs should set; the yolks should remain liquid.)

Place the remaining watercress sauce over low heat, whisk in ½ cup milk, and bring to a boil. Remove the pan from the heat and, bit by bit, whisk in 6 tablespoons of butter. Taste for seasoning.

Pour the sauce onto 4 warm dinner plates. Set a baked egg in the middle of each sauced dish and garnish the plates with fresh sprigs of watercress. An elegant presentation.

SERVES 4

EGGS ON A GRATIN

Here "gratin" is used in the traditional sense of the word to mean a crusted layer against the surface of the cooking dish proper. The eggs are broken directly onto the top of a bready undercrust, and by the time they have finished cooking, the dish will present a sliceable whole—a kind of fried eggs on green toast—with the liquid yolks serving as a sauce for the undercrust.

> 4 slices firm but not dry crustless white bread
> 3 tablespoons softened unsalted butter
> A large handful of parsley, leaves and stems
> 2 anchovy filets
> 4 shallots
> 1 large garlic clove
> 8 eggs plus 2 egg yolks
> Salt and pepper

If you have a food processor, combine bread, 2 tablespoons of butter, the parsley, anchovy filets, shallots, garlic clove, 2 egg yolks, and seasoning in the work bowl. Blend the mixture to a fine and fragrant mash. To mix by hand, mince parsley, anchovies, shallots, and garlic together. Crumble the bread into crumbs and work into the parsley mixture, softened butter and egg yolks with your hand.

Lightly butter a 9- or 10-inch frying pan or gratin dish that can be placed over flame. Pack the bread mash over the bottom and up the sides to a height of no more than ¼ inch.

Place the pan over medium-low heat and allow a toasted crust to form over the bottom—a matter of 6 to 8 minutes. Break the eggs carefully over the surface, season with salt and pepper, and place a small shaving of butter on each yolk. Cover the pan and let the eggs cook for 3 or 4 minutes until the whites are completely set and a film has formed over the yolks.

Uncover (be careful not to allow the water accumulated on the lid's underside to rain down on the eggs) and serve at once from the pan. Cut the gratin into serving slices, 2 eggs per portion. A light first course or a breakfast dish.

SERVES 4

GRATIN OF SCRAMBLED EGGS
AND ARTICHOKES

> 4 large artichokes
> ½ lemon
> 1 stick melted unsalted butter
> 8 to 12 eggs, depending on appetites
> 1 garlic clove, peeled
> Salt and pepper
> ½ cup grated Parmesan cheese
> ½ cup heavy cream, heated
> ⅓ cup fine, dry bread crumbs

Break off the stems and any undersized leaves at the bases of the artichokes. Slice off the upper third of the artichokes evenly and snip all remaining sharp points from the leaves with scissors. Rub each artichoke as it is finished with the cut lemon half to avoid discoloration. Peel the stems (there is no sense in wasting their tender interiors). Bring a large pot of salted water to the boil and squeeze the juice from the half lemon into it. Place artichokes and stems in the water, cover the pan, and cook the vegetables until the sharp point of a knife can pierce the stem end easily. (It is better to under-cook rather than overcook here, however.) Remove the arti-chokes from the pan and leave them to drain upside down on a paper-towel-covered platter.

Tear off the leaves from the artichokes and dig out the bristle-like center core. The resultant "hearts," along with the stems, should then be cut into cubes. Using a small spoon, scrape the tender bit of flesh from the inner surface of each large leaf. Melt 2 tablespoons of butter in a small pan and briefly sauté all the edible artichoke bits. Season and set aside.

Crack the eggs into a mixing bowl, spear the clove of garlic on a fork, and use the fork to thoroughly mix and blend the eggs. Season the eggs well and stir in half the cheese. Melt 4 tablespoons of butter in a heavy saucepan, pour in the eggs, and over very low heat continually whisk the eggs until they evolve, over a period of time, into a custard-smooth scramble. (If, at any point, egg coagulates on the sides or bottom of the pan, turn the heat down still further.) At the precise moment when the eggs have thickened but before they start to dry, pour in the heated cream (this will stop the cooking).

Preheat the broiler. Lightly butter a small gratin dish. Spoon in half the eggs. Spread the artichokes over the surface and top with the remaining eggs. Mix the rest of the cheese with the bread crumbs and strew them over the eggs. Dot with the remaining melted butter and place the dish under the broiler until a nicely browned gratin forms over the surface. Serve at once.

SERVES 4

SCRAMBLED EGGS WITH SMOKED SALMON
AND RYE CROUTONS

    2 slices dark rye bread, crusts removed
    1 stick unsalted butter
    8 to 10 eggs, depending on appetites
    1 small garlic clove, peeled
    2 to 3 ounces quality smoked salmon, cut in small dice
Salt and pepper
    3 ounces cream cheese
    ⅓ cup heavy cream
    1 tablespoon minced parsley
    1 tablespoon minced tender scallion greens *or* chives

Cut the rye bread into ½-inch cubes. Melt 1½ tablespoons of butter in a frying pan and fry the croutons. Shake the pan and turn the bread with a fork until the cubes are crisp and brown on all sides. Wrap the croutons in two layers of paper towels and keep warm until needed.

Break the eggs into a bowl. Spear the garlic clove with a fork and use the fork to beat the eggs until well blended. In order to have the smoothest, most elegant scramble possible, pass the eggs through a sieve. (This step strains out shell, chalaza, and the garlic clove if it gets lost; and it permits a perfect amalgamation of yolk and white.) Add the salmon to the eggs and season with pepper.

Note: the quality of the fish should determine the amount of both salmon and salt added. The more refined the salmon, the more can be used in the eggs. If the salmon is strong and/ or salty, use it sparingly and add no salt at this point. The final scramble should be one of subtle distinction.

For the best results, cook the eggs in a *bain-marie*. Half fill a large pan with hot water and heat the water to just below the boiling point. Place a saucepan containing the remaining butter in the water. When the butter has melted, add the eggs and whisk and stir constantly until the eggs evolve, over an unhurried period of time, into a perfect, custard-smooth scramble.

Heat the cream cheese and cream in a small saucepan until hot, and add to the eggs just when they are perfectly cooked. This will immediately stop the cooking process. Taste carefully for seasoning. Pour the eggs into a heated serving dish, scatter the croutons over the top, and finish with a flourish of parsley and scallions. Serve at once.

MAKES 4 TO 6 PORTIONS

ON POACHING EGGS FOR AN ENGLISH BREAKFAST

One mid-winter morning in December, I slip from my snug covers at 5:00 A.M., dress quickly in the chill of an English bedroom, and set out walking across a still sleeping London town. Curious the silence, the heavy dark of the city, the damp fog about the streetlamps their light angling silently through the thick, the great calm. It is a long walk to the Connaught Hotel, where I am going to spend the morning with the breakfast chef.

By the time I reach the hotel, I am chilled through. Down the back steps and into the kitchen, past the vegetable bins and dark larder, the chef's office and the ranks of stoves I go toward the circle of warmth and light at the front of the kitchen. The breakfast chef, already busy at his task, gives me a smile, then goes about his work. I pull up a stool, sit in half shadow, and watch him.

He is a giant of a man, this white Russian, with a full red beard. Every morning he single-handedly cooks breakfast first for the staff, then for the hotel's guests. After that, when the kitchen quickens, he moves to a far corner and cooks the

noon meal for the hotel's fifty maids, waiters, doormen, recep-
tionists . . . something like an Irish Stew or Steak and Kidney
Pie . . . good British fare . . . and then his shift is over.

But now he uses two full stoves. On the burners are large
pots of water which hiss and steam when he removes their
covers. The ovens are at low temperatures; still, when he
opens one, its heat breathes out and warms me. The other
stove is toasting (split muffins and toast points) and grilling
(trays of tomato halves and bacon strips and bangers). Then
into the ovens the trays go, next to the stack of heating plates.

What remains is to poach the eggs. There, in our cozy and
detached microcosmic world-within-a-world, in the infusing
warmth, the chef starts breaking eggs, each one laid delicately into a saucer, then slipped into a very large pot of
steaming, salted, vinegared water. The eggs are impeccably
fresh. The white clings to the yolk and the creature egg, creation and re-creation in a shell, floats into the water, sinks,
then hovers halfway in the depths. The chef slips in more and
more eggs—they pattern in the pot and in his mind so that he
lifts each one out in order. Out comes the first egg, raised on
a thin strainer, then he dips it briefly in another pot of water,
just at the side but unvinegared, to rinse away the acid.
Quickly, he lifts the broad clean towel twisted into his apron
strings, covers his great-knuckled hand and tenderly, as if he
were caressing a small fledgling bird, he nestles the egg, its
yolk quivering, onto the towel for a brief instant where it
blots and dries, its ragged trailing feather white remaining
on the towel, and then he moves the egg oh so gently with his
sure hand onto a warm plate, adds a tomato, two bacon strips,
a banger and some toast, and offers me the first hot breakfast
of the day.

When a massive assembly line for poached egg production
is not in order, it is perhaps easiest to poach a small quantity
of eggs (such as the four called for in each of the following

recipes) in a 9- or 10-inch skillet that has a close-fitting lid. In this case, it is not necessary to break the eggs first into a saucer—simply crack them lightly on the edge of the pan and slip each egg directly into the salted, steaming water.

The fresher the egg, the less the white will spread and trail. Unless, however, someone I know brings me eggs from their chickens, I always assume my eggs, store-bought, to be questionably fresh. I do add a tablespoon of wine vinegar to the water and it does make for a more cohesive white. You can test this out right before your eyes by breaking an egg into salted water. If the white spreads unduly, add some vinegar and then break in another egg and watch the obviously different result. The slight vinegar aftertaste will be lost in the following recipes so it is not necessary to rinse these eggs. Large eggs take about 3½ minutes for a perfect poach.

POACHED EGGS EN MATELOTE

> 3 cups red wine
> 1 cup water
> 1 small onion, quartered
> 3 garlic cloves, peeled and crushed
> A bouquet garni (bay leaf, parsley, thyme)
> 2 cloves
> Salt and pepper
> 4 slices firm bread, crusts removed
> 8 tablespoons unsalted butter
> 8 eggs
> 1½ tablespoons flour
> Minced parsley, for garnish

Combine wine, water, onion, 2 garlic cloves, the bouquet garni, cloves, and seasoning in a medium-sized saucepan or frying pan. Bring to a light boil and let cook, covered, for 15 minutes. During this time, fry the bread slices in 4 tablespoons of the butter until crisp and brown. Rub the croutons over lightly with a crushed garlic clove and keep warm until needed.

Strain the wine through a sieve (discard the debris) and return the liquid to the pan. Regulate the heat until the liquid is just below the simmering point, then slip in the eggs, a few at a time, and poach them. (Keep the pan covered during poaching.) Place 2 eggs on each crouton and hold in a warming oven. Strain the poaching liquid again to remove any particles of egg.

Bring the strained liquid to a fast, rolling boil and reduce it down until there remains only half the initial volume. Take the remaining 4 tablespoons of chilled butter and knead it together with the flour until it is a smooth paste. (This *beurre manié* or "worked butter" will be used to thicken the sauce.)

Over low heat, whisk the *beurre manié*, bit by bit, into the wine. Check the sauce carefully for seasoning, then pour it over the eggs. (Service is greatly simplified by composing each portion in a small, individual gratin dish if possible.) Garnish with parsley.

SERVES 4

POACHED EGGS IN THE MANNER OF LYON

4 large onions, sliced thin
4 tablespoons unsalted butter
3 tablespoons flour
1½ cups chicken stock
About 2 cups milk
Salt, pepper, nutmeg, a pinch of paprika
8 poached eggs
¼ cup grated Parmesan cheese
Chopped parsley, for garnish

Put the onions to stew in the butter in a covered pan. Let them cook over very low heat for close to 30 minutes. Stir occasionally and let the onions cook until they turn a pale straw color. Sprinkle the flour over the onions, continue stirring and cooking for another minute, then slowly add the stock and 2 cups of milk. Add seasoning, then let the sauce simmer gently, stirring from time to time, for 20 minutes. (Add a bit more milk if necessary to keep the consistency within the general range of a medium-white sauce.)

Preheat the broiler. Lightly butter a small gratin dish and spoon half the onion sauce into the bottom. Place the cooked eggs over the sauce, then cover with the remaining onions. Scatter the grated cheese over the surface and place the gratin to brown briefly under a broiler. Garnish with chopped parsley and serve. (Large croutons on the side are welcome.)
SERVES 4 OR 8

POACHED EGGS WITH A JULIENNE OF VEGETABLES AND BUTTER SAUCE

1 medium zucchini
1 medium carrot, scraped
1 small sweet red pepper
2 scallions
2 tablespoons unsalted butter
A scant ¼ cup slivered almonds, lightly toasted
Butter Sauce (see following recipe)
8 eggs
1 tablespoon red or white wine vinegar
Salt and pepper
1 tablespoon minced parsley

Cut the green skin from the zucchini in long strips and cut the bright green strips into inch-long julienned matchsticks. Cut the carrot lengthwise into strips matching the zucchini in size. Cut the red pepper into short strips, and trim the scallion whites and tender greens into inch-long julienne, also.

Melt 2 tablespoons of butter in a frying pan. Add 3 tablespoons of water and cook the carrot strips over medium heat until the water evaporates. Turn the heat to high and immediately add the zucchini, red pepper, scallions, and almonds. Toss and stir the vegetables until everything is mixed and tender crisp. Set aside, then warm before use.

Start the Butter Sauce (see the following recipe), and poach the eggs in salted water with a tablespoon of added vinegar.

Arrange the eggs, two to a serving, on warmed plates or in individual cocottes. Season the eggs. Finish the Butter Sauce by whisking in the chilled butter, then mask the eggs with the sauce. Scatter the warm crisp vegetables over the top and garnish with minced parsley.

SERVES 4

BUTTER SAUCE

    2 tablespoons unsalted butter
    2 level tablespoons flour
    1½ cups boiling water with ¼ teaspoon added salt
    Pepper
    2 egg yolks
    1 tablespoon heavy cream, heated
    1 tablespoon lemon juice
    6 tablespoons unsalted butter, chilled and cut
      into chunks

Melt 2 tablespoons of butter in a small saucepan, whisk in the flour and stir for 3 minutes over low heat. Pour the boiling water into the flour and whisk hard until the mixture is as smooth as possible. Add pepper. Stir the egg yolks and warm cream together in a bowl and gradually whisk in the hot sauce. Return the sauce to the heat briefly, whisking all the while, but do not allow it to come anywhere near a boil. When the sauce has thickened, strain it through a fine sieve. (The sauce can sit in a pan of hot water for 15 minutes at this point, if necessary.) Whisk in the lemon juice and butter, taste for seasoning, and make sure the sauce is hot. Serve at once.

HOT TERRINE OF FISH WITH SAFFRON SAUCE

   1 pound skinless white fish filets
     (flounder, bluefish, trout, bass, etc.)
   3 cups loosely packed fresh bread crumbs
  ¾ cup milk
   2 eggs plus 2 egg yolks
   3 tablespoons unsalted butter, softened
Salt, pepper, a small pinch of nutmeg
   2 tablespoons minced parsley
   1 cup chilled heavy cream
Butter for mold
A double recipe of Butter Sauce (see preceding recipe)
¼ teaspoon powdered saffron
Lemon wedges and whole saffron stamens dipped briefly in boiling water until limp, then blotted dry, for garnish

Cut the fish into small pieces and pound them with a pestle in a mortar or grind them in a food processor to a smooth paste.

Soak the bread crumbs in milk, then squeeze them dry. Add the damp crumbs to the fish and stir in the eggs and yolks and softened butter. Press the mixture through a large sieve (preferably a drum sieve) to strain out any bits of fishy connective tissue and to assure a homogeneous blending of ingredients.

Stir in the seasoning and parsley. Cover and refrigerate the fish for 1 hour.

Butter an 8-cup terrine or soufflé dish. Cut a piece of brown paper to fit the top of the dish and butter one side.

Preheat the oven to 350°. Whip the cream until thickened but still runnably loose. Fold the cream into the fish and spoon the mixture into the terrine. Give the dish a smart tap on a towel-covered countertop to settle the contents, then place the paper lightly on top, buttered side down.

Cook the terrine in a *bain-marie* (a larger pan containing enough water to come halfway up the terrine's sides). The dish should bake for about 50 to 60 minutes, at which point the terrine should feel firm to the touch in the middle.

Make a double batch of Butter Sauce as in the preceding recipe, but add ¼ teaspoon saffron to the boiling water. Serve slices of terrine on individual plates. Ladle sauce over the fish and let it float out to the rim of the plate. Scatter 5 or 6 saffron stamens over the sauce and place a lemon wedge on each plate.

SERVES 8

COUNTRY TERRINE WITH HAZELNUTS

> 8 to 10 chicken livers
> 4 slices firm bread, crusts removed
> 5 ounces salt pork (freeze ½ hour before use)
> 1 medium onion, chopped fine
> 1 large garlic clove, minced
> 1 pound ground veal
> 1 pound ground chicken (preferably dark meat)
> ¼ cup chopped parsley
> Salt
> Fresh-cracked pepper
> 1 teaspoon mixed thyme and savory
> 2 tablespoons cognac

3 pulverized juniper berries
⅓ cup coarsely chopped hazelnuts
Butter for mold
3 large hazelnuts and juniper or hemlock sprigs,
    for garnish

Look over the chicken livers and trim them of any fat and green portions. Place them on a cutting board and slide a knife through the mass repeatedly until the livers are well chopped.

Soak the bread slices in water until soft, then squeeze them until only a damp mass remains. Crumble bread into a large mixing bowl and add livers.

Cut the salt pork into small dice. (The easiest method is to have the block of fat well chilled before dicing. Cut the dice directly against the rind then slice off the small cubes.) Place the salt pork in the mixing bowl and add all other ingredients except the garnish. Mingle everything well with the hands.

Preheat the oven to 325° to 350°. Lightly butter a terrine or soufflé dish (about 5 cups in capacity) and pack in the mixture. Cover the terrine lightly with aluminum foil and place in a *bain-marie* (a larger pan holding an inch or so of water). Bake for 1 hour. The water should steam but not bubble.

Remove the terrine and tip it slightly to drain off any liquids. Place a double thickness of aluminum foil on top and weight the loaf with canned goods. When cool, place the weighted terrine in the refrigerator overnight.

To garnish, arrange 3 whole hazelnuts in a centered triangle and place 2 small sprigs of piney green on either side.

MAKES A GOOD 10 SERVINGS

Note: for a more finished look, or if the terrine is not to be eaten soon, a thin layer of aspic quickly composed from clarified chicken stock and gelatin can be poured over the surface. Another attractive preservation method, which will hold any terrine for 10 to 12 days, is to pour melted butter into the dish until it forms a solid protective layer over the meat. Chill, then coat the butter with a mixture of dried herbs. Cover and refrigerate until needed.

FOUR AND TWENTY MEATBALLS
BAKED IN A PIE

2 pounds ground veal
2 pounds ground pork
¼ cup chopped parsley
2 garlic cloves minced
Salt and pepper
Pinch of ground cloves
1 tablespoon pulverized mixed dried herbs
(thyme, savory, etc.)
¼ cup cognac
⅓ cup white wine
Heavy cream, as needed
Flour
A mixture of butter and oil for frying

Puff pastry, or plain pastry given 3 turns
1 egg yolk beaten with 1 tablespoon water for glaze
2 tablespoons flour

FOR THE SAUCE:

½ cup thin-sliced shallots
4 tablespoons unsalted butter
¼ cup minced parsley
2 cups firm bread crumbs
½ cup white wine
Juice of ½ lemon
Salt and pepper
2 tablespoons red wine vinegar
About 1½ to 2 cups chicken stock

Parsley or watercress, for garnish

Mix the veal, pork, parsley, garlic, seasoning, spice, and herbs together. Add the cognac and wine, then cover and let the mixture marinate in the refrigerator from 8 hours to overnight. Before making the meatballs, add a touch of heavy cream to the mixture if need be—just enough so that the meat is succulently moist. Shape into 24 meatballs. Roll the balls lightly in flour and fry them, a few at a time and over brisk heat, in a mixture of oil and butter. When the meatballs are crisply browned, drain them on paper toweling.

Cover the exterior of a 9-inch round cake tin (or casserole) with aluminum foil. Place the pan upside down on a baking sheet with no raised lip. Roll out the pastry and drape it over the foil-covered pan. Cut off the extra dough neatly, and reserve the scraps. Let the pastry rest for 20 minutes, then brush it over with egg glaze and put to bake in a 350° oven for 20 to 25 minutes or until the pastry has expanded, firmed, and just begun to brown. Lift off the cake tin, gently reverse it onto the baking sheet, and remove the dish and foil.

Place the meatballs in the pastry "dish," heaping them in the center. Make a small paste with 2 tablespoons of flour and a bit of water. Moisten the rim of the "dish" with the paste. Roll out the reserved pastry and cover the pie. Cut off extra pastry and press and pinch the edges of the dough together gently.

With the tip of a knife, trace a shallow circle 5 inches in diameter in the center of the lid. Do not let the knife penetrate the dough—it should simply crease a line. Poke 3 or 4 small holes in the lid, then use the remaining pastry scraps to decorate the lid (I like to do a fanciful "Wedgwood" design, with a small knobbed handle in the center). Brush the top of the pie with egg yolk glaze and put to bake in a 350° oven for 35 minutes.

Make the sauce. Cook the shallots in the butter until tender but unbrowned. Add parsley, bread crumbs, wine, lemon juice, and vinegar, then season, and moisten with stock. Let the sauce simmer for 10 minutes until thick and creamy. Add enough stock as the cooking progresses so that the sauce remains of medium pouring consistency.

Take the pie from the oven. Cut carefully around the outlined circle and remove the center lid from the pie. Pour in the sauce, replace the lid, and bake another 20 minutes. (Protect the pastry from overbrowning with foil.)

To serve, gently slide the pie onto a platter. Surround it with greenery and place the lid on a tilt by the side. Put a handsome serving spoon into the center and let people dish out their own servings.

SERVES 12 TO 15 AS AN HORS D'OEUVRE;

FEWER AS A FIRST OR MAIN COURSE

Soups and Stews

HEREIN are a variety of simple and complex soups built upon
a variety of foundations. The progression of this chapter is a
gradual movement from thin to thick; from lean to fat. There
are, first, traditional soups built upon the easiest of bases,
water and the thickening of water with the addition of gelatinous animal carcass rendered into consommé. Thickened
further with egg drops and pasta, these soups are the kinds
most people find of comfort. Easily digestible, they fall into
the analeptic ranks of restorative foods.

A slightly more complex base, yet not so very, is the simple
milk soup which thickens first with bread, or evolves into a
chowder or, with further complication, thickens with flour
into a sauce base so that the final soup is white and richly
creamed. (A puréed vegetable or fish soup is of much the same
complexion.) Most of these varieties are still simple in that

they are usually stock in combination with one other element and they are usually quickly composed so that those elements remain clear, sharp, distinguished.

As soups become more complex, dense with a variety of foodstuffs, the cooking times become longer, the end results advance, the ingredients metamorphosing into new beings that stand, whole yet intricately formed, upon the involutions of their elements. Pot herbs, stock, meat, vegetables combine, giving up their souls to the greater glory of the cause. In such a dish as a minestrone, a Provençal *pistou,* a *hochepot,* a gumbo, the whole concept of soup totters on the very brink of its nomenclature. There is the perfect form, the balancing mix of liquid and solid. Condense that liquid any more and soup slides into *potée* and *potée* into stew. It is a natural progression then, in this book, from the minestrone at the center of the chapter to the *garbure* following. Almost the same elements are present, but the cooking time is longer, the liquid less apparent, the solids larger, more imposing so that they are taken out and eaten separately, or at least it is necessary to cut them up within the large soup plate. The solids are eaten, the liquid is polished off at the end in one long quaff. The *pot-au-feu* condenses equally, the *daube* even more so. One has to press down upon the stewed elements to receive a spoonful of liquid. And finally there are those stews (like fricassees, *matelotes,* blanquettes) which, though they do not necessarily contain a plethora of ingredients, are still so full of liquid essence that they move upon the plate. These later dishes are main courses, of course—the only differentiation I make to place them within this chapter is that, each having a liquid base, they *do* move upon the plate.

Of all the food contained within this book, the recipes in this chapter are most open to adaptation and whatever inspiration the cook can creatively bring to the cooking process. Most of the soups are of the type that I would best call "intuited." When my mother, for instance, was asked to recall how she made her bean soup, she was at a loss for specific amounts though she could describe perfectly the exact density, the sensate heaviness in the mouth of that soup which she must have made a hundred times. Grandmother Olney's soup is best made by eye and feel rather than precise measurement —it is certain that *she* made it in no other way. And above all, one truism should hold for any soup recipe: you can always thin faster and more easily than you can thicken. So it is best perhaps to withhold the full complement of any recipe's liquid until one tastes and knows the soup on the edge of its completion.

———

Because many soups are based upon a stock (and even water-based soups can be enriched with stock substitution if so desired), the following recipe presents a rich broth that will be worlds better than any canned or cubed product. Particularly in uncomplicated soups, where, for instance, a simple pasta stands in relief against its background consommé, the weak quality of a purchased product will be glaringly apparent. This homemade stock is especially luxuriant, enhanced as it is by a veal knuckle or the feet of a chicken. There is no reason not to make a very large batch, then condense it somewhat and freeze it in portions so that it can be thawed and used, with an addition of water, as a base whenever needed. Never throw away bones and carcass from a bird that is roasted or broiled. Instead, wrap the bones and place them in the freezer until needed for stock. Hold aside the necks and wingtips for that purpose, also.

HOMEMADE CHICKEN SOUP BASE

About 2½ pounds cheap chicken (carcasses, backbones,
    wingtips, necks—a turkey neck may be added)
2 or 3 pairs of chicken feet (toenails removed)
or
1 veal knuckle (cut by the butcher into small pieces)
1 large onion, quartered, each quarter stuck with a clove
2 carrots, scraped and sliced thin
1 garlic clove, peeled
1 stalk celery with leaves
1 small turnip, quartered
1 large bay leaf
Several sprigs each of fresh thyme and parsley
1 teaspoon salt, preferably sea salt
8 peppercorns

Rinse the chicken parts and chicken feet (or the veal knuckle)
under cool water. Rinse especially those portions of the
chicken which are ribbed to draw off any residual blood.
Place the meat in a large, heavy stockpot and add 3 quarts of
cool water. Let the pot sit for a half hour, then bring it slowly
to a low boil. As this point is reached, an eruption of albumin
will occur which will cover the crest of the boil with eddies of
gray-brown scum. Using a large spoon or close-wired skim-
mer, lift off this scum continually. When the scum seems to
abate, pour a small glass of cold water into the pot, joggle the
bones slightly, and let the water again return to the boil.
Skim and repeat this step until the surface is entirely clear,
then add vegetables, herbs, and seasoning. Simply drop them
in the pot with no attempt to mix the ingredients. Again, let
the mixture boil up and again skim; then cover the pot, regulate the heat down until only an occasional bubble breaks
and there is the merest hint of agitation to the liquid. Continue cooking for 1½ hours. (Veal knuckle if used, usually
cooks a longer time, but here it need lend only its gelatinous

qualities to a stock that should be predominately poultry-flavored.)

Line a large sieve with cheesecloth, pour the stock through carefully, avoiding the last sullied bit. Use, or cool and freeze. Stock to be kept more than a week should be frozen.

YIELDS ABOUT 2½ QUARTS

VERMICELLI SOUP

2 tablespoons unsalted butter
1 large onion, sliced thin
3 ounces vermicelli
4 cups salted water (or 4 cups defatted chicken stock)
  at a boil
4 slices dry bread, trimmed of crust and cut into rounds
½ cup grated Gruyère cheese

Melt the butter in a saucepan and cook the onion over low heat until it turns a straw gold. Break the vermicelli into small pieces, then add them straight into the onion. Continue cooking, moving the contents of the pan about, gently and carefully, with a wooden spatula, until the vermicelli takes on a light golden tinge. Stir in all at once the boiling water or chicken broth, cover the pan, and simmer for about 8 to 10 minutes or until the pasta has cooked to your taste.

Spread the grated Gruyère cheese on top of the bread slices and place them under a broiler briefly to melt the cheese.

To serve the soup, place a slice of toast on the bottom of each soup plate and pour the hot vermicelli soup over it. A wedge of Gruyère may be placed on table, and each person can supplement his broth with additional cheese if so desired.

SERVES 4

PFANNKUCHEN (PANCAKE) SUPPE

Pfannkuchen Suppe (or *Frittatensuppe* as it is sometimes called) is an Austro-German variation on the vermicelli theme. Instead of purchased pasta, a small eggy pancake, fried then cut into noodle-wide strips, is used to give the broth body. This nourishing soup can be used as an elegant first course or as an analeptic.

FOR THE PANCAKE:

> 2 level tablespoons flour
> ¼ teaspoon salt
> 2 eggs, lightly beaten
> 1 tablespoon melted unsalted butter
> Milk
> 1 tablespoon butter for frying
>
> 5 to 6 cups beef broth
> Pepper
> Chopped chives

To make the pancake, mix together the flour and salt. Make a well in the middle and pour in the eggs, 1 tablespoon melted butter, and a bit of milk. Smoothly blend the liquid into the dry, then add more milk until the batter is the consistency of very thick, half-clotted cream. (This batter should be a good deal thicker than standard crêpe batter.)

Melt a tablespoon of butter in a 9-inch frying pan and pour in the batter. Make one thick pancake, fried nicely brown on both sides. Cut the *Pfannkuchen* into short, noodle-like strips.

Heat the beef broth to boiling, check it carefully for seasoning, and add the pancake strips. Serve out into warmed bowls immediately and sprinkle each serving with chopped chives.

SERVES 4 TO 6

AVGHOLÉMONO WITH FLOATING CUSTARDS

The rich, tart egg and lemon soup from Greece, with an addition of more egg in the form of round, buoyant custards.

FOR THE CUSTARDS:

  1 egg plus 2 egg yolks
  ½ cup heavy cream
  ¼ teaspoon salt
Pepper
  1 large tablespoon fine-minced parsley
Softened butter for the mold

  4 cups Homemade Chicken Soup base (see page 94),
     well seasoned and defatted
  ¼ cup long-grained rice, rinsed and drained
  2 eggs
Juice of ½ lemon, or to taste
Salt and pepper

To make the custards, beat the egg and egg yolks until just blended, then add the cream, seasoning, and parsley. Butter 8 indentions in a muffin tin and divide the custard among them. Place a larger pan, containing an inch of hot water, into a 300° oven. Set the muffin tin into the larger pan, then let the custards bake until firm to the touch (about 12 minutes—test with the fingers).

Bring the chicken broth to the boil and add the rice. Turn the heat down, cover the pot, and let the rice simmer about 20 minutes or until *al dente*. Whip the eggs together with the lemon juice until they are slightly frothy, then start ladling hot broth into the eggs, whisking as you go. When the eggs are heated, pour them into the soup pot and heat well until the soup thickens, but do not allow it to boil. Season carefully with more salt, pepper, or lemon as needed.

Ladle the soup into heated soup plates. Turn out the custards and let them float, two to a dish, with their parsleyed sides up.

SERVES 4

PÉRIGORD SOUP

A sort of French egg drop soup . . .

2 tablespoons lard or butter
8 garlic cloves, peeled and lightly crushed
   with a knife blade
1 large onion, sliced
2 level tablespoons flour
5 cups water (or chicken stock), at room temperature
Salt
2 whole eggs, separated, plus 1 egg yolk
2 tablespoons white wine vinegar
Dried bread slices or Miques (see page 44)

Melt the fat in a saucepan. Add the garlic cloves and onion, then let them sweat, covered and over low heat, until soft (do not allow them to brown). Drop in the flour and stir the resulting roux with a wooden spoon for 3 or 4 minutes over very low heat. (Again, do not allow the roux to brown.) Whisk in water (the traditional liquid) or stock (nontraditional but enriching); add salt and bring to the boil.

Beat the egg whites with 2 tablespoons of water until they are loose and liquid, then drop them slowly into the boiling broth, stirring all the while. Regulate the heat to low and simmer for 5 minutes. Lift out the garlic cloves with a strainer.

Mix the egg yolks with 2 tablespoons of vinegar in a bowl. Slowly whisk in a ladleful of hot soup, then pour the warmed yolks into the soup. Stir briskly until the soup thickens slightly, but it should not boil after this point.

Pour the soup into large heated bowls, each containing bread or sliced, toasted *miques.*

SERVES 4

ENGLISH MILK SOUP

> 1 quart whole milk
> 1 teaspoon sugar
> 2 bay leaves
> Pinch of cinnamon
> Pinch of salt
> 4 thick slices homemade bread, toasted
> 2 egg yolks
> Butter

Place the milk in a saucepan. Add sugar, bay leaves, cinnamon, and salt and bring to the boil. Cut the toast into 1-inch squares and add them to the milk. Simmer briefly until the bread is soft. Slowly beat ½ cup of hot milk into the egg yolks, then add the yolks to the "soup" so that they may thicken it slightly. (Do not let the soup boil at this point.) Remove the bay leaves, serve the soup out into heated bowls, and let each person stir a lump of butter into his little mess.
SERVES 3 OR 4

CREAMED STEW OF SCALLOPS

> 1½ cups whole milk
> 2 cups heavy cream
> A bouquet garni (bay leaf, parsley, leek greens *or* scallions, thyme, a leafy celery stalk)
> Salt, pepper, cayenne
> 1 pound fresh bay or sea scallops
> 4 large, crustless croutons, rubbed lightly with a garlic clove
> Chopped parsley and 4 lemon slices, for garnish

Combine milk, cream, bouquet garni, and seasoning in a saucepan. Bring just to the boil, then remove the pan from the heat, cover, and let the milk and herbs steep for 20 minutes, then remove the herbs.

Rinse the scallops, dry them well, and if using sea scallops, cut them into thin slices. Bring the milk back to a boil, then regulate the heat to a simmer. Let the milk reduce and thicken for 10 minutes or so. Add the scallops, cover the pan, and cook for another 15 minutes. Place the croutons in warmed soup plates and pour the stew over the bread. Scatter some parsley on top and serve each bowl with a lemon slice cut through and straddling the rim of the dish.

SERVES 4

SAFFRON SOUP WITH BREAD AND SHALLOTS

> 5 cups Homemade Chicken Soup Base (see page 94)
> 1 large carrot, scraped and diced
> 1 medium onion, chopped
> 2 garlic cloves, minced
> 1 medium potato, peeled and diced
> 1 medium turnip, with a thick peel removed, diced
> 2 leeks, the tender whites sliced thin
> A bouquet garni (parsley, thyme, bay leaf,
>   a 2-inch piece of orange peel)
> 5 thick slices firm white bread, crusts removed, diced
> A generous ¼ teaspoon powdered saffron
> 6 large shallots, chopped
> 3 tablespoons olive oil
> Salt and pepper
> Saffron pistils for garnish (optional)

Bring the chicken stock to a simmer. Add carrot, onion, garlic, potato, turnip, leeks and bouquet garni. Cover the pan and let the vegetables simmer until they are just tender.

Add the bread cubes and saffron and simmer, covered, for another 15 minutes.

In a small frying pan, cook the shallots in the olive oil over gentle heat until they are limp but unbrowned.

Remove the bouquet garni from the soup, and pass the soup through a sieve. Press down on the ingredients with a pestle and force everything through. Place the soup back in a saucepan. Add the shallots and taste for seasoning. The soup should be the consistency of a thick creamed soup—add a small portion of stock or water if it seems too thick. Heat the soup well and serve it out in large, rustic bowls. Garnish each serving with several pistils of saffron.

SERVES 4 OR 5

CREAM OF MUSHROOM AND HAZELNUT SOUP

A rich and flavorful soup, yet of the creamed variety, so that it combines the hearty and the elegant as one; the toasted hazelnuts and nut-brown butter steer this simple mushroom soup toward rustic ground.

6 tablespoons unsalted butter
3 level tablespoons flour
4 cups defatted chicken stock
10 hazelnuts
4 ounces mushrooms, cleaned, trimmed, and
    chopped fine
Salt, pepper, nutmeg
3 egg yolks
About ½ cup heavy cream, as needed
1 large, perfect mushroom, sliced thin, and
    chopped parsley or chives, for garnish

Melt 3 tablespoons of the butter in a heavy saucepan and stir in the flour all at once. Over low heat, continue to stir the flour and butter roux together for 4 or 5 minutes. Allow the roux to color just slightly, so that it turns a medium beige. Whisk in 3 cups of the chicken stock and when the liquid is quite smooth, bring it almost to the boil, then regulate the heat so that the broth is just at a very low simmer. Cover and allow to cook for about 20 minutes.

Roast or grill the hazelnuts until their skins are crisp and dark, then rub them roughly with a kitchen towel to remove the skins. Grind the nuts to a powder in food processor, blender, or mortar and set aside.

Melt 1 tablespoon of butter in a frying pan and sauté the mushrooms over brisk heat until they are cooked and very dry.

When the soup base has simmered its 20 minutes, carefully draw off the thin layer of condensed skin on the surface. Add the hazelnuts and the mushrooms and let the whole cook for another 10 minutes. Stir frequently now, to avoid scorching. Pour the thick base into a sieve and press the entire mass through with a pestle. Return the puréed soup to a clean saucepan and dilute it with the remaining cup of stock. Season carefully.

Beat the egg yolks and cream together, then whisk in a small amount of hot soup. Pour the eggs into the soup and allow the soup to heat (but not approach a boil) until it is very hot. If this soup seems a bit thick, adjust the consistency by adding appropriate cream or even milk and taste again for seasoning.

Melt the remaining 2 tablespoons of butter and let it heat until nut-brown. Stir the butter into the soup and then pour the soup into heated plates. Decorate each surface with 2 or 3 slices of raw mushroom and a sprinkling of green herbs.

SERVES 4

CREAM OF JERUSALEM ARTICHOKE SOUP

The rather pungent sweetness of Jerusalem artichokes, when diluted with a purée of potato and sharpened with a bit of onion, makes a richly filling soup. Jerusalem artichokes (sometimes called "sunchokes") should feel firm to the touch when purchased, never sponge-like.

> 2 large all-purpose potatoes, peeled and diced
> About 9 ounces Jerusalem artichokes
> 1 medium onion, chopped fine
> 4 tablespoons butter
> 1 tablespoon flour
> 1 cup chicken stock
> 1 cup milk, plus more as needed
> 1 cup heavy cream, heated
> Salt and pepper
> Small crouton cubes, well buttered, for garnish

Boil the diced potatoes, and, while they are cooking, scrub the unpeeled artichokes lightly with a vegetable brush.

Strain out the potatoes when they are cooked and add the artichokes to the potato water. When the artichokes are tender, drain them from the water and peel.

Cook the onion in 2 tablespoons of butter until it is very soft but unbrowned. Sprinkle the flour over the onion and stir the mixture for a few minutes, then slowly add the stock, potatoes, and artichokes. Bring to a boil, then purée the mixture in a food processor or blender, or press it through a sieve. Season well.

Place the purée in a saucepan along with the milk, and let the soup simmer for 10 minutes. Add the heavy cream, and when the soup is hot and just ready to be served, stir in the remaining 2 tablespoons of butter and adjust the seasoning. If a thinner consistency is desired, more milk may be added. Serve sprinkled with a great plenty of croutons.

SERVES 4

CARAWAY SOUP

From Austria, a soup blending milk and broth bases.

    3 large all-purpose potatoes
    ½ teaspoon caraway seeds
    1 cup buttermilk
    1 heaping tablespoon flour (preferably quick-blending)
    Salt and pepper
    1 cup sour cream
    Chopped parsley, for garnish

Peel the potatoes and cut them in half. Put 5 cups of cold salted water in a saucepan, add the potatoes and caraway seeds, and bring to the boil. Cook the potatoes until they are just tender, but do not let them disintegrate at all. Strain out the potatoes and use the remaining cooking water as the base for the soup.

Stir the buttermilk into the potato broth. Place the flour in a cup and blend in broth until the flour forms a smooth, liquid paste. Stir the flour into the soup and bring to a boil. Allow the soup to simmer for 15 minutes. Dice the potatoes into large cubes and add them to the soup. Taste the broth for salt and add pepper. When the soup is very hot, remove it from the heat, stir in the sour cream, and allow to heat again, but do not let it boil. Serve out in warm soup bowls and garnish each dish with parsley.

SERVES 4

When I was cold or sick, my mother always made soothing potato soup. The potatoes were quickly boiled, peeled and cut in cubes. Over the whole was poured rich, hot milk, then I added salt, pepper, and a lump of butter. Nothing could be better.

MARY JANE POOLE

GRANDMOTHER OLNEY'S NOODLE SOUP

This is a soup famous in the Olney family, and there exists a bowl that belonged to Grandmother, which she kept and used always for this recipe, that is passing its way down the generations.

FOR THE NOODLES:

> 2 egg yolks and about a tablespoon of white
> 1 teaspoon butter, melted
> ¼ teaspoon salt
> Flour (a quick-blending variety makes the
>   smoothest dough)

> 4 cups lightly salted water
>   (or homemade chicken stock)
> 1 large onion, chopped
> 4 slices lean bacon, cut into small pieces
> 4 medium-large potatoes
> Unsalted butter
> A pepper mill

To make the soft yellow noodles, mix together in a small bowl the egg yolks, about 1 tablespoon of egg white, the melted butter, and the salt. Stir in flour until the dough can be formed into a soft mass, then turn it out onto a lightly floured surface and knead, adding flour as necessary, until the dough has a somewhat elastic, nonsticky texture. (If kneading by hand, do a thorough job at this point. If you have a pasta machine, it can do some kneading later.) Wrap the dough in plastic wrap and let it rest for 30 minutes.

Using a pasta machine, knead the dough a few times until it is very smooth, then work the dough down through the kneading blade until it is as thin as possible. (Or roll the dough out by hand, again as thin as humanly possible.)

Cut the dough by hand into ½-inch-wide noodles about 2 inches long. Sprinkle the noodles lightly with flour and then give them a few light tosses to shake off the excess. Cover with a towel and set aside until needed.

Bring 4 cups of lightly salted water (or untraditional but very enriching chicken stock) to a boil. Add the onion and bacon and simmer until the onion is tender. Peel the potatoes and cut them into ¾-inch cubes. Add them to the soup, cover the pot, and continue simmering. The final consistency is what is now important. The potatoes will cook, soften, impart their starch to the reducing broth. The broth will thicken and, at the last moment, the noodles should be thrown in so their final 3-minute simmer will again thicken the soup to the point that a spoon will stand up in it—this is quite necessary. (The total cooking time can be an adaptable 40 to 55 minutes.) Divide the soup into 2 heated soup bowls. At table, each person will stir into his soup a large chunk of sweet butter and grind on pepper to taste.

SERVES ONLY 2

BLÒ BLÒ

Here is another soup much in the same spirit, though from Italy. The onomatopoetic title is equivalent to the English sound for a heavy soup cooking in a pot: blub, blub.

> ¼-pound slab of lean bacon
> 1 large garlic clove, minced
> 1 teaspoon mixed dried marjoram and oregano
> Salt and pepper
> A 28-ounce can tomatoes drained to a dry pulp
>   and chopped
> Fresh pasta made from 1 egg *or* 1½ cups
>   small, dried pasta of choice
> A small pitcher of olive oil

Cut the bacon into small, thin squares and fry until crisp and brown. Strain out onto paper toweling and blot dry. Place the bacon in a large saucepan and add the garlic clove, herbs, seasoning, and tomatoes. Stir over low heat until the mixture is simmering, then add 5 cups of hot, salted water. Stir the soup, cover it, and let it simmer for 30 minutes. Bring to a boil and add the pasta. Stir, recover, and cook until the pasta is tender. Serve in deep soup bowls and place a pitcher of olive oil on table so that each diner can drizzle some into his soup.

SERVES 2 OR 3

RICOTTA AND TOMATO SOUP

A curious mixture to be called a soup, this same formula was given to me by three different Italian friends who all relate having had it as children.

> 1 cup fresh, loose ricotta
> ¼ cup fresh-grated Gruyère or Cheddar cheese
> 1 to 1½ cups thin homemade tomato sauce
> Grated Parmesan cheese
> Toast rubbed with garlic

Mix the ricotta and grated Gruyère or Cheddar cheese in a saucepan. Add tomato sauce until the cheese becomes thick and soup-like. Let the mixture heat over a low flame and when the cheese has melted and the "soup" is hot, serve it in a warmed soup bowl with grated Parmesan on top and a garlic-rubbed toast on the side.

SERVES 1

COCK-A-LEEKIE SOUP

This famous soup (famous in the British Isles for its restorative powers after a long day of riding to hounds) can be made in a number of ways. The whole chicken, covered in water to make its own stock (or covered in stock for an even richer version), is first poached, then the meat is picked from the bone and returned, along with leeks, to the broth. Or leftover chicken may be used up in previously made stock. Sometimes a small amount of rice is added, which gives a thickened, slightly creamed appearance to the final product. The following version calls for a whole chicken and provides its own stock. The breast of the bird is set aside to be used in some later guise.

A 3½-pound chicken
1 medium onion, quartered
1 large carrot, sliced thin
An abundant bouquet garni (leek greens,
    parsley, bay leaf, celery stalk, thyme)
Salt and pepper
4 large or 6 to 8 smaller leeks
2 tablespoons melted, unsalted butter
4 large croutons (or dry bread) and
    chopped parsley, for garnish

Cut the chicken into serving pieces. (Either you may set aside the breast at this point to cook as suprêmes another time, or the breast can be poached in the soup and then set aside to be used as leftovers.) Rinse the pieces well, particularly the ribbed and backbone portions, and pat dry.

In a heavy pot, place the onion, carrot, and bouquet garni. Arrange the chicken sections on top (add also the deskinned neck and the heart and gizzard); then add just enough water to cover the bird. Salt lightly, place the pot over medium heat, and bring slowly to the boil. Observe now the niceties of making stock. Just as the water comes to the boil, skim off the scum that forms until there is none left, then lower the heat so that the liquid agitation nearly stops. Cover the pot and let the chicken cook for about 1 hour over very low heat. (It may be necessary again to remove a bit of scum during this time.)

Cut the white parts only of the leeks into thin julienne. Shortly before the chicken has finished cooking, simmer the leeks in 2 tablespoons of melted butter and a small ladleful of the chicken stock. Cook the leeks briefly to *al dente* stage.

Lift out the chicken portions from the soup and when they are cool enough to handle, divest them of skin and bones and cut the meat into strips. Strain the cooking stock, stopping short at that last bit of flecked gray liquid. Place the stock back in a saucepan, add the leeks and chicken, then heat until very hot. Season with pepper. (This soup should be exceedingly thick.) Ladle into heated soup bowls, float a crouton on top, and sprinkle with parsley.

SERVES 4

DUCK SOUP

"Duck soup" is what should always happen to the leftover carcass of a roasted bird, for its cooking perfumes a day so nicely. The name, however, is purely generic, and "duck soup" is more likely and frequently to be made from a chicken or the abundant remains of a turkey. Serving amounts will depend on the quantity of leftovers. The following recipe is a procedural outline only.

The leftovers of a roasted, stuffed bird
A large bouquet garni (bay leaf, parsley, celery, thyme)
Salt
1 large onion, sliced thin
About ⅓ cup barley, rinsed under running water
   and drained
Unsalted butter
Pepper
Chopped parsley, for garnish

Spoon out and set aside any stuffing that remains in the bird. Strip the meat from the carcass and cut it into small slivers. Break the carcass into small portions at the joints, then place the bones in a pan and cover completely with cold water. Add the bouquet garni and season lightly with salt. Cover and bring to a soft boil, then skim off any scum. Immediately reduce the heat to low and allow the stock to cook at a bare simmer for a minimum of 1 hour for a small carcass or up to 4 hours for larger carcasses. Continue removing any scum that forms from time to time, and add water to maintain the level.

Carefully strain the broth through a sieve (reject the final clouded portion). Place the stock back in the pot and add onion and barley. Simmer for 40 minutes, then add the chicken and stuffing and simmer for a final 15 minutes. Extra water can again be added so that the final consistency is thicker or thinner, as you please. Or a ladleful of cooked barley can be removed just before the chicken pieces are added and the grain puréed and used to thicken the soup, giving it a creamed appearance. Add any final seasoning, then serve out each portion with a lump of butter, a grinding of pepper, and a sprinkling of parsley. Again, serving amounts will depend on the quantity of leftovers and the amount of barley used.

GREEN BARLEY SOUP

6 cups defatted Homemade Chicken Soup Base,
  well seasoned (see page 94)
⅔ cup barley
1 medium onion, sliced thin
1 celery stalk, sliced
1 carrot, scraped and sliced
4 garlic cloves, minced
6 ounces spinach, washed and stemmed
A few slices of Polish sausage (kielbasa)
Salt, pepper
2 tablespoons mixed parsley and chives,
  in an exceedingly fine mince
Large croutons, rubbed with the cut edge
  of a garlic clove
Unsalted butter

Heat the stock to a boil. Wash the barley well under cold, running water; drain completely, then add barley, onion, celery, carrot, and minced garlic to the stock. Cover the pan and simmer for 30 minutes or until the barley is tender.

While the soup is cooking, prepare the spinach. Bring a pot of salted water to the boil. Throw in the spinach and cook briefly until it has wilted and just gained an edge of tenderness. Strain out the spinach while it is still a bright green and refresh it under cold water. Wring the mass very dry.

When the barley is tender, lift out about half of the grain with a slotted spoon or strainer (remove any carrot slices and put them back in the soup) and purée it along with the spinach, in a food processor or blender, or press it through a sieve with a wooden pestle. Stir this thick green cream back into the soup. Add the sausage slices and let the soup reheat until very hot. Adjust seasoning and liquid if necessary (the soup should be of medium thickness).

At the last moment, stir in the fine mince of herbs. Place a crouton on the bottom of each soup plate and ladle soup over the top. Place a chunk of butter in the middle of each portion.

SERVES 4

MOTHER'S NAVY BEAN SOUP

½ pound dried navy beans
½ teaspoon baking soda
4 tablespoons peanut oil
1 large onion, chopped
1 carrot, chopped
1 celery stalk with leaves (strings removed), sliced thin
Soy sauce
Salt and pepper

Pick over the beans and discard any that are damaged and all small stones that are posing as beans. Rinse the beans under running water, then place them in a large pot. Cover with cold water and add 1 teaspoon of baking soda. Let the beans soak overnight.

The soup can cook from 3 to 4 hours in all. Approximately 3½ hours before you plan to serve, drain the beans from their soaking waters. Rinse them well, then place them back in the pot and re-cover with a good 2 quarts of fresh cold water. Bring slowly to the boil and skim off any frothy albuminous scum from the surface. Lower the heat to the barest simmer, cover the pot, and let the beans cook for 2 hours.

Heat 2 tablespoons of peanut oil in a frying pan. Add the onion, carrot, and celery and cook over low heat until the vegetables are soft but unbrowned. Stir the vegetables into the beans. Continue cooking for another 1 to 2 hours. Keep an eye on the water level and add a bit more water as needed, so that the final soup will have about it the air of a clear broth with beans in it rather than a thickened mass of just beans.

Stir in the remaining 2 tablespoons of oil, the soy sauce (just enough to uplift flavor but not reveal its own identity), and salt and pepper to taste. Serve in large warmed soup bowls and accompany with a basket of whole-wheat croutons.

SERVES 4

Chill any leftover beans and eat them for lunch the next day on hot buttered toast.

BROTH WITH BRIGHT VEGETABLE BALLS

A fast and easy soup that can be turned in either an Oriental or Occidental direction. For an Eastern dish, use soy sauce, dried wood mushrooms, bok choy, and rice thread noodles. For a Western dish, season with salt and use fresh white mushrooms, spinach, and vermicelli.

    3 large carrots, scraped clean
    2 large turnips, heavy peel removed
    3 tender scallions
    20 to 24 small firm button mushrooms, cleaned and cut
        off at the stem or several dried Japanese wood
        mushrooms, soaked, reconstituted, and sliced thin
    2 tablespoons butter or peanut oil
    1 garlic clove, minced
    4 cups defatted Homemade Chicken Soup Base
        (see page 94)
    A handful of vermicelli or Japanese rice thread noodles
    2 cups of torn spinach leaves (carefully washed
        and stemmed) or 2 cups of bok choy greens, well
        washed
    Salt and pepper or soy sauce and ¼ teaspoon sesame oil
    2 hot hard-boiled eggs, sliced in half

Cut the carrots and turnips into balls. Use either a melon baller or cut the vegetables into roughly ¾-inch cubes and round the edges with a paring knife. Parboil the vegetables in boiling, salted water until they are almost tender, then drain well. (This step can be done ahead of time.)

Cut the scallions, including as much of the dark green leaf as possible, into very thin cross slices. Trim the mushrooms so that they are all of a size. Heat the butter or peanut oil in a large frying pan or saucepan and when it is hot, add the scallions, mushrooms, garlic, and vegetable balls and sauté briefly. At the same time, bring the stock to a boil and add the noodles. Just as the noodles are tender and the scallions a bright, crisp green, throw the spinach or bok choy onto the vegetable balls and pour the boiling stock over the vegetables—which will immediately wilt the greens.

While the entire soup takes a last brief heat, season with salt and pepper or, for an Oriental taste, soy sauce and sesame oil. Taste carefully, then divide the soup among 4 soup bowls and float half an egg in each.

SERVES 4

MINESTRONE IN A CABBAGE LEAF

Minestrone is usually built upon a beef or veal stock, but there is no reason not to vary the broth and use a Homemade Chicken Soup Base (see page 94).

> ½ cup dried lima, kidney, or navy beans
> 1 large onion, chopped
> 2 leeks, cleaned, the tender parts sliced
> 2 garlic cloves, minced
> 2 tablespoons olive oil
> A 1-pound can of tomatoes, partially drained of juices
> Salt, pepper
> 1 teaspoon mixed herbs (thyme, oregano, marjoram)
> 1 bay leaf and 1 sage leaf
> 2 quarts stock

¼ pound salt pork, chilled and then diced
2 leafy celery stalks, sliced
2 carrots, scraped and sliced
1 large savoy cabbage
1 large all-purpose potato, peeled and diced
½ cup pasta (broken spaghetti or ziti or
    elbow macaroni)
1 cup zucchini, in medium dice
½ cup fresh green peas
A pot of unsalted butter
A wedge of Parmesan cheese

Cover the beans with boiling, salted water and let them sit for 1 hour. Drain well.

In a large heavy pot, cook the onion, leeks, and garlic in the olive oil over low heat until they are tender. Add the tomatoes, seasoning, and herbs, then cook the mixture for 10 minutes. (Break up the tomatoes with a spoon and discard any tough stem ends.)

Add the stock and bring to the boil. Add salt pork, celery, carrots, and beans, then cover the pot and simmer very slowly for 20 minutes. Remove and wash the outer leaves of the savoy cabbage (they will be used later for decor), and shred 2 cups of the remaining tender, stemless cabbage. Add the shredded cabbage and diced potato to the soup and simmer for another 15 minutes.

Add the pasta and then, 5 minutes later, the zucchini and peas so that those fragile vegetables will cook the shortest time. Simmer another 10 minutes or so. Adjust the seasoning carefully during this time. The consistency should also be watched at this point. Be particular about the density of the soup—it should be very thick but there should be always broth within the thickness. As the pasta absorbs liquid, the vegetables may be in danger of sticking to the pan's bottom, so maintain the liquid level with additions of water or broth if necessary.

To serve, place a large savoy cabbage leaf or two in each

heated soup dish, with a portion of the frilly leaf edge deco-
rating the rim of the dish. Ladle the soup into the bowls and
the heat will steam the cabbage somewhat, so that it provides
a bright, bordering green. Place on table a pot of unsalted
butter, pepper and salt mills, and a wedge of Parmesan
cheese with a grater so that each person can doctor his soup
to taste.

SERVES 6

GARBURE

The famous *garbure* from the Béarnais district of south-
western France is a well-known and popular Sunday meal.
Cooked in an accommodating glazed earthenware *toupin* or
"belly jar" (that utensil so named for its quaintly rounded
shape) and containing an abundance of potatoes, beans, and
cabbage, the traditional *garbure de Béarn* usually counts
within its elements a preserved section of goose. For everyday
fare, however, the meat additions tend to revolve around
bacon, ham, or sausage, and our recipe includes the easier
ingredient. Serve with the dish a hearty red wine, perhaps
Châteauneuf-du-Pape, or from closer to the region, wines
from Corbières or Minervois, so that the final ritual of the
goudale can be tastily executed.

> 1 cup Great Northern beans
> 1 pound sausage (kielbasa or Spanish chorizos)
> 2 medium potatoes, peeled and sliced thick
> 1 small rutabaga, peeled and sliced thick
> 2 large carrots, scraped and sliced
> 1 large onion, cut in thick slices
> 2 large leeks, washed, the tender parts chopped
> A large bouquet garni (bay leaf, thyme, parsley, leek
>   greens, a 2-inch section of orange peel, a celery
>   stalk)

Salt, pepper, cayenne
  2 crushed garlic cloves
1½ pounds savoy cabbage
  3 slices lean bacon, very cold
Parsley
  2 whole garlic cloves
  1 cup green peas, fresh if possible

FOR THE CROUTONS:

A recipe of Garlic Toasts (see page 39)

Look over the beans, remove any bits of stone or damaged beans, rinse them well, then cover with cool water and, following package directions, bring them to a boil. Off the heat, let them sit for 1 hour, then change the water and cook the beans until tender. Drain well and set aside.

In a large stew pot (a glazed earthenware *daubière,* an enameled iron pot, or failing those, a heavy stainless one), place the sausage and 2 quarts of cold water. Bring to the boil, then add potatoes, rutabaga, carrots, onion, leeks, and bury the bouquet garni in their depths. Add seasoning (coming down heavy on the cayenne if you like it) and 2 crushed garlic cloves. Let the mixture stew at a good simmer for about 45 minutes.

Meanwhile, prepare the cabbage. Remove any damaged outer leaves, cut the cabbage into quarters, and trim out the tough cores and ribs. Slice the cabbage into large chiffonade (shreds) and parboil in salted water for 10 minutes. Drain the cabbage and refresh under cold water, then gently press the mass dry.

Mince together the bacon, a handful of parsley, and 2 garlic cloves. When they are a fine paste and the cooking vegetables are tender, add to the pot the cabbage, the bacon mixture and the peas. Let the stew simmer for another 15 minutes. Make the garlic toast.

Purée half the beans (in a food processor or press them

through a sieve). Add the beans, both whole and in purée, to the stew. Add at the same time 2 of the garlic toasts cut into small squares and let them dissolve into the soup and contribute body. Taste carefully for seasoning now and give the soup many stirrings. It will cook another 15 minutes, during which time it may be in danger of sticking. Watch the final density so that the stew remains slightly liquid yet thick enough to support upright a ladle plunged into its depths.

To serve, place the garlic toasts into heated soup plates. Remove any obvious surface fat and the bouquet garni from the stew. Ladle stew into the bowls, then lift out the sausage and divide it into portions. Make sure that some broth stays in the pot.

When the solids of the stew have been consumed, divide the remaining stock among the plates and allow everyone to *faire la goudale*. Each person pours an amount of red wine equal to the volume of broth remaining into his soup plate. All stir the broth and wine together, then toast one another and drink up directly from their dishes.

SERVES 4 TO 6

BAECKAOFFA

Baeckaoffa, an Alsatian dish the name of which translates as "baker's oven," is a compilation of potatoes and gelatinous portions of beef, lamb, and pork set to stew in the area's famous Riesling wine. Traditionally, each housewife composed the dish at home and carried it to the large ovens of the local baker where it baked, along with the *baeckaoffas* of other families, for Sunday dinner. A long, slow, 3-hour stew, during which time the pot is tightly sealed against escaping steam, is necessary if this dish is to form a rich, correctly gelatinous unctuosity.

1½ pounds trimmed beef shank
  2 pounds shoulder of lamb
  1 pig's foot
1½ pounds shoulder butt of pork
  1 pig's tail *or* 1 pound oxtail (trimmed of fat)
A bouquet garni (bay leaf, thyme, celery, leek greens,
    parsley
  2 large leeks, trimmed and washed, the white parts
    only
  2 medium onions, chopped
Salt and pepper
  1 bottle good-quality Riesling wine
  1 tablespoon red wine vinegar
  6 medium all-purpose potatoes

Flour, water, oil for the sealing paste
A strip of clean sheeting

Fit the beef shanks, the shoulder of lamb (trimmed of fat but left in its entirety as much as possible), the whole pig's foot, the trimmed shoulder of pork, and the pig or oxtail into a ceramic or stainless mixing bowl. Bury the bouquet garni in the center of the meats. Add the sliced leek whites and chopped onions and season well. Pour over the bottle of wine, the vinegar, and enough extra water so that the meats are almost covered. Turn the ingredients well with the hands, then cover the bowl with plastic wrap and leave to marinate in the refrigerator for 24 to 36 hours.

Bring a pot of salted water to a boil. Fish the pig's foot and tail or oxtail out of the marinade and let them blanch in the water for about 8 minutes. (This process helps cleanse the meat and allows the skins to tighten and firm so that they do not disintegrate when baked.) Drain well. Strain out the solids from the marinade and reserve the liquid.

Peel the potatoes and cut them into ¼-inch-thick slices. Spread the slices out and wipe them with paper toweling to remove some of their starch. Layer half the potatoes into an earthenware *poêlon* or enameled iron casserole (either dish must have a tight-fitting cover). Arrange the meats and vegetables in the center, then place the remaining potatoes on top. Reserving the bouquet garni, pour the marinade juices over the potatoes. Pluck the bay leaf and a sprig of thyme or parsley from the bouquet and place them on top of the potatoes for a decorative touch. Cover the dish.

Mix 3 tablespoons of flour with 1 teaspoon of oil and enough water to form a glue-like paste. Cut a 2-inch-wide strip of cloth to fit the circumference of the dish. Dip the cloth in the paste until it is totally saturated, then drape it around the lid and tuck it down and over the sides of the pot. Place the *baeckaoffa* in a 325° to 350° oven for a good 3 to 3½ hours. The cloth strip will dry and solidify during baking, thus ensuring that the top does not jar loose and that no steam escapes.

To serve, carry the dish to table, rip the cloth from around the edge, and release the aromatic steam. Serve out portions of potatoes into large soup bowls, then lift out the various meats onto a cutting board and slice them at table into serving portions. Divide the meats among the bowls and finish the servings with more potatoes and broth.

SERVES 5 TO 7

Perhaps nowhere in literature is there a more evocative description of food as a source of comforting stability and harmonious unity with things past, present, and future, than in Virginia Woolf's *To the Lighthouse*. It would, of course, involve a stew. In this excerpt, Mrs. Ramsay gives a dinner party and serves a "perfect triumph" of a *boeuf en daube*.

. . . an exquisite scent of olives and oil and juice rose from the great brown dish as Marthe, with a little flourish, took the cover off. The cook had spent three days over that dish. And she must take great care, Mrs. Ramsay thought, diving into the soft mass, to choose a specially tender piece for William Bankes. And she peered into the dish, with its shiny walls and its confusion of savoury brown and yellow meats and its bay leaves and its wine, and thought. This will celebrate the occasion. . . .

And at this moment, "Everything seemed possible. Everything seemed right" to Mrs. Ramsay and a great feeling of security rose within her.

. . . it arose, she thought, looking at them all eating there, from husband and children and friends; all of which rising in this profound stillness (she was helping William Bankes to one very small piece more, and peered into the depths of the earthenware pot) seemed now for no special reason to stay there like a smoke, like a fume rising upwards, holding them safe together. Nothing need be said; nothing could be said. There it was, all around them. It partook, she felt, carefully helping Mr. Bankes to a specially tender piece, of eternity; as she had already felt about something different once before that afternoon; there is a coherence in things, a stability; something, she meant, is immune from change, and shines out (she glanced at the window with its ripple of reflected lights) in the face of the flowing, the fleeting, the spectral, like a ruby; so that again tonight she had the feeling she had had once today, already, of peace, of rest. Of such moments, she thought, the thing is made that endures.

"Yes," she assured William Bankes, "there is plenty for everybody."

OXTAIL DAUBE

About 3 pounds oxtail
A large handful of parsley
 2 garlic cloves
 1 tablespoon mixed dried herbs (thyme,
    oregano, savory, etc.)
 3 large onions, cut in thick slices
 2 carrots, scraped and sliced
Salt, pepper, allspice
 3 cups red wine
 2 tablespoons cognac
⅓ cup red wine vinegar
 2 tablespoons olive oil
A bouquet garni (parsley, celery stalk, bay leaf,
    a 2-inch piece of dried orange peel)
A small handful black Niçoise olives, for garnish

Chopped parsley, for garnish

AS A SIDE DISH :

Small quality pasta, either homemade spaghetti *or*
    elbow macaroni, shells, bows, etc, *or*
Pulled Bread (see page 26) dipped in fat from
    the daube and browned in the oven

Trim the oxtail sections of any overabundant fat. There should
be only a thin encircling of fat around the meat. Mince the
parsley and garlic together and rub it over the meat. Place
the oxtail in a large bowl and add herbs, onions, carrots, seasoning, wine, cognac, and vinegar. Turn the meat to moisten
it well and leave to marinate in the refrigerator from 4 hours
to overnight. (Rearrange the sections during this period so
each has time to remain fully covered with the marinade.)
    Remove the oxtail, strain the marinade liquid into the pot
that will hold the stew (preferably an earthenware casserole,

but any kind of enameled iron pot will also work) and reserve the solids. Bring the marinade to a boil and reduce by half.

Pat the meat sections dry. Heat the olive oil in a sauté pan, add the oxtail, and let the sections brown. Remove them from the pan, then sauté the carrots and onions from the marinade until lightly browned. Place meat and vegetables into the reduced marinade juices, nestle the bouquet garni into their midst, pour over enough boiling water to just skim the surface of the ingredients, and cover the pot tightly. Let the daube simmer gently for about 3½ hours in a 325° oven.

When the cooking is finished, skim all fat from the surface of the stew. (If, at this point, the juices seem at all watery, they should be drawn off with a bulb baster and put to boil until reduced to an unctuous and lightly coating consistency.) Serve the daube, sprinkled with garnishing parsley and olives, from its stewing pot. Place pasta or bread in large soup bowls and ladle meat, vegetables, and juices out at table.

SERVES 4 TO 6

IRISH STEW

An Irish stew in Ireland is made with mutton. Lamb will produce a taste more to Americans' liking.

    2 pounds lamb (breast, shoulder, neck), cut into
        generous 2-inch cubes of meat, with no fat
    ¼ cup flour
    Salt and pepper
    3 tablespoons olive oil or peanut oil
    1½ cups sliced onions
    2 cups peeled, sliced, all-purpose potatoes
    1 cup peeled, sliced turnips
    A bouquet garni (bay leaf, celery stalk, thyme, parsley)
    Chopped parsley

Pat the sections of lamb dry with paper toweling. Give the meat a good dredging in seasoned flour. Place the meat in a small paper bag, add flour, some salt and pepper, and give the bag several shakes.

Heat the oil in a large sauté pan and when it is quite hot, add the meat and allow it to sear and brown lightly on all sides. Add the onions and continue to cook them until they begin to soften and absorb some of the meat's caramelized brownings.

In a heavy casserole, place first a layer of sliced potatoes and turnips. Then add the meat and onions and bury the bouquet garni in the central depths; place the remaining turnips and potatoes on top.

Add just enough water so that the contents of the dish are well covered. Season again with salt and pepper, then bring the dish to a boil. Regulate the heat to a simmer, cover the pot and cook, either on top of the stove or in a 375° oven, for about 1½ hours.

At the end of this time, the potatoes and turnips will have thickened the loose dish into a stew, bathing and coating the solid meat with their rich, rendered starch. Sprinkle the parsley on top of the stew and serve from the cooking pot into deep, heated dishes.

SERVES 4 TO 6

MARINATED CHICKEN IN FRICASSEE

A particularly flavorful fricassee, with the uplift of wine, vinegar, and herbs to flavor and enhance the lightly bound sauce. If this same stew is prepared with a substitution of veal or lamb, it would be called a blanquette. The theory of the dish is then an important and versatile one, a technique that should be committed to memory. The fricassee/blanquette can contain additions of pearl onions softened by a long stewing in butter or small whole mushrooms rapidly tossed in butter.

FOR THE MARINADE:

    2 garlic cloves, minced
    3 shallots, minced
A bay leaf
    2 tablespoons chopped parsley
    ¼ teaspoon dry, or several sprigs fresh, thyme
Salt, pepper, nutmeg
    1 tablespoon cognac
    1½ cups dry white wine
    1 tablespoon red wine vinegar

A 3-pound chicken, cut into serving pieces
    3 tablespoons unsalted butter
    3 egg yolks
    ⅓ cup heavy cream
A pinch of sugar
Chopped parsley, for garnish

Combine the elements of the marinade in a mixing bowl. Place the chicken portions, shriven of any pockets of excess fat and blotted dry, into the marinade. Mix the pieces with your hands so that the liquid and herbs impregnate all surfaces of the meat, then cover the dish and refrigerate for 36 to 48 hours. (A few times during this interval, move the chicken and turn it about so that all pieces remain moist.)

Remove the chicken from the marinade and blot the sections well. Melt 3 tablespoons of butter in a sauté pan and fry the pieces until they are a nice brown. Place the browned portions on a serving platter as they are finished.

Using a bulb baster or paper towels, draw off as much fat as possible from the sauté pan, then pour the marinade into the pan and allow its acid to deglaze the caramelized pan juices. Stir with a wooden spatula to scrape up any deposits.

Place the chicken back into the pan, add ½ cup of water, cover the pan, and cook at a simmer until the chicken is tender (about 30 minutes). Remove the chicken to a heated platter and keep warm. Strain the cooking liquid, then return it to the same pan and bring to a simmer.

Mix together the egg yolks, cream, and sugar in a small bowl. Start whisking in small spoonfuls of the hot liquid, then pour the warmed eggs into the pan. Shake the pan, stir the juices rapidly, and they should soon thicken into a loose, coating sauce. Do not allow the sauce to boil. Check carefully for seasoning, then pour the sauce immediately over the chicken, strew on parsley, and serve (perhaps with rice or noodles).

SERVES 6

MATELOTE

A variety of fish stews called *matelotes* (that French word also meaning "sailor") exists in the different provinces of France. Sometimes made with white wine, sometimes red, the stews consist of slices of fish (either sea or fresh water) or eel cooked in wine which has been aromatized then thickened with *beurre manié* (kneaded butter) or, less frequently, egg yolks. It is a fine and hearty dish, garnished as it is by small onions, mushrooms, garlic-rubbed croutons, even crisp lardoons of pork. This particular version, from the Franche-Comté region, most often contains carp, pike, or mullet.

4 serving portions (slices or filets) of any fresh fish or eel
1 large onion, cut in thin rings
3 tablespoons unsalted butter
2 level tablespoons flour
2 cups red wine
1 garlic clove, minced
2 shallots, minced
Salt and pepper

1 teaspoon minced dried thyme and parsley, mixed
A bay leaf
1 cup sliced mushrooms
3 egg yolks
About ½ cup heavy cream
Minced parsley and large croutons, rubbed over on
   either side with a cut garlic clove, for garnish

In a large sauté pan, cook the onions in 2 tablespoons of butter over medium-low heat until they turn a straw gold. Sprinkle the flour over the onions and continue stirring them for another few minutes so that the flour, forming a soft roux, cooks and disappears into the butter. Stir the wine into the onions, and then 1 cup of water. Add the garlic, shallots, seasoning, and herbs, then allow the mixture to simmer, uncovered, for 20 minutes.

Add the slices of fish, cover the pan, and let them stew over low heat for 15 minutes. (Eel will need to persist for 30 minutes.)

As the fish is cooking, sauté the cup of mushrooms rapidly in the remaining tablespoon of butter and make the croutons.

When the fish is done, remove the slices to heated dinner plates or individual gratins and keep them warm while you thicken the sauce. Fish out the bay leaf. Mix the egg yolks with the cream in a small bowl, then slowly add some of the hot purple sauce to the eggs. Pour the warmed eggs into the wine sauce and shake the pan back and forth over medium heat for a brief time until the sauce thickens again (do not allow it to boil). The consistency should be that of a medium thin white sauce. Thin with more cream if necessary. Pour the sauce over the fish, garnish each portion with mushrooms and parsley, and arrange the croutons at the side.

Note: if you have very fresh fish (that is caught that day), it is nice to follow that old-fashioned English technique of "crimping" fish or eel before putting it to stew. Simply soak the slices covered in ice cold water for 30 minutes before cooking. This stiffens the flesh, even crisps it somewhat if we can stretch that word, so that the slices remain particularly firm throughout their stew.

SERVES 4

THE POT-AU-FEU PRINCIPLE

In that great and famous stew the *pot-au-feu*, which graces so many French tables of a Sunday, we have a dish which Escoffier always maintained proclaimed the very essence of the family in its unifying concept. Once again, it is a dish providing a first course consommé in which is cooked the beef and vegetables eaten as a second course. Sometimes a stuffed chicken (such as that on page 155) is added to the dish, in which case the *pot-au-feu* becomes a *poule-au-pot*. To the consommé can be added small-grained pasta and toasts with melted Parmesan cheese. And always accompanying the meats, which are sliced at table, are cornichons, mustards, horseradish sauce, and a dish of coarse salt so that one can make rough sandwiches, if so desired, at table.

Throwing traditional ingredients to the wind, it is also possible to think of a *pot-au-feu* in seafood terms, and in so doing, one comes up with a dish much more rapid in its composition than the beef-laden relative, which must stew a good four hours before its meat is tender enough to be eaten. In a "pot-au-seafood," a rich fish stock is prepared. A large fish is poached in it; perhaps some shrimp in shells and mussels are added at the last moment. Leeks, celery, potatoes (all complementary to fish) are cooked separately. The fish soup, floating with croutons, is eaten first, then a large platter brought to table on which is centered the fish and, around it in piles, the other seafoods and vegetables. For condiments, a homemade tartar sauce.

The following recipe upholds tradition, however.

POT-AU-FEU

    2 pounds rump steak
    1 pound shank bones, cut in 2-inch sections
    1 quart Homemade Chicken Soup Base (see page 94)
    Salt, peppercorns
    4 medium carrots, scraped
    4 medium leeks, the white lengths only
    2 medium turnips, peeled and cut in half
    4 medium onions, peeled and each stuck with a clove
    A bouquet garni (parsley, bay leaf, thyme, leek greens)
    ½ cup small-grained pasta
    Dried bread slices or croutons
    A wedge of Parmesan

TO ACCOMPANY:

    Mustards, cornichons, coarse salt

Rinse the rump steak. Tie the bones up in a little bundle of cheesecloth so that the agitation of cooking will not wash away the tender marrows.

Place the piece of rump steak in a large heavy pot. Cover it with the stock and 1 quart of cold water. Bring the liquid slowly to a boil, and just as the boil breaks, skim the surface. Add a small glass of cold water, bring to the boil again, and skim anew until no scum remains. Let the meat simmer, over a very low flame indeed, for 3 hours.

At the end of this time, add the bones, peppercorns, carrots, leeks, turnips, onions, and bouquet garni. Continue simmering (remember that boiling will only lead to tough meat) for another hour. Check the water level and add more during this time if necessary.

Remove the meat and bones from the pot and place them on a heated platter. Lift out the vegetables and place them around the meat. Hold the platter in a warming oven. Skim off some of the fat from the surface of the broth (leave an enriching thin layer, however). Drop the pasta into the broth and when it softens, after a short time, ladle the soup into bowls and serve it with a bowl of croutons and a wedge of cheese, allowing people to grate at table the amount they might wish on their soup.

Serve the meat, vegetables, and bones (each person must suck out the luscious marrow) as the second course. Cut the meat into serving portions at table and hand around a small tray holding mustards, cornichons, and coarse salt.

SERVES 4

NEW ENGLAND BOILED DINNER WITH BEEF SUET DUMPLINGS

To solidify this chapter, a recipe for a New England Boiled Dinner (or Corned Beef and Cabbage, as it is more prosaically known). It is, in effect, a dry *pot-au-feu*, with no attempt to make a soup from the briny cooking juices of the pickled beef. In all other ways it resembles its paternal dish, and it should be accompanied with all those same mustards and pickles that will even better complement corned beef.

A 3- to 3½-pound brisket of corned beef
A 1½-pound savoy cabbage, quartered
    4 medium carrots, scraped and stemmed
1½ cups pearl onions, peeled, with a small X
      cut in the stem ends
    4 medium turnips, heavy peel removed
    8 small new potatoes, peeled
    4 tablespoons unsalted butter
A pinch of sugar
Salt, peppercorns
    1 tablespoon chopped parsley

FOR THE DUMPLINGS:

About 4 ounces beef suet, minced with a cleaver
2 cups flour
A scant teaspoon of salt
Pepper
1 tablespoon minced parsley

Chopped parsley, for garnish

Rinse the corned beef under cold running water, then place the meat in a bowl and cover it with cool water. Let the meat soak for an hour to partially remove its brininess. Drain well, then place the meat in a pot, cover generously with cold water, and slowly bring to a low boil. Skim until no more scum appears, then lower the heat, cover the pot, and let the meat cook for a good 4 hours at a bare simmer. Keep the meat covered as necessary by adding more water.

Core the cabbage, remove any damaged outer leaves, and cut out obvious tough ribs. Bring a pot of salted water to the boil. Tie up the cabbage in some cheesecloth, then parboil for 10 minutes. Change the water and cook the cabbage until tender. At the same time, cook the carrots and onions in boiling water for 10 minutes.

A half hour before the beef has finished cooking, put the turnips (cut into quarters) and the potatoes on to boil. Melt 2 tablespoons of butter in a frying pan. Add the onions and carrots, a pinch of sugar, seasoning, and a few tablespoons of water. Cover the pan and let the vegetables cook until tender, allowing them to glaze nicely in the process. Place the bundled cabbage in with the beef to reheat. When the potatoes and turnips are just tender, drain them well, then put them back in their saucepan with 2 tablespoons of butter, some seasoning, and chopped parsley. Keep them warm until needed.

To make the dumplings, work together the beef suet, flour, salt, pepper, and parsley with your fingers until you have a flaky substance of oatmeal consistency. Bind the dough together with about ¾ cup of ice water—the final mixture will have the consistency of a completely moistened but not soggy pie dough. On a floured surface, roll small pieces of dough, each the size of a fifty-cent piece, into balls. Drop the dumplings onto the surface of the simmering beef, cover the pan, and let them steam for 10 minutes. Warm a large serving platter.

To serve, lift off the dumplings and place them at one end of the platter. Remove the beef, cut it into slices, and arrange them down the middle. Place the potatoes and turnips at the other end, then garnish the long edges with glazed carrots, onions, and cabbage. Over all, sprinkle chopped parsley.

SERVES 4 TO 6

Main Courses

THREE PRETTY PASTAS

THE FIRST PASTA RECIPE that follows is an excellent dish for entertaining economically but elegantly, and if you enjoy finishing off a dish at table, this one can be so compiled. With each of the three binding sauces given, one should keep in mind that the more sauce served in relationship to pasta, the more refined becomes the dish. A handful of homemade fettuccini with an abundance of other solids, binding cream and cheese so that, in effect the pasta is used as the excuse on which to drape a sauce, can easily be served in individual gratins as a first course. (I think with particular fondness of a small round casserole offered at the restaurant Hiely in Avignon which contains delicate pasta, crayfish, scallops, and mussels all knee-deep in a Nantua sauce.) Use more pasta in proportion to the sauce and you still will have a marvelously flavorful dish, but one at once more economical and less sumptuous.

I should only add that homemade pasta, with any of these preparations, is to be hoped for above any commercial product, but if you must use a purchased pasta, it is best to buy an Italian-made brand such as DeCecco.

PASTA IL FORNO

FOR THE TOMATO SAUCE:

> 3 tablespoons mixed olive oil and butter
> 1 large onion, chopped
> 1 carrot, scraped and diced
> 2 garlic cloves, minced
> 1 teaspoon mixed thyme and oregano
> A 28-ounce can of crushed tomatoes in purée *or*
>   a 28-ounce can of whole tomatoes, half drained
> A handful of chopped parsley
> A bay leaf
> ¼ teaspoon sugar
> Salt, pepper, a touch of cayenne

> About 1½ pounds eggplant (choose several
>   long, thin specimens)
> 3 to 4 medium zucchini, again, long, small, thin
> 3 medium, fresh tomatoes
> 1 cup heavy cream
> 4 to 5 tablespoons olive oil
> Homemade pasta (based on 1 whole egg plus 3 egg
>   yolks and cut in noodle width) *or* about ¾ pound of
>   purchased fettuccini
> 1 cup fresh-grated Parmesan cheese
> 4 tablespoons unsalted butter
> Salt and pepper
> Chopped parsley

To make the tomato sauce, heat the butter and oil in a sauce-pan and add onion, carrot, and garlic. Cook over medium heat until the vegetables are soft but unbrowned. Add herbs, tomatoes, parsley, bay leaf, sugar, and seasoning, then cover the sauce and let it simmer for 40 minutes. Press the sauce through a sieve so that it is perfectly smooth.

Prepare the vegetables. Wash and dry the eggplants and zucchini. With a paring knife, cut off the peels of the vegetables in ⅓-inch-thick strips. Cut these peels into julienne strips about 2 inches long and ¼ inch wide. With a tomato knife, cut the skin from the tomatoes and trim it also into julienne size. (Reserve all vegetable interiors for another use.)

Have the tomato sauce heated and the cream half whipped to a thickened sludge.

Bring a large pot of salted water to the boil for the pasta.

Heat 3 tablespoons of olive oil in a very large sauté pan or saucepan (it should be large enough to hold the entire finished dish). Sauté the eggplant peel first, adding enough oil to keep it from sticking. When the eggplant is just tender, throw in the zucchini peel and continue cooking, shaking the pan to mix and move the elements. Cook the pasta, and just as the vegetables and noodles are *al dente,* drain the pasta well, then add it to the vegetables.

Immediately add the cheese, tomato strips, tomato sauce, whipped cream, butter, and seasoning (grind on plenty of fresh pepper). Lift and turn the pasta with two wooden spoons or forks, all the time keeping it over low heat, until the elements are nicely melted, the sauce smooth and plentiful. Scatter parsley over the top and serve at once from the pan.

SERVES 6 AS A MAIN COURSE

Note: for entertaining, prepare the tomato sauce, grate the cheese, and pare the vegetables ahead of time. (The interiors of the vegetables will have to be used another time in ratatouille; or slice them, fry them, and make a gratin of layered tomatoes, vegetables, ricotta, cream, and cheese.)

To do this dish at table, as it is done at the Ristorante Il Forno in Venice, simply have situated around one the various bowls containing tomato sauce, cream, cheese, and butter. Hold the cooked pasta in a strainer set in a bowl of hot water. Sauté the vegetables over a hot plate, then combine with the other ingredients for all to see.

PASTA WITH CHICKEN LIVERS, ONIONS, AND CREAM

FOR THE SAUCE:

4 tablespoons unsalted butter
2 large onions, chopped
5 chicken livers
4 shallots, minced
1 cup heavy cream
2 sage leaves
2 tablespoons chopped parsley
A 28-ounce can of tomatoes, completely drained, *or*
    4 large fresh tomatoes, the flesh cut into strips
Salt and pepper
Homemade pasta (based on 1 whole egg plus 2 egg yolks) *or* 8 ounces of any purchased pasta of choice (fettuccini, spaghetti, shells, etc.)
4 tablespoons unsalted butter, cut in dice
A wedge of Parmesan cheese

Melt 2 tablespoons of butter in a large frying pan and cook the onions over very low heat until they are completely tender but unbrowned. Remove the onions and turn up the heat. Quickly sauté the chicken livers, allowing them to remain a rosy pink on the interior. (If you are a fancier of chicken livers, more can be added than this recipe calls for. The given amount will add only a slight, meaty quality to the sauce.)

Combine the livers and onions and purée them together (adding a touch of the cream to smooth the process) in blender or food processor.

Melt the remaining 2 tablespoons of butter in a saucepan and cook the shallots until limp. Add cream, the onion purée, sage leaves, parsley, tomato strips, and seasoning. Let the sauce simmer and reduce over medium-low heat until the cream thickens slightly. Remove sage.

Cook the pasta *al dente,* then mix the sauce and the diced butter into the pasta and serve at once. Place a wedge of Parmesan and a grater on table for those who wish to add a garnish of cheese.

This dish is less of a company production than the preceding one.

SERVES 4

ORIENTAL PASTA WITH SHRIMP

Oriental noodles, sold fresh in the produce departments of many grocery stores, are not more difficult to make than Italian-style pasta if you have a machine. Chinese noodles may or may not contain egg; if they don't, the ingredients are simply water, a soft flour (all-purpose flour with a bit of cornstarch added will do), and salt. The noodle dough should be rolled in a light dusting of cornstarch before it passes through the machine. Knead the dough until smooth, then work it down through the kneading process to three notches from the end. Cut the dough on the thinner blade. A homemade egg pasta will taste barely different, however.

8 to 10 dried Oriental (wood) mushrooms
½ pound shelled shrimp
¼ teaspoon salt
2 teaspoons cornstarch
3 scallions, shredded
1 garlic clove, minced
½ cup fresh green peas, or, if necessary, frozen peas
A handful of snowpeas, strings removed
1 small sweet red pepper, cut in thin strips
4 fresh water chestnuts, peeled and sliced thin
(optional)

FOR THE SAUCE:

⅔ cup sieved tomato sauce
3 tablespoons soy sauce
1 tablespoon rice or white wine vinegar
1 cup mushroom-soaking water
Salt and cayenne pepper
1 tablespoon sugar
2 tablespoons sesame oil

⅓ cup peanut oil
1 tablespoon cornstarch diluted with
2 tablespoons water
About 1 pound fresh noodles

Soak the dried mushrooms for 30 minutes in cool water. Drain and cut out the tough stem centers. Cut the mushrooms into thick shreds and reserve the soaking liquid.

Rinse the shrimp well under running water. Drain, then sprinkle them with ¼ teaspoon salt and 2 teaspoons cornstarch. Turn and mix well, then let them sit for 20 minutes.

Prepare all the vegetables and place them on separate small dishes.

Combine all the ingredients for the sauce.

Cook the noodles until they are soft, in a pot of boiling,

salted water. Drain well, then sprinkle them immediately with 2 tablespoons of peanut oil.

Place the remaining oil in a hot wok or a large, heavy sauté pan and heat until very hot. Fry the shrimp until they are a bright orange. Strain out the shrimp and, in the oil that remains, fry the scallions and garlic briefly, then add quickly the mushrooms, peas, snowpeas, red pepper strips, and water chestnuts. Throw ¼ cup of water into the pan, cover, and let the vegetables steam briefly until barely tender. Test by tasting.

Pour in the sauce and bring to a boil. Add noodles and shrimp. Lift and turn the noodles with two wooden spoons or forks until everything is well mixed. Continue cooking the noodles over heat. Stir the cornstarch and water together again (the cornstarch will have settled to the bottom) and pour it into the noodles. As soon as the sauce thickens lightly, dish the noodles into soup plates.

SERVES 4

SEAFOOD AND SPINACH CANNELLONI

This is a good and rapidly made dish that can be composed ahead and refrigerated for a few hours before cooking. If time is limited, make 10 large cannelloni wrappers. For a more delicate presentation, take the time to prepare 20 wrappers.

FOR THE PASTA:

1 egg
Pinch of salt
Flour (a quick mixing variety) like Wondra
2 tablespoons oil

> 1 slice fresh white bread, trimmed of crust
> ½ pound shelled shrimp *or* flounder filet (skinless)
> 5 ounces fresh spinach (cooked, squeezed dry,
>   and chopped)
> 1 tablespoon chopped parsley
> 1 egg
> 3 tablespoons unsalted butter
> Salt, pepper, nutmeg
> 1 pint heavy cream
> Fine, dry bread crumbs

Make the pasta. Break the egg into a small bowl, add the salt, and stir until well mixed. Start stirring in flour until the dough becomes compact enough to gather up into a mass. Turn the mass out onto a floured surface and knead the paste, adding more flour as necessary, until the dough is no longer sticky, and it feels elastic and softly smooth. Cover the dough with plastic wrap and let it rest for 30 minutes.

Roll the dough out very thin by hand or run it through a pasta machine. (Little kneading should be necessary. Simply thin it progressively down to the thinnest opening.) Cut the pasta into 10 strips (for large cannelloni) or for a more delicate dish cut these strips across to make 20 pieces.

Bring a pot of salted water to the boil. Add 2 tablespoons of oil to the surface so the pasta will not stick together. Cook the pasta (in 3 or 4 batches) for about 1 minute. Lift out the pasta on a strainer, run it under cold water, and spread the portions out flat on a kitchen towel to drain.

For the filling, soak the bread briefly in cold water and wring it dry. Combine bread, fish, spinach, parsley, egg, 2 tablespoons butter, seasoning, and ½ cup cream and purée in a food processor or, bit by bit, in a blender.

Lightly butter a large gratin dish or baking tin, and preheat the oven to 350°. Divide the filling among the pasta squares. Align the fish down one edge, then roll the pasta into tubes.

Place the cannelloni in the buttered dish. Pour all the remaining cream over the pasta and top each cannelloni with some dry bread crumbs. Cut the remaining tablespoon of butter into thin shavings and place them on the crumbs. Bake for 35 to 40 minutes.

SERVES 5

SEAFOOD RISOTTO

Seafood Risotto (any risotto for that matter), is a greatly soothing composition that seems, in winter time, the perfect consolation for inclement weather. The following recipe, with its cream addition, is not the traditional way in which to form a risotto, but I do admire the way in which the cream expands upon the already exuded starch and binds, with the last addition of Parmesan, into a comforting mess. This is a dish that must be "intuited." If clams or mussels are added, for instance, they can render, upon opening, a tremendous amount of liquid which must be reckoned with as the dish composes itself. There must be no watery quality to the finished product—just a dish smooth to the point of seeming sauced. Read this recipe carefully beforehand. Risottos invite a careful watchfulness and a keen sense of timing.

½ pound shrimp, in the shell
1 tablespoon olive oil
5 tablespoons unsalted butter
½ pound filet of flounder or trout, skinless
1 medium onion, chopped
½ cup dry white wine
⅔ cup arborio rice
A large pinch of powdered saffron
A 10-ounce can of tomatoes, well drained, the tomato
  mass squeezed dry and chopped
Several mussels, clams, or sliced scallops, or
  a mixture of same
Salt and pepper
Heavy cream
½ cup fresh-grated Parmesan cheese
Chopped parsley

In a heavy, medium-large sauté pan (the risotto will be presented in its cooking dish at table), sauté the shrimp in a tablespoon of oil and one of butter. When the shrimp are cooked, the shells a vivid pink, remove the shrimp to a bowl, add a bit more butter as necessary, and fry the fish. Remove the fish and, without cleaning the pan, add the onion and ¼ cup white wine. Scrape the bottom of the pan with a wooden spatula to loosen any congealed bits, then reduce the heat and let the onion simmer until tender. Add the rice and stir it continually until it attains a milky white opacity.

Bring a small pan containing 2 cups of salted water to a simmer. Add saffron.

Add the remaining white wine to the rice and keep the heat very low. The rice will gradually absorb the liquid and as it does, add a ladle of simmering saffroned water to the rice. From now on, as the rice absorbs, swells, grows, a continuous supply of liquid must be added so that the rice remains moist. As soon as one ladle fully disappears, replenish the dish with another.

After the rice has cooked for 15 minutes, add the tomatoes
—they will also produce liquid. Stir frequently and, toward
the end of cooking, constantly, so that the rice moves about
the pan in restless effort to escape the sticking point.

Flake the fish apart with a fork. Peel the shrimp. Place all
shrimp shells, any juices, and 4 tablespoons of butter in a
food processor, blender, or mortar. Grind the shells until
pulverized, then place the mass in a small sieve and press all
the lovely pink shrimp butter through the wire. Scrape the
butter from the back of the sieve and set aside.

If the dish is to contain shellfish, cook the mussels or clams
in a separate pot. Place them in a saucepan, splash a small
amount of water on them, and let them steam open over heat.
When they are cooked, remove them from the pan, strain the
juices (which should be pure sea essence) through a fine
cloth, and add them to the risotto. Add any scallops directly
to the rice. You will need to estimate time carefully, gaging
the time for the seafood into the entire risotto schedule of 25
to 30 minutes cooking time.

When the risotto has cooked for about 20 minutes, make a
moisture addition of ½ cup heavy cream. Stir continually now
(a wooden fork does the least grain-breaking damage).

Observe and taste the rice. Season if necessary. When it is
moist, just tender, melting, add shrimp, cheese, flaked fish,
shrimp butter, some chopped parsley and a bit more cream as
necessary. Stir lightly, place any shellfish on top, sprinkle with
more parsley, then cover the dish and let it rest, off the heat,
for five minutes.

Carry the dish to table and serve from the cooking utensil.
The final consistency should be loose and creamy, but just
short of being able to move and run on the plate.

SERVES 4 TO 5

SAFFRONED GRATIN OF LEEKS AND SCALLOPS

FOR THE COURT BOUILLON:

2 cups dry white wine
1 cup water
1 large carrot, sliced
A few sprigs of fresh thyme or 1 teaspoon dried thyme
A bay leaf
Salt
¼ teaspoon peppercorns

4 medium-large leeks
1 pound scallops
3 tablespoons unsalted butter
Juice of ½ lemon
5 ounces small mushrooms, trimmed and wiped clean
1 generous tablespoon flour
¼ teaspoon powdered saffron
⅔ cup heavy cream
1 cup dry bread crumbs
½ cup grated Parmesan cheese

Combine all ingredients for the court bouillon in a stainless steel pan and bring to a simmer. Slice the tops of the leeks off at the point where the green begins. Trim the ends and remove an outer layer of leaf. Slit the leeks lengthwise to within 2 inches of the root. Gently spread the leaves apart and rinse well under cold water. When the stock is simmering, add the leeks and let them cook, covered, for 20 minutes.

Remove leeks from the broth, pressing them carefully to remove excess water, and set aside. Rinse and dry the scallops and place them in the court bouillon. Cover and poach for 8 minutes. Place a large sieve over a bowl and turn the scallops into it to drain. Reserve the court bouillon.

In a small saucepan, melt 2 tablespoons butter and add

lemon juice and a small ladleful of bouillon. Over high heat, add the mushrooms and quickly cook them until they give off their juices. Remove mushrooms with a slotted spoon, regulate heat to low, and whisk in the flour, stirring continuously until a soft roux has formed. Let the roux cook over very low heat for 2 or 3 minutes, then slowly whisk in the rest of the court bouillon. Add saffron. Let the sauce simmer, unstirred, for 15 minutes. (Twice during this period the thin crusted film which will form over the surface should be pulled to the side of the pan and lifted off.)

Stir in the cream and let the sauce cook, stirring from time to time, at medium heat for another 15 minutes, or until it has thickened to the consistency of a medium-thick white sauce. Taste for seasoning.

Preheat the oven to 350°. Lightly butter a 10-inch gratin dish. Cut the leeks into 2-inch sections and, if they are large, slice the scallops across into thin rounds. Mix leeks, scallops, and mushrooms in the dish. Season, and strain the sauce over the top. Mix bread crumbs and cheese together, scatter them over the surface, and dot the crumbs with the remaining tablespoon of butter cut in thin shavings. Bake for 25 minutes, then turn on the broiler and briefly brown the crumbs. Serve with an attendant rice pilaf.

SERVES 4

BREADCRUSTED FISH WITH VEGETABLE STUFFING

A pretty presentation, with the thinnest of bread-crumb crusts encasing a fish whose boned interior is filled with gentle vegetables.

2 tablespoons unsalted butter
2 medium carrots, scraped and cut into dice
2 celery stalks, strings removed, diced
1 medium onion, chopped
¼ teaspoon thyme
1 tablespoon parsley, chopped fine
Salt and pepper
4 ounces mushrooms, cleaned and chopped
A lemon wedge
A 2–2½ pound fish, neatly gutted, whole and fresh
   (trout or bluefish will be easiest to bone)
Fine, dry bread crumbs
1 egg, beaten
Melted, clarified butter
Lemon wedges and parsley or watercress, to garnish

In a frying pan, melt 2 tablespoons of butter. Add carrots, celery, onion, thyme, parsley and seasoning, and let the vegetables stew over low heat for 20 minutes. Add the mushrooms and a squeeze of lemon, and continue cooking the mixture for another 15 minutes.

Prepare the fish for stuffing. Place the fish on its side, facing away from you. Insert a small, sharp knife straight down into the fish at a point one inch from the beginning of the tail. Draw the knife along the backbone toward the head, using short, smooth cutting motions and feeling always along the backbone of the fish. (Do not, of course, plunge in the knife so far that it cuts through the other side.) When the one side of the central bone is completely exposed to within an inch or so of the gills, turn the fish over and cut the bone free along the other side. When the flesh is separated from the bone, take a pair of poultry scissors and snip out the bone at the tail and again toward the head so that the fish presents a boneless, open pocket, with tail and head intact, and the central body free and ready to accept stuffing. Rinse the fish well and pat it dry with paper toweling. Season the interior.

Spoon the vegetables into the fish and, using a trussing needle and kitchen thread, run 4 or 5 large running stitches along the top to enclose the stuffing.

Choose a large gratin or baking sheet that can hold the fish. Butter the dish generously and scatter dry crumbs over the portion where the fish will rest. Place the fish on the dish. Brush it over on the top side with beaten egg, then pat dry crumbs over the fish and press them firmly into a good thick layer with a dry, clean knife blade. Sprinkle melted butter over the crumbs until they are slightly damp. Press them down again, then using the rounded tip of a spoon, make indentions over the creature, starting from the head and working back, in fish scale pattern. Clean away any excess crumbs.

Place the fish in a 350° oven and bake it for about 40–45 minutes. During this time, it should be basted frequently with clarified buter. Let the crust turn a good gold, but protect the tail and head from overbrowning, if necessary, by placing on them a portion of aluminum foil.

Serve the fish, surrounded by lemon slices and greenery, from the gratin; or transfer it from the baking sheet to a serving platter by running a flexible spatula under the fish then easing it off onto the dish.

SERVES 4–6

Note: to make clarified butter, place a stick of unsalted butter in a small pan and melt it over low heat. Do not allow to brown. Spoon off any foam on the surface then let the butter solidify in the refrigerator or freezer. Lift off the hard butter and wipe it clean. This is now clarified butter. The still liquid pale white whey can be discarded.

Frequently in cooking, the simplest dish is the most comforting and, at the same time, the most common. I am thinking of the good wives of France and the gentle, well-known dishes named and garnished in their honor. No fancy *à la financière* or *à la Rothschild*, no foie gras or truffles, but rather simple potatoes, onions, carrots, that stand the tests of time and digestibility.

The thrifty housekeeper (*ménagère*), the good wife (*bonne femme*), who peel and round potatoes, chop some bacon, slice a few onions, perhaps add mushrooms, and put the lot to braise along with chicken; the baker's wife (*boulangére*), who slices potatoes and onions and meat, layers them in a deep dish, and puts them to bake in her husband's oven; the farmer's wife (*fermière*), and the gardener's good woman (*jardinière*), who braise a vegetable mélange or pull sweet vegetables from the fertile earth, trimming and turning them carefully, then arrange them in piles around the roasted meat. The thrifty miller's wife (*meunière*), who coats a sole in her husband's flour and frys it to inviting brown; and the mariner's wife (*marinière*), selecting from her husband's catch of fish then, compounding fish with seafood, garnishing her dinner dish with a pretty musseled sauce.

SOLE IN THE MANNER OF
THE MARINER'S WIFE

    1 large sole or flounder (a generous 2 pounds),
      trimmed and gutted
    1 stick unsalted butter, chilled
    2 tablespoons shallots, minced
    ½ cup dry white wine
    Salt and pepper
    10 or 12 mussels
    ¼ cup heavy cream
    Chopped parsley and lemon wedges, for garnish

Preheat the oven to 350°.

Rinse the fish and dry it well. In a copper or enameled iron gratin dish large enough to hold the fish, melt 2 tablespoons of butter and add the shallots. Let the shallots cook over low heat until they are limp. Add the wine and ½ cup water, then arrange the fish on top of the shallots. Season well and cover the dish with aluminum foil. Put to bake for 20 minutes.

Scrub the mussels under running water, thoroughly and with a stiff brush. Pull out any portions of whisping beard. After the fish has cooked for 20 minutes, lift off the foil and ring the mussels around the edge. Put the fish back in the oven, uncovered, for another 10 minutes.

Slide the fish onto a heated platter, surround it with mussels in the shell, and hold in a warm oven. Strain off the juices into a saucepan, and reduce them rapidly over a brisk heat. When only a half cup of liquid remains, remove the pan from the heat. Whisk in 6 tablespoons of butter bit by bit and then the cream. Keep the sauce very warm but never so hot that it melts the butter. The sauce should, instead, build into a creamy emulsion. Taste for seasoning.

Intersperse the lemon wedges between the mussels, pour the sauce over the fish, and sprinkle the whole with parsley.
SERVES 4 TO 6

CHICKEN IN THE MANNER OF THE THRIFTY HOUSEWIFE

2½ cups pearl onions
1 small chicken, cut into serving pieces
4 tablespoons flour
Salt and pepper
4 tablespoons unsalted butter
16 small, new potatoes, peeled and rounded
Several sprigs of thyme, or 1 teaspoon leaf thyme
5 or 6 bay leaves
8 lean rashers of bacon
⅓ cup white wine
1 cup mushrooms, minced fine
Chopped parsley

Peel the onions (placing them in a bowl of cold water during peeling facilitates the process). Cut a small "X" in the bottom of each stem end. Bring a pan of salted water to the boil and parboil the onions for one minute. Drain well.

Pat the chicken sections dry with paper toweling. Place the flour and a generous amount of salt and pepper in a paper bag. Add the chicken pieces and give the bag some gentle shakes so that the chicken coats evenly.

In a large pan with a cover, melt 4 tablespoons of butter. When it is hot, add the chicken and sauté the sections until they are nicely browned. Scatter the potatoes, onions and herbs over and around the chicken. In particular, allow the potatoes to reach the bottom of the pan. Place the breast sections of chicken on top so they will not tend to overcook. Season well. Pour ⅓ cup of water over the ingredients, turn down the heat to low, and cover the dish. Let the chicken cook, the vegetables steam, for about 20 minutes. From time to time, uncover the pan, tip it slightly, and baste everything with the buttery juices. (Don't allow the water on the lid to drip back into the dish.)

At the end of 20 minutes, remove the cover, turn up the heat to medium, and allow the water to evaporate until the chicken is cooking in pure fat. Move and shake the pan, rearrange the vegetables, and let the potatoes and onions brown for another 10 minutes.

Fry the bacon strips until crisp.

Have a rustic platter heated, and when the chicken and vegetables are tender and brown, remove them to the dish, the chicken in the center; the vegetables and herbs around the edge; the bacon, broken into pieces, scatter over the lot. Spoon off any fat in the pan, then add the white wine and deglaze, using a wooden spatula to scrape and loosen any congealed juices. Pass the pan juices through a sieve, then put them into a small clean pan and bring to a boil. Add the mushrooms, and when they have cooked, spoon the sauce over the chicken. Scatter chopped parsley over all.

SERVES 4

CHICKEN LOLLIPOPS

A dish of mixed cultural sensibilities featuring a Chinese technique (but a decidedly Provençal flavor) and an amusing shape which children like to gnaw on.

FOR THE FRYING BATTER:

½ cup sifted flour
¼ teaspoon salt
1 tablespoon olive oil
2 egg whites

16 chicken wings
3 tablespoons pitted, chopped black olives
1 small garlic clove
¼ cup dry white wine
2 tablespoons olive oil
1 tablespoon chopped parsley
1 tablespoon mixed dried oregano and thyme
Salt and pepper
1½ quarts peanut oil or olive oil for deep-frying

To make the frying batter, sieve flour and salt into a bowl and make a well in the middle. Add olive oil and ½ cup lukewarm water. Using a whisk, gradually incorporate the flour into the liquid until it is a smooth paste. Cover the bowl with a towel and let rest for 1 hour. Beat the egg whites to firm peaks, fold them into the batter, and use immediately.

The "lollipops" will be formed from the upper "drumstick"

length of wing and stuffed with a fragrant mash of olives. Sever through the "elbow" joint, cutting off the double-boned middle joint and the wingtip. (Reserve these for stock.)

Starting at the smaller, less fleshy end of the bone, cut through the skin and tendons with a sharp knife, then push and scrape the flesh cleanly down the length of the bone toward the "shoulder" end. Using the fingers, pull the mass of meat up and over the bone's end. The wing should now resemble a small lollipop, with a clean bone/stick and a fat rounded mass of meat on top. Trim off any ragged bits of skin.

Chop the olives and garlic clove to a fine mince and stuff a small portion of the mixture into the center of each fleshy wing. Place the wings in a bowl, sprinkle them with wine, olive oil, herbs, and seasoning; leave to marinate for ½ hour.

Heat the oil in a deep-fryer or high-sided pot. Pat the chicken wings dry with paper towels and line a cookie sheet with several layers of paper toweling to receive the fried wings. Test the oil by dropping in a small amount of batter. When it slowly sinks, then bobs sizzling to the surface, the oil is ready. Dip the stuffed ends of the wings into batter and let them fry to a deep golden brown. Do not overcrowd the pan. Remove the wings as they cook, blot gently with paper towels and put them, on the towel-covered cookie sheet, into a warm oven until all are finished.

Serve, if you like, with a small dipping pot of thick, flavorful tomato sauce tangy with cayenne pepper.

MAKES 4 SERVINGS OF 4 WINGS EACH

CHICKEN IN CHICKEN WITH LEMON AND CAPER SAUCE

The following presentation, mounted and dependent on a clay pot meant to hold a chicken, is adaptable to almost any chicken recipe wherein the bird is left whole. It consists of a sculpted, placid, and maternal hen (formed from bread dough) affixed to the upper half of the pot while the lower half roasts and holds a whole bird. The bird is then surrounded by a brood of rice, noodles, or sautéed vegetables.

To make a bread chicken, compact aluminum foil into a smooth semblance of a chicken head and neck. Fix it to the upper half of the clay pot with tape. Make a batch of bread dough from 1½ cups water, 1 teaspoon yeast, ⅓ cup salt, and enough flour to bind into a firm dough. Knead until smooth and let rise for an hour, then punch down. Place the upper half of the clay pot on a baking sheet and mold the top half

of a nesting chicken over its form. (See drawing.) Brush over with egg yolk and water glaze and put immediately into a 325° oven. Let the chicken bake a good hour or until nicely browned. When cool, preserve the bird with polyurethane if desired. For further verisimilitude, form an oval nest from dried herbs and grasses in which the whole "bird" can rest.

The following recipe is basically a plain roasted chicken with bordering rice, but the more complexly stuffed bird in the next recipe can also be presented in this disguise, though the extraneous presentation is not a necessary part of any dish, of course.

A 3½-pound chicken
Salt and pepper
Thyme, a bay leaf
2 tablespoons butter
1 tablespoon capers
⅓ cup pitted, chopped Niçoise olives
2 tablespoons fine-chopped parsley
1 cup rice, cooked

FOR THE LEMON SAUCE:

2 egg yolks
Juice of 1 medium lemon
Zest from 1 lemon
Salt and pepper
1 cup heavy cream, heated
2 tablespoons cold butter, cut in chunks
1 tablespoon capers

Season the chicken cavity with salt and pepper and place the herbs and butter inside. Truss the bird and roast it for about an hour at 350°. Baste frequently. (Use the bottom half of the clay pot for roasting.)

Stir capers, olives, and chopped parsley into the rice. Place the rice around the roasted chicken and hold in a warming oven until the sauce is finished. (Place the sculpted bread chicken on top just before serving. It will keep the real bird warm for a good period of time.)

To make the sauce (which is essentially a "Hollandaise" made with cream), whisk together egg yolks, lemon juice, zest, seasoning, and 2 tablespoons cream. In a double boiler or over very low heat, whisk until the mixture turns thick and frothy. Slowly add the warm cream, bit by bit, and finally the butter. Continue whisking until the mixture is steaming hot, but do not allow to boil. Stir in capers and adjust seasoning.

To serve, quarter the real chicken and serve out a portion

with a scoop of rice on each of four dinner plates. Pass the sauce separately.

SERVES 4

MASTER PLAN FOR A STUFFED BIRD

The following full-meal proposition for stuffing a bird is adaptable to special dinners and holiday meals. The rustic thrust and balance of the bird will necessarily change the remainder of the meal, relaxing it into a more provincial (though just as festive) framework than might be usual in such a situation.

What should be aimed for here is a first full meal for a determined number of guests and then enough leftovers for Duck Soup (see page 109). With smaller birds of course, the more bones that can be removed to make way for stuffing, the more people can be served from the bird. A 4-pound chicken, deboned except for its wings and drumsticks, will serve 8 to 10 people (with no leftovers). A duck, partially deboned, will serve 6 people. A goose or turkey will not have to be deboned (except for the wishbone, which greatly facilitates carving), as their cavities are large enough to hold sufficient stuffing for many people.

Whatever the choice of the bird, the meal consists of:

—a fowl stuffed with mushrooms, pistachio nuts, spinach, giblets, etc.

—a thin pasta of semi-soup consistency cooked in stock (the stock can be made from removed bones or from home-made stock composed earlier and frozen)

—a piquant sauce, basically a vinaigrette, bound with egg yolks and thickened with a purée of the bird's liver

—a small, slightly ribald sausage made from the neck skin of the bird and containing garlic-buttered crumbs

For the sake of convenience, let us choose a 4-pound chicken for the following recipe.

A 4-pound chicken

FOR THE STOCK:

The removed bones and interior neck section
1 onion, sliced
1 carrot, scraped and sliced
Parsley sprigs, a bay leaf, thyme
Judicious salt

FOR THE STUFFING:

10 ounces fresh spinach, washed and parboiled
1 tablespoon olive oil
1 small onion
4 ounces mushrooms, cleaned and chopped
The giblets (except for the liver), chopped fine
¼ cup shelled pistachio nuts
1 egg plus 1 egg yolk
1 small garlic clove, pressed
1 teaspoon mixed dried herbs
  (thyme, oregano, savory)
Salt and pepper
2 slices soft bread, crusts removed, soaked in water
  and wrung dry
Olive oil for basting the bird

FOR THE SAUSAGE:

3 tablespoons unsalted butter
1 small garlic clove, minced
Around 1 cup of firm, coarse bread crumbs
Salt and pepper
Neck skin of the chicken
Oil

3 egg yolks
¼ teaspoon salt
Pepper
¼ cup red wine vinegar
3 shallots, minced fine
2 scallions, white and tender green, sliced thin
1 small garlic clove, minced
1 tablespoon minced parsley
1 hard-boiled egg, diced
The chicken's liver
Olive oil
Lemon juice

About 2 cups of small dried pasta
Whole and chopped parsley, for garnish
A piece of grating Parmesan to place on table

Partially bone the chicken. Place the bird breast up, and locate the wishbone immediately at the front of the body cavity and just under the soft flesh of the breast. Using a small sharp knife, outline the bone, then push the flesh back with the fingers and pry it out. Locate the two larger bones next to be felt running to either side of the cavity and attaching themselves to the wing bones. Cut and loosen these bones all around the wing joints, severing cartilage as necessary, until the V-shaped bone is free. Hook a finger through this bone, loosen the flesh along its upper length, then pull and snap it out. (What should remove itself is the long bone plus its attached, free-floating shoulder blade.) When both are removed, continue running a knife and a finger around the slender rib cage of the bird until you can loosen it to the middle back. Twist and tear it out. The pelvic structure, lower backbone, leg bones, and wing bones can all remain in the bird.

Use the removed bones for stock. Run a finger around the

neck bone and strip off the skin. Use this internal neck section
for stock also, and reserve the skin for the "sausage." To make
the stock, place in a saucepan the bones, onion, carrot, herbs,
a light seasoning, and 1 cup of water for each person to be
served. Slowly bring to a boil, skim off any scum, and regulate
immediately to the barest simmer. Cover the pan and cook,
undisturbed, for 50 minutes. This broth will be strained and
later used to cook the pasta.

Make the stuffing. Squeeze the cooked spinach very dry and
chop it well. Heat 1 tablespoon of olive oil and sauté the onion
until tender. Turn up the heat, add the mushrooms and giblets, and let them cook. The mushrooms will expel their
juices then reabsorb them. When the mixture is very dry, add
it to the spinach.

Place the pistachio nuts in a small pan of water and bring
to a boil. After 1 minute, strain the nuts out, place them in a
kitchen towel, and rub them briskly. Remove the green nutmeats from the rubble of skins and add to the spinach. Add
the eggs, garlic, herbs, seasoning, and crumble in the damp
bread. Mix everything until it is well homogenized. Season
the interior of the bird, then stuff in the green mixture. Sew
the neck opening neatly shut. Tuck the wings under the back
and truss the bird. Rub the chicken with 2 tablespoons of oil
and put it to roast in a 350° oven. Bake for 1 hour, basting it
frequently with juices in its last ½ hour.

Make a small, garlic-crumbed sausage. Heat 3 tablespoons
of butter in a small frying pan. Add the minced garlic and the
bread crumbs. Season. Stir and fry the crumbs until they
entirely toast and brown. Turn the neck skin inside out. Pull
off any fat, then turn the skin right side out and tie one end
tightly shut with kitchen string. Fill the neck with crumbs
(it should be loosely packed) and tie the other end shut. Rub
the skin with oil and put it to roast along with the chicken
for about 40 minutes. (Turn the sausage frequently so that it
will brown evenly.)

Make the sauce. Place the egg yolks, salt, pepper, and vinegar in a small saucepan. Over very low heat, whisk the yolks until they thicken. Off the heat, add shallots, scallions, garlic, parsley, and the hard-boiled egg. Sauté the chicken liver in a bit of oil. Pass it through a sieve and stir the purée into the sauce. In a thin stream, add enough oil so that the mixture turns into a sauce the consistency of a thick vinaigrette. Taste and add more oil, more seasoning, and lemon juice as needed to bring the sauce to a rich, peppery, rather acid piquancy. Place on table in a sauceboat.

Ten minutes before the chicken is finished, strain the chicken stock and spoon off any fat from its surface. Place the stock in a pan, bring to the boil, and add pasta. Cover the pot and simmer and steam; the final consistency should be thick and stew-like.

Serve the dish as follows. Ladle the soupy pasta into large, heated bowls and place them on table. Place a wedge of Parmesan cheese and a grater on table. Carry on the roasted chicken and sausage, garnished with parsley. People can either grate cheese over their pasta and eat it as a first course, with the meat and sauce following after as a separate second course. Or, a slice of chicken can be placed atop the pasta, the sauce added, the cheese grated over the whole, and the whole eaten in a lovely muddle. Slice the "sausage" into a bite for everyone.

SERVES 4 TO 6 (WITH LEFTOVERS) OR
6 TO 8 (WITHOUT LEFTOVERS)

BEEF RIBS WITH MUSTARD AND ONIONS

3 pounds beef ribs
3 tablespoons flour
Salt and pepper
3 tablespoons olive oil
3 very large onions, sliced thin
1 teaspoon mixed dried herbs (thyme, oregano,
savory, etc.)
2 small bay leaves
⅓ cup Dijon-style mustard
1½ cups white wine
4 large slices of bread *or* 2 halved Italian rolls
Minced parsley, for garnish

Remove the fat from the bony sides of the ribs. Season the flour with salt and pepper and roll the ribs in the flour, knocking off any excess that may cling. Heat the oil in a frying pan and brown the ribs on all sides.

In a round or oval cocotte or baking dish, both rustic and suitable for service, spread a layer of sliced onions, then a layer of ribs, then another layer of onions. Season well. Sprinkle half the herbs over the top and place a bay leaf in the middle. Add the rest of the ribs, then cover them with the remaining third of the onions and season yet again.

Place the mustard in a small bowl and stir in ½ cup of wine. When the mustard is thinned and smooth, add the remaining wine, then pour the mixture over the meat and onions. Sprinkle with the remaining herbs and center the bay leaf. Cover the dish and bake in a 325° oven for 2½ hours. (This is a good holding dish—one that will not suffer from remaining in the oven another half hour or so at warming temperature.)

Fifteen minutes before serving, remove the cover and press the bread slices, one at a time, on the surface of the dish. Allow the breads to blot up fat, mustard, and a few onions. Place the slices in a baking tin and let them bake and brown, along with the uncovered meat, for another 15 minutes.

Just before carrying the dish to table, press down on the mass of onions and meat and spoon off any surface fat. Scatter parsley over the top and serve from the baking vessel. Place a bowl on table to receive empty bones.

SERVES 4

ON GRILLING STEAK FOR
A FRENCH BREAKFAST

The time is late October. A group of forty, multi-national people has gathered to tour the wine country of Bordeaux, and it is the morning of the tour's third day. It sounds an easy thing to do, to step into a bus; to be driven to the great chateaux; to be fêted and wined and greeted by the owners in their cavernous *chais;* to taste and savor the wealth of vineyards; but on this, the last day, the group is tired and out of spirits. The French among us are peevish, the Americans subdued, the Germans liverish, and the English not speaking. We have been working hard, seriously tasting, thinking, and absorbing. Everyone offers us food everywhere. We have eaten too much, and there are a few among us who should have done more spitting—on a wine tasting you do not really drink, you taste, savour in the mouth and judge, then judiciously expectorate into a cask of sawdust. Two days have taken their toll and the overindulgers have, as the French would say, *gueules de bois* (wooden throats) on this morning after.

And so the bus pulls out at 7:30 A.M., through the center of Bordeaux, past the outskirts of town to Chateau Haut-Brion, just at the beginning of Graves. We pass down a long drive, through the barren vineyards in the famously flinty soil, toward the Chateau. When we dismount, the first thing that strikes us is the smell of grilling meat. We look at each other in dismay—steak for breakfast?

There, in a large pit outside the kitchen, the cooks have put thick slabs of *entrecôte* to grill over glowing embers formed, we learn, from gnarled *sarment*, the pulled, discarded vines no longer needed for production.

The chill of the morning soon drives us into the long dining hall. Stretched down the length of the room are white-clothed tables loaded with plates and baskets of bread. We seat ourselves, have a small comparative tasting of Haut-Brion, that "King of Graves," and then comes, whether we are ready or not, platter upon platter of breakfast. The steak has been smothered with a pale, purple sauce, a reduction of wine swimming with coarse gray shallots, mounted with a quantity of butter, and garnished with cèpes. The cooks slice the steak across the grain into thin strips and then proceed to load our plates. There is no stopping them and we, resigned, begin to eat in silence.

It is a strange experience, steak for breakfast, when one does not expect it, but somehow, in the process of masticating the tough, flavorful beef, we revive, the meat and potent sauce combining to shake us from our lethargy. The French regain their composure; the Americans slap each other on the back; the Germans break into song, and the pallor of those among us who have been indiscreet disappears in the face of the vigorous strength of the beef. We eat all the meat, then swab the platters clean with chunks of bread. We board the bus again in high spirits, and continue the day in mutual, fortified accord.

FLANK STEAK IN THE MANNER OF BORDEAUX

16 to 20 slices beef marrow (optional)
1 can cèpes or 1 small package dried cèpes
A large handful parsley
1 garlic clove

Olive oil
1½ cups red Bordeaux wine
⅔ cup sliced shallots
Salt and pepper
A bay leaf
1½ pounds flank steak
1½ sticks chilled unsalted butter, cut in small chunks
Chopped parsley, for garnish

If beef marrow is easily obtainable, by all means include it, for the unctuous garnishing texture it provides happily and traditionally enriches this dish. Have a butcher cut shank bones into 2-inch sections. At home, push the central marrow from each bone. Cut the marrow into inch-thick slices. Bring a small pot of salted water to the boil, regulate the heat to low, and poach the marrow in the quiet water. In a matter of a few moments, the marrow will have lost all pinkness and turned a translucent gray. Drain and set aside.

Prepare the mushrooms for sautéeing: if using canned cèpes, drain them from their juices and let them soak briefly in cool water and lemon juice to mitigate any canned and tinny flavor; if using dried cèpes, reconstitute them by soaking in cool water, then trim the stem bases of tough fibers. Dry the mushrooms well.

Chop a handful of parsley and a garlic clove together to a fine mince. Sauté the cèpes in a minimum of olive oil and, when they are lightly browned, throw in the parsley mixture. Shake the pan to disperse parsley over the mushrooms and set aside. Preheat the broiler.

Place red wine, sliced shallots, salt, and a bay leaf in a small saucepan. Reduce over medium heat. At the same time, brush the steak with oil and put it under the preheated broiler. Turn the steak once and cook to your personal degree of doneness.

When the wine has entirely evaporated, leaving only a dried bed of stained purple shallots on the pan's bottom, remove from heat and take out the bay leaf.

Cut the meat across the top grain in thin slices almost

horizontal to the steak, and arrange the slices down the middle of a platter. Season with salt and pepper. Place the cèpes around the edge of the meat and scatter on the marrow. Put the platter in a warming oven until the sauce is finished.

Put the reduced shallots back over low heat and, a few chunks at a time, rapidly whisk in the butter. Move the pan back and forth over the heat source, if necessary, to ensure that the butter does not melt but builds instead into a thick, creamy emulsion. Taste the sauce for heat (it can safely be quite warm but never will it be truly hot) and seasoning. Take the platter from the oven, sweep the sauce down the center of the meat, and scatter on parsley.

SERVES 4–6

GRILLED OXTAIL WITH MUSTARD SAUCE

This oxtail preparation, similar in spirit to grilled pigs' feet, is a succulent and ice breaking dish to serve at an informal dinner party. There is no way it can be eaten with dignity— it is quite necessary simply to pick up the bones and gnaw on them. Offer finger bowls or fragrantly heated damp washcloths in the Japanese manner after the feast.

> 4 pounds skinned oxtail, cut into joint sections
> (or figure 1 pound per person)
> 1 large onion, sliced
> 2 carrots, sliced
> A bouquet garni (bay leaf, thyme, parsley, celery,
> large strip of orange peel)
> Salt and pepper
> Dijon-style mustard
> Fine, dry bread crumbs
> 4 tablespoons butter, melted

> 2 medium onions, chopped
> ½ cup white wine
> 2 tablespoons red wine vinegar
> ⅔ cup cooking broth
> A large tablespoon of mustard
> Pepper
> Cayenne
> About 5 tablespoons chilled, unsalted butter,
> cut in small cubes
> 1 tablespoon fine-minced parsley

As a side dish: a tasty mash up of half potatoes and half turnips *or* rutabaga.

Trim any excessive fat from the oxtail sections. Place the meat in a large pan along with the onion, carrots, bouquet garni and seasoning. Just cover the ingredients with water and bring to a boil. Skim any frothy gray scum from the surface and regulate the heat so that the oxtail cooks at a bare simmer. Stew the meat for 2½ hours in the covered pan.

Lift off as much fat from the surface as possible with a large spoon, then remove the oxtail sections and let them cool. Strain the broth through a large sieve, discard the vegetable matter, and retain the richly gelatinous stock.

Spread a coating of mustard over each piece of oxtail. Roll the sections in crumbs, dip them quickly in melted butter, and roll in crumbs again. (The meat can be covered and refrigerated for a few hours at this point, if so desired.) Heat the broiler, place the meat on a baking sheet covered with aluminum foil, and grill slowly, at some distance from the heat, until the sections are crisp and brown on all sides.

For the sauce, place onions, wine, vinegar, ⅔ cup of the meat's defatted cooking broth, and salt in a small saucepan. Reduce the liquid over medium-high heat until there remains only a thick, syrupy gravy of onions and condensed liquid.

Stir in mustard, pepper, and cayenne to taste. Off the heat, start whisking in the butter, bit by bit, until a thick, emulsified sauce forms. (Place the pan off and on a moderate heat source during this time—the sauce should be very warm but never truly hot.) Taste carefully for seasoning—make sure the sauce is positively piquant. Serve the sauce in a boat or in individual dipping pots.

Heap the grilled oxtails into a heated serving bowl. Let diners serve themselves and place a dish on table to receive bones.

SERVES 4

Note: make sure to keep the cooking stock. Refrigerate it, lift off the surface fat when it has congealed, and use the stock to cook Little Stuffed Lettuces (see page 172).

BRAISED SHANK OF VEAL WITH OLIVES

> 4 large slices of veal shank
> Flour
> Salt and pepper
> 1 stick unsalted butter, chilled
> 1 tablespoon oil
> 3 cups white wine
> 1 large onion, chopped
> 1 large lemon, cut in thin slices
> A bouquet garni (bay leaf, parsley, thyme,
>   dried leek greens)
> 5 ounces Spanish olives, pitted

Trim the veal of any extra fat around the edges of the slices. Flour the slices lightly and sprinkle with seasoning. Heat a tablespoon of butter and one of oil in a heavy casserole. Brown the veal on both sides over medium-low heat, being careful not to dislodge the marrow at the bone's center. Remove the slices from the dish, pour off all fat, and deglaze the casserole with ½ cup of white wine. Off the heat, place half the lemon slices in the casserole and top with half the onion. Place the meat on this bed and then the remaining onions and lemon slices. Bury the bouquet garni in the middle.

Pour the remaining wine over the meat, season lightly with salt, and add enough water so that the liquid comes just to the top of the meat. Cover the dish and let it cook at the barest simmer for 1½ to 2 hours.

Drain the olives from their brine. Place them in a small saucepan and cover with cold water. Bring to a boil. Drain the water off, then repeat the boiling step three more times, using fresh water on each occasion. Drain and dry the olives well.

When the meat has cooked, first put the olives and a table-spoon of butter in a small frying pan and let them fry over low heat until needed. Then, remove the slices of veal from the pan and place them on a serving platter in a warming oven. Pour the cooking liquids through a strainer. Lift out the bouquet garni and the spent lemon rings from the flotsam in the strainer, then press the remaining onions through with a pestle and add the purée to the juices. Place the juices in a medium-sized pan and reduce them over a brisk heat until only a good ½ cup remains. Lift the pan from the heat, let it cool a moment, then drop the remaining 6 tablespoons of butter (chilled and cut into small dice) into the pan all at once. Whisk hard and when the butter has melted, taste the sauce for seasoning, then pour it over the veal. Garnish the meat with the olives and serve with a pilaf of rice.

SERVES 4

CALVES LIVER WITH VINEGAR AND BRAISED TURNIPS

A good and rapid meal, the whole of which can be prepared in an hour's time.

> 3 pounds firm turnips
> 1½ sticks unsalted butter, chilled
> Salt and pepper
> 8 thin slices of rosy calves liver, no thicker than ½ inch
> Flour
> 3 tablespoons minced shallots
> ⅔ cup red wine vinegar
> Parsley *or* watercress, for garnish

Cut a thick peel from the turnips and pare the vegetable into roughly rounded balls more or less 2 inches in diameter. Melt 3 tablespoons butter in a sauté pan, add the turnips and then ½ cup of water. Cover the pan and let the turnips simmer until just tender, then lift the lid and let the water evaporate. The turnips can now continue frying, over low heat, in butter alone. Let them turn a crusted brown on one side, then give the pan a shake and a twist so that the balls will roll and expose an unbrowned side to the heat. Continue in this manner and the turnips should be crisp and well gilded after a total of 35 to 40 minutes' cooking. Season them well with salt and pepper.

Fifteen minutes before the turnips are done, prepare the liver. Trim off any visible parchment-thin outer membrane. Flour the slices lightly, then fry the liver quickly in 2 tablespoons of butter. Allow the exteriors to turn a light gray-brown, but make sure the interiors are still a light pink. (Press a thumb on the slices—just as the juices change from red to pink the liver should be removed from the pan, a matter of 3 or 4 minutes.) Place the slices on a platter and hold them in a warming oven.

Work rapidly now. Cut the remaining butter into small dice. (Make sure the butter is cold before you try to cut it.) Add the shallots to the pan and let them cook over medium heat until just tender. Pull the shallots to one side of the pan with a slotted spoon and pour off all juices. Add the cup of vinegar and deglaze the pan, stirring up from the bottom any tasty brownings that may have congealed there. Reduce the vinegar until it feels and looks the consistency of corn syrup. Take the pan from the heat, add all the butter, and whisk furiously as it melts. Season with salt and pepper. Pour the sauce over the liver slices and set the golden turnips, interspersed with greenery, around the edge of the meat.

SERVES 4

CALVES LIVER FLAN WITH TOMATO CREAM

3 slices fresh bread
½ cup milk
½ pound calves liver, sliced thin
Salt and pepper
A large handful parsley
4 large shallots
Butter for mold
2 eggs, separated, plus 1 egg white

FOR THE SAUCE:

2 tablespoons red wine vinegar
A 10-ounce can tomatoes, well drained
1 small garlic clove, minced
½ cup cream
1 tablespoon unsalted butter

Minced parsley, for garnish

Crumble the bread into the milk and let it stand for 5 minutes. Squeeze the bread, ridding it of excess moisture, until it remains only a damp mass. If you have a food processor, combine bread, liver, seasoning, parsley, shallots, and egg yolks in the bowl and blend to a well-combined and fairly fine-textured mixture. Or, chop the liver well by hand (cut slices into thin strips, then chop the meat with a cleaver or two heavy knives). Mince the parsley and shallots and combine all the same ingredients in a mixing bowl.

Preheat the oven to 325° to 350°. Generously butter an 8- or 9-inch cake pan. Cut two circles of brown paper to fit the bottom and place one in the pan. Butter the top of the paper very generously. Beat the egg whites to firm but not dry peaks. Stir half the whites into the liver, then fold in the remaining half. Spoon the liver into the pan.

Butter one side of the other paper round with a good 2 tablespoons of butter and fit it lightly on top of the filling. Put the dish to bake in a *bain-marie* (a larger pan holding water) for about 45 minutes, or until the flan feels firm to the touch in the center and a knife inserted in the middle comes out clean. Remove the top paper and let the cake sit briefly before turning it onto a heated platter. Remove the bottom piece of paper.

For the sauce, place the vinegar in a small saucepan and heat briefly until it almost evaporates. Add tomatoes, mashing and pressing them with a fork into small sections. When the tomatoes come to a boil, stir in garlic, cream, salt, and pepper. Let the sauce stew briefly over medium heat until the cream thickens somewhat. Remove from heat and stir in butter to gloss the sauce. Mask the flan with the vivid tomato sauce and sprinkle with parsley.

SERVES 4 TO 6

ROASTED, STUFFED HEART OF VEAL

Heart of veal is a delicious meat that centers somewhere in spirit between calves liver and tongue for it possesses the splendid and delicate flavor of near-liver yet the texture of the denser, firmer tongue. It can be fried or stewed, stuffed and braised . . . the later method, when the heart is sliced, produces a delicately sculpted encasement of pale meat around a vivid central filling.

> 2 small calves' hearts
> Olive oil
> A wedge of lemon
> Salt and pepper
> 1 medium onion, minced
> 4 tablespoons unsalted butter
> ½ teaspoon mixed herbs (thyme, savory, a touch of sage)
> 2 tablespoons parsley, minced very fine
> 2 slices of fresh bread, crust removed, crumbled
> 6 or 8 large slices of barding fat (or rinsed salt pork)
> Oil for basting
>
> A crock of mustard

Remove all veins and fatty membranes from the exteriors of the hearts. Slice them halfway open, then rinse any clotted blood from the interiors and pat the hearts dry with paper toweling. Sprinkle with olive oil, a bit of lemon juice and seasoning, then leave them to marinate while the stuffing is prepared.

Sauté the onion in 4 tablespoons of butter. When it begins to soften, add herbs and seasoning, then turn the heat down and let the onion continue to cook over low heat. When the onion is tender, add the bread crumbs and stir well until the bread has absorbed all butter and the stuffing is moist and well mixed.

Pat the hearts dry. Fill the central cavities with the stuffing. Using a small trussing needle and kitchen string, sew up the hearts. Place the slices of barding fat around the plump globes and tie the fat on, again using the kitchen string to wrap around the hearts and secure the fat.

Place the hearts in a small baking pan, oil them liberally, then set them to roast in a 325° oven for about 50 minutes to an hour.

To serve, untie the hearts and pull out the basting strings. Cut the hearts in thin cross-slice, and arrange the slices around a crock of mustard on a heated serving platter.

This is very good served with a dish like Colcannon (see page 211), or a Turnip and Potato Gratin (see page 217). Leftovers make excellent sandwiches.

SERVES 4 TO 6 OR PERHAPS MORE

LITTLE STUFFED LETTUCES

> 4 large Boston lettuces
> 1 pound chopped or ground veal or pork
> 3 tablespoons softened butter
> 2 cups fine-shredded raw spinach or beet greens
> ½ cup thin-sliced scallions, the white parts and tender greens
> 2 tablespoons minced parsley
> ½ cup bread crumbs
> 2 tablespoons heavy cream
> 1 egg
> 1 small garlic clove, pressed
> Salt, pepper, nutmeg
> 4 cups soup broth or chicken or veal stock
> A bouquet garni (bay leaf, parsley, celery stalk)
> ½ teaspoon sugar
>
> Cheesecloth, string

Wash the lettuces under cold water, removing any damaged outer leaves and trimming the stems. Reserve 8 perfect large leaves. Cut out the very small central hearts of the lettuces and reserve them for salad.

Bring a large pot of salted water to a slow boil. Gently lower each lettuce, one at a time, into the water and press it under the surface with a spoon. In 30 seconds, lift it out and leave it to drain. When all the lettuces have been blanched, dip the 8 perfect leaves in the water until they turn bright green. (Spread each of these leaves out flat on paper toweling and blot it dry; they will be used later for presentation.)

Cut four 14-inch squares of cheesecloth. Place each lettuce head on one, stem end down. Gently peel back the leaves and spread them out into full petals.

Combine meat, butter, greens, scallions, parsley, crumbs, cream, egg, garlic, and seasoning in a bowl. Mix them well, kneading the ingredients between the fingers until well amalgamated. Divide the meat into 4 portions and shape each into a round ball. Place one ball in the middle of each lettuce, then form the leaves over the meat until it is entirely enclosed. Gather the cheesecloth up and tie it tightly at the top so the lettuce forms a neat package. Cut off excess cheesecloth.

Bring 4 cups of stock plus 4 cups of water to a boil. Add the bouquet garni, sugar, and salt. Place the stuffed lettuces in the broth, adding enough hot water to just cover them, and place the lid on the pan. Turn the heat to low and cook the vegetables, at a simmer, for 1½ hours.

Lift out the letuce balls and remove the cheesecloth. Wrap two of the bright green lettuce leaves around each ball to brighten the presentation. Using the point of a knife, carefully scrape back the lettuce in a small circle at the top so the pink meat will be decoratively exposed. The lettuces should be served with rice and can be presented in two ways. Either place each one in a bowl, add a serving of rice and enough boiling broth so the dish becomes, in effect, almost a soup; or serve each lettuce on a dinner plate with a scoop of rice and a spicy tomato sauce.

SERVES 4

LAMB AND RED PEPPERS WITH PULLED BREAD

Although this dish could properly be called a stew, the two composing elements, lamb and peppers, are cooked separately then combined only toward the end so that the single flavors of meat and vegetables remain more vividly individualistic than if they had married early on in the cooking process. The Pulled Bread, served on the side in a large bowl, is eaten along with the stew and serves to sop up juices—a tasty and useful addition and the only one needed to make a meal.

About 2 pounds boneless lamb (shanks, neck, shoulder, breast)
5 tablespoons olive oil
A bouquet garni (bay leaf, thyme, celery, parsley)
3 medium onions, sliced thin
3 garlic cloves
Salt and pepper
1½ cups dry white wine
5 sweet red peppers, seeded and cut in strips

Pulled Bread (see page 26); count 3 or 4 pieces per person
4 tablespoons unsalted butter
1 garlic clove, crushed
¼ teaspoon rosemary, pulverized in a mortar

Trim and cut the lamb into 2-inch pieces, then brown the meat in 3 tablespoons of oil, stirring and shaking the pan constantly. When the cubes are well browned on all sides, add the bouquet garni, half the sliced onions, and 2 crushed garlic cloves to the pan. Season with salt and add a cup of white wine. Cover the pan tightly and let the meat stew, over very low heat, for 1 hour.

Thirty minutes after the meat has been put to stew, heat

2 tablespoons of oil in a sauté pan and cook the remaining onions (covered and over low heat) for 15 minutes. Add a garlic clove, the red pepper strips, and seasoning. Cover the pan and stew the combined vegetables for another 15 minutes.

When the lamb has cooked, strain out the cubes and add them to the peppers. Remove the bouquet garni and pour what remains in the lamb's cooking pan through a strainer. Discard the oily juices. Deglaze the pan with the rest of the wine. Using a pestle or wooden spoon, press the onions through the strainer into the wine. Stir the sauce, let it come to a brief boil, then pour it onto the red peppers. Season the stew generously with fresh-ground pepper and let it simmer uncovered for 10 minutes before serving.

SERVES 4 OR 5

For the Pulled Bread, melt the butter in a saucepan and add the crushed garlic clove and rosemary. Let steep for 20 minutes, then strain. Dip the bread in the aromatic butter before its brief bake.

LEG OF LAMB WITH GARLIC CLOVES AND BREAD SAUCE

For solid comfort, there is nothing better, more reassuring, than a succulent roast of beef or lamb, the whole joint offered simply in its savory natural state and carved at table. Henry James, in his *Autobiography*, remembers such an occasion from childhood:

. . . the thick gloom of the inn rooms, the faintness of the glimmering tapers, the blest inexhaustibility of the fine joint, surpassed only by that of the grave waiter's reserve —plain, immutably plain fare all, but prompting in our elders an emphasis of relief and relish, the "There's nothing like it after all!" tone, which re-excited expectation, which in fact seemed this time to re-announce a basis for faith and joy.

As an alternative to the standard (but hard to better) roasted leg of lamb, the British frequently boil or braise the leg. The following hearty presentation, with garlic and a classic English bread sauce expanding that expensive meat until a half leg will easily feed 6 to 8 people, should be accompanied simply with boiled new potatoes tossed in parslied butter.

> 1 half leg of fresh lamb, about 3½ to 4 pounds
>   (avoid frozen lamb)
> 1 medium onion, sliced
> 1 large carrot, sliced
> 1 tablespoon mixed dried herbs
>   (thyme, oregano, savory, etc.)
> 2 tablespoons olive oil
> 2 tablespoons flour
> 1½ cups dry white wine
> 2 large whole heads of garlic
> Salt and pepper
> A bouquet garni (parsley, bay leaf, celery,
>   a 2-inch strip of orange peel)
> ¾ cup fresh bread crumbs
> 2 tablespoons butter

Trim the lamb of all noticeable fat and fell. Choose a covered casserole just large enough to hold the lamb and place in the meat. Scatter onion, carrot, and herbs over the lamb and dribble the olive oil over all. Place the covered dish over medium-low heat and let the lamb cook for 30 minutes (turn the meat over after 15 minutes).

Lift the lamb out onto a platter and sprinkle the flour over the onions and carrots. Stir over heat for 3 to 4 minutes until a soft, light gold roux has formed. Whisk in the white wine and 1½ cups of water, bring to a simmer, then strain through a sieve into a waiting bowl. Press the vegetables well to release all juices.

Return the lamb to the pan and pour the strained sauce over it. Press down on the garlic heads with the flat of the hand to divide them into cloves (remove any loose, papery skins) and place the unpeeled cloves around the lamb. Season and add the bouquet garni. Either place the casserole in a 350° oven for 1 hour or continue cooking on top of the stove with the pan tightly covered and the liquid at the barest simmer.

Remove the lamb to a serving platter. Fish out and discard the bouquet garni and lift out the garlic cloves with a slotted spoon. Scatter the garlic over the lamb and place the meat in a warming oven. Skim off any fat accumulated on the surface of the sauce and bring the sauce to a boil. Throw in the bread crumbs and let them cook for 10 minutes at a good clip. Stir in the lump of butter for gloss, and taste the sauce for seasoning.

Serve out slices of lamb (each with several garlic cloves) and place the bread sauce on the side. Accompany with boiled potatoes, garnished with butter and chopped parsley. The diners can either suck out the mild garlic purée from the cloves' interiors or they can press out the soft garlic with a fork and mash it and the sauce into their potatoes.

SERVES 6 TO 8

FOUR CLEVER WAYS TO USE/DISGUISE LEFTOVERS

Nothing, I think, in the realm of home cooking makes one feel more economically virtuous or more culinarily clever than skillfully using up leftovers in a tasteful and well-devised manner. Leftovers need not be looked upon with inevitable boredom nor should they be ignored, abandoned in the refrigerator until beyond use then guiltily disposed of. And above all they must not be thought of as mere "family fare"—something to be sloughed off on long-suffering loved ones but never offered to guests.

If leftovers occur too frequently or with surprising and unplanned regularity, then one might wish to examine the cost, quality and consumption of food as, it affects one's immediate family but, in fact, life can be greatly simplified at times if there are leftovers to deal with and if one knows what to do with them. It is sometimes reasonable to make extra, to actually desire a surplus of meat or vegetables, particularly when days ahead are busy and offer no time for involved cooking.

Many obvious ways occur to use leftovers. In summer, when food tends to be prepared simply and less in combination, a large, accommodating salad can be composed to hold all manner of cold meats and most plain-cooked vegetables; or a simple flat or rolled omelet might do the honors. In winter it more frequently happens that complex foods (those consisting of a variety of ingredients) are converted again into complex foods, e.g., a bit of leftover stew is chopped and loses itself in a meatloaf; some creole shrimp or creamed chicken with certain judicious care enters into the construction of a risotto. And, of course, there is the ubiquitous and catch-all casserole, a concept made more pure and palatable by thinking "gratin" instead, by binding together chosen ingredients with a thick tomato or properly made Béchamel sauce and crusting them over with bread crumbs, cheese, and a dribble of oil—never cereals or such.

There are also certain traditional ways to use leftovers in most cultures. Italian *avanzi* are chopped and find their way back into disguising lasagna or cappelletti. Leftover spaghetti is often mixed with a mash of anchovies, capers, and olives, then spread in a frying pan containing a thick layer of oiled crumbs. The cake is heated and browned and turned out, crust up, on a platter. Chinese leftovers frequently reappear, along with that soft rice gruel, congee, to be eaten the next morning for breakfast as, occasionally, does a Britisher's roast of beef from the night before. (Indeed many an old-school Sahib attributes the decline of the Empire to the fact that Englishmen no longer eat roast beef *every* morning for breakfast.)

Les restes, as they are known in France, receive special consideration. There are those dishes, such as *pot-au-feu* and *bouillabaisse,* that are positively looked forward to in their leftover state, for these remains, which gel upon refrigeration, can be sliced and eaten cold the next day for lunch. For leftover meats there exists an entire series of *émincés*—a generic name for thin-sliced meat (be it pork, veal, lamb, beef, or chicken) covered with an infinite variety of sauces and put to heat until just warmed through, the best known of which is the *miroton,* a layer of beef ensconced between thick blankets of an onion-rich *sauce lyonnaise.* The corresponding *émincé* of chicken is called a *capilotade* but its bedclothes might range from a cayenne-sharp *sauce à la diable* to a mild, mushroom-laden Béchamel.

The four following recipes are all intended as special treatments for leftovers, lifting those mundane remainders from the everyday to company fare if need be. They present master plans for using a single leftover; two items in combination; and a series of odds and ends. They all involve some molding, encasing additional element that inexpensively expands quantity, and they range in difficulty from an easy, quickly made all-purpose roulade to a spectacular but complex pasta beehive.

THE ALL-PURPOSE ROULADE

The most delicate disguise—an enfolding sheet of egg that puffs and expands into a golden roll. Use for a single leftover.

Possibilities: onions, mushrooms or duxelles; zucchini; dry tomatoes; ham; spinach; cheese; asparagus; seafood.

> 5 tablespoons unsalted butter
> 5 eggs, separated
> Salt and pepper
> 3 tablespoons flour
> About 2 cups of fine-chopped or grated leftovers,
>   seasoned well
> 1½ cups heavy cream
> ½ cup grated Parmesan or Gruyère cheese
> Chopped parsley *or* watercress stalks, for garnish

Cover a baking sheet or jelly roll pan with a layer of kitchen parchment or waxed paper. Grease the paper with 1 tablespoon of butter.

Preheat the oven to 350°. In a large bowl, beat the egg yolks until thick and light in color. Beat the whites until stiff, then fold them gently onto the yolks. Season with salt and pepper and sieve the flour over the whites. Rapidly, carefully, fold yolks and whites together, then spread the mixture evenly onto the baking sheet in a rectangle approximately 10 by 14 inches. Bake for 7 to 8 minutes. The eggs should be firm and just beginning to turn golden.

Spread a kitchen towel on a counter and flip the egg sheet over onto it. Peel off the paper. Scatter the leftovers over the egg, dribble ½ cup of cream over the surface, and dot with 2 tablespoons of butter cut in thin shavings. Roll up the egg sheet to make a short, rather than long, length. (Use the towel to firm and guide the roll.)

Lightly butter a 10-inch gratin or quiche dish. Carefully lift one edge of the roulade into the dish, then slide in the whole roll. Trim a small diagonal slice from both ends to neaten the roulade. Pour the remaining cream over the top (the egg will act as a sponge, absorbing the cream and swelling in the baking process). Disperse the grated cheese down the length of the roll, dot with thin slices of butter, and bake

in the same 350° oven until brown and bubbling (about 30 minutes). Give the dish some garnishing green.
SERVES 4 TO 6

THE PASTA SNAIL

Use the pasta snail for a combination of two or three items: mixtures of vegetables; meatloaf and mashed potatoes; mushrooms and macaroni and cheese; ratatouille, etc. Because the thin layer of dough holding the ingredients together is particularly nonobtrusive, the leftovers themselves can be of the roughest or most flavorful sort.

FOR THE PASTA:

> 1 egg plus 1 egg yolk
> ¼ teaspoon salt
> About 1½ cups quick-blending flour (like Wondra)

> 4 to 5 cups of relatively dry leftovers
> Salt and pepper
> Appropriate herbs, chopped parsley
> 1 cup grated Parmesan or Gruyère cheese or
>   a mixture of the two
> 2 cups very thick Béchamel or tomato sauce
> 1 egg
> 1 cup heavy cream
> 1 cup chicken stock

To make the pasta, mix whole egg, yolk, salt, and enough flour to make a dough of firm consistency. Knead until elastic, either by hand or through a pasta machine. Cover the dough with plastic wrap and let it rest for 30 minutes. On a floured surface, roll the dough out thin and trim it to a rectangle approximately 10 by 15 inches. (If you are running the pasta through a machine, roll two strips 15 inches long, overlap them ¾ inch on one long side, moisten the edges, and firmly press the two strips together.)

Mix leftovers, seasoning, half the cheese, the sauce, and an egg together. Spread the mixture evenly over the pasta and carefully roll it up lengthwise into a loose, 15-inch-long cylinder. Transfer one end of the pasta into a round, lightly oiled 10-inch gratin or quiche dish, and carefully lift and coil the rest of the roll into the dish. (Any small tears will disappear during cooking.) Coil the roll loosely as it will swell while baking. Pour the cream and stock over the top and sprinkle the remaining cheese along the spiraled surface. Bake in a 350° oven for about 50 minutes or until the creature is puffed and golden. Spoon up sauce and baste it over the "snail" several times during cooking. (If the top threatens to overbrown, cover it lightly with aluminum foil.)

Cut large wedges from the coil, serve them out with a spatula, and add a spoonful of sauce to each portion.

SERVES 6 TO 10 DEPENDING ON ACCOMPANYING DISHES

THE BEEHIVE

This classic design, adapted from the famous chef Antonin Carême, is the most involved of our leftover disguises. In his early nineteenth-century book *Le Cuisinier Parisien,* Carême presented a dish called *timbale à l'Indienne.* First a mold was lined with macaroni, half of which was yellowed with saffron. A chicken forcemeat was spread over the interior, acting as mortar to hold the macaroni in place, then a thick ragout of cocks' combs, kidneys, truffles, and morels bound with a cayenne-spiced sauce was used to fill the center. Though circumstance and availability may necessarily change the timbale's interior ingredients, the basic concept remains valid and attractively amusing. The "beehive" can be made adaptably larger or smaller depending on the amount of leftovers to be had, and extra diced pasta can always be used in supplemental quantity. It seems to me best to head this dish in one of two directions: either toward the Indian—fish, meat (lamb is nice), leftovers, eggplant, with almonds, plumped raisins, and a curried sauce; or toward the Provençal/Italian—meat (or just vegetables), peppers, zucchini, onions, pasta, tomatoes, garlic, herbs, etc., bound mainly with eggs, then served with a thin but flavorful tomato sauce on the side. But it is also possible to think along the more delicate lines of fish, seafood (forcemeat and leftovers), spinach, mushrooms, Nantua-type sauces, and uncolored pasta. The molding dish could be a soufflé or charlotte mold, but a 1½- to 2-quart stainless mixing bowl or tinned dome mold makes a perfect "beehive."

FOR THE FORCEMEAT:

½ pound raw fish or seafood *or*
½ pound uncooked chicken
    (use with poultry leftovers)
        or
½ pound uncooked veal
    (use with red meats)
 1 egg white
¾ cup heavy cream, chilled
Salt, pepper, a nutmeg scraping

Around ⅔ pound ziti macaroni (available in
    gourmet or Italian produce stores)
Powdered saffron
Softened butter
 4 to 5 cups leftovers and solids
Salt and pepper
Chopped parsley
Appropriate herbs and spices

TO BIND THE INGREDIENTS:

1½ to 2 cups thick white sauce (Béchamel)
or
Velouté sauce (replace the Béchamel's milk with
    stock) with an added egg or two
or
Eggs and cream (as for a quiche)
or
Just eggs

To make the forcemeat, pound the raw fish, chicken, or veal together with the egg white in a mortar, or purée it in a food processor until the meat is soft enough to press and pass through a sieve. (This will allow any bits of connective tissue to be filtered out.) Pack the sieved meat into a small bowl, press plastic wrap directly over the surface of the flesh in an airtight seal, and refrigerate for at least 1 hour. Immediately before the forcemeat is needed, whip half the cream until thickened but not firm. Take the flesh from the refrigerator, stir in the unwhipped cream first, add seasoning, then fold in the whipped cream.

Cook half the macaroni in boiling salted water until tender. Lift out the pasta with tongs and slotted spoon. Add enough saffron to turn the water a positive yellow, then cook the other half of the pasta. Lay the strands out carefully, one by one, so they do not stick together, and blot them dry. Grease the mold with a thick and generous layer of softened butter. When the pasta is cool, coil a yellow strand into a tight ring and center it on the bottom. Continue coiling a white strand or two, and then yellow strands. Alternate with thick stripes of color to the top of the mold (you can always remove a band or two of pasta if the leftover filling is not sufficient to complete the mold.) Chill the dish until the butter has solidified. Spread the forcemeat mixture over the pasta with a rubber spatula. Press it well into the strands, for the forcemeat will expand and, in effect, cement the coil together. Replace mold in refrigerator.

Preheat the oven to 350°. Combine any remaining force-meat, leftovers, diced macaroni, seasoning, herbs, and binding ingredients. Fill the mold. Place a buttered round of brown paper or kitchen parchment over the top. Place bowl in a larger pan containing hot water (a *bain-marie*) and bake for 1 hour.

Remove mold from oven, place a slotted grill or cake rack over the top, and reverse the dish over the sink to allow any accumulated liquids to drain away. Turn mold right side up, then cover and leave to settle for 5 minutes. Unmold onto a heated platter. Can be garnished with parsley or watercress. Cut in pie wedges to serve.

A FULL 1½-QUART MOLD MAKES 6 TO 8 PORTIONS

ROPEY PIE

Ropey pie is a comfortably hearty way to use all plain-cooked meats and even some in more complex forms (thick leftover stews would be a distinct possibility). A dish that traces back to Nova Scotia (and probably even further back to the Lancashire hot pot's lamb, potato and kidney stratas) this pie consists of a dense layer of potatoes and onions topped by meat and then another potato layer. Because the potatoes are grated then pressed until they have lost a good deal of moisture, much of their starchy bulk is lost. It is therefore necessary to think in terms of cooking this dish in a deep and narrow vessel rather than a gratin dish. A soufflé dish would work, as would an enameled casserole or a deep pie dish of the English type. Though the following recipe gives some specific amounts, think *concept* here, for the dish is very quantitatively adaptable.

5 pounds all-purpose potatoes
1 large onion, chopped fine
Salt and pepper
4 tablespoons unsalted butter
Leftover meat cut in cubes (the layers can be either
    thick or thin)
Watercress, for garnish

Peel the potatoes and grate them through the large holes of a
hand grater or the medium blade of a Mouli-julienne (the
food processor grates too fine here). Mix potatoes and onion.
Place a large sieve over the sink to catch any dropped shreds
and begin squeezing handfuls of potatoes over the sieve.
Squeeze the potato mass twice in this way. Season with salt
and pepper.

Grease a baking dish with 1 tablespoon of butter. Place a
scant half of the potatoes on the bottom, press them down
well, then pour over enough hot water or stock to just moisten
the potatoes. Arrange the leftovers in the middle, then top
with the remaining potatoes, pressing and compacting them
to a firm layer. Melt 3 tablespoons of butter and drizzle it
evenly over the top.

Note: it is particularly important that the layers of potatoes
be *thick*. They shrink again in cooking and unless they are
dense enough to protect the enclosed leftovers, the meat can
dry.

Put the pie to bake in a 350° oven for 45 minutes to 1 hour
(depending on the size of the dish). The top crust should be
thick and crisply brown. Serve out large portions and garnish
each plate with watercress. Let every diner add a good chunk
of butter to melt into his serving.

SERVES 4 TO 6 DEPENDING ON AMOUNT OF LEFTOVER MEAT

Vegetables and Salads

FLAN OF ARTICHOKES

8 large artichokes
½ lemon
3 eggs
1 cup heavy cream
1 large garlic clove, pressed
3 tablespoons olive oil
Juice of ½ lemon
1 teaspoon mixed dried thyme and oregano
Salt and pepper
⅓ cup grated Gruyère cheese
Olive oil
Fine-minced parsley, for garnish

Cut off the top third of the artichokes and remove any small leaves at the base of the stems. Break off the stems and peel them, cutting away the thick, stringy outer casing and reserving the tender inner nucleus. Rub over these small but tasty cores with the cut lemon half.

Bring to a boil a large pot of salted water and, at the last moment, acidulate it by squeezing in the juice from the rubbing lemon. Cover and cook the artichokes and trimmed stalks until a fork thrust into the stem end pierces the hearts easily. Remove artichokes from water and leave them to drain upside down on a platter.

When cool enough to handle, peel back all the leaves and remove the thistle-like choke from the hearts. With a small spoon, scrape the edible flesh from the base of each leaf, a tedious project perhaps, but one which results in a tidy heap of delectable meat. Add the stem cores to this pile. Trim the hearts and slice them crosswise into thin rounds. Put aside the most perfect slices as garnish. Add the remaining imperfect trimmings to the "scraped" pile and purée this flesh in a food processor or, bit by bit, in a blender.

Mix artichoke purée (which should be very smooth), eggs, cream, garlic, olive oil, lemon juice, herbs, and seasoning together and pour into a lightly oiled, round gratin or quiche dish. Place the perfect slices of artichoke on top (do not overlap them). Sprinkle on the cheese and dribble 2 tablespoons of oil over the surface. Put to bake in a 350° oven for about 30 minutes or until the custard has set.

Garnish the dish by trailing the minced parsley around the artichoke slices and filling the small spaces between circles. Good with lamb.

SERVES 6 TO 8

ARTICHOKES BARIGOULE

    ½ cup olive oil
    2 tablespoons chopped shallots
    1 garlic clove, minced

8 ounces mushrooms, cleaned and chopped
3 ounces chopped ham
Salt, pepper, nutmeg
3 tablespoons minced parsley
2 medium onions, chopped
2 carrots, cleaned and chopped
1 teaspoon mixed dried herbs (thyme, oregano, etc.)
4 large artichokes
½ lemon
⅓ cup dried bread crumbs
4 slices barding fat
3 cups white wine

Heat 2 tablespoons olive oil in a frying pan and add the shallots, garlic, mushrooms, ham, seasoning, and 2 tablespoons of parsley. Cook and stir over high heat while the mushrooms give off their liquid. When the mixture appears quite dry and the mushrooms squeak in the pan when stirred, remove from heat and set aside.

Heat the remaining olive oil in a casserole that has a cover and is just large enough to accommodate 4 artichokes. Add the onions, carrots, 1 tablespoon of parsley, and the mixed herbs. Let the vegetables stew over low heat for 20 minutes until they are soft but unbrowned. The artichokes will cook on this braising bed.

Prepare the artichokes. Break off the stems and even the ragged edges with a stainless steel knife. Cut off the top 1½ inches of each artichoke and trim off the sharp leaf tips with scissors. Using a spoon, dig out the central thistle-like choke with its covering purple leaves, exposing the smooth, clean white heart surrounded by edible leaves. Rub each artichoke over with the cut lemon half and squeeze some juice into the heart's crevice.

Stuff the artichokes with the mushrooms, then pat the dried bread crumbs on top of the stuffing. Tie a slice of barding fat over the top of each vegetable with kitchen string, then place the artichokes on their braising bed of onions and carrots.

Pour over the white wine and squeeze in whatever juice remains in the lemon. Add enough water to bring the level of the liquid halfway up the artichokes' sides. Bring to a boil, then cover the pan and continue cooking the artichokes in a 350° oven for 45 minutes.

Uncover the pan, remove the string and barding fat, then return the artichokes to the oven for another 15 to 20 minutes so that the crumbs can brown. Lift out the artichokes and keep them warm. Strain the casserole juices through a sieve. Press down lightly on the vegetables to drain them of their essence, then throw them away (they've given their soul). Reduce the juices over very high heat until only 1 cup of liquid remains. Season with salt, pepper, and lemon juice if needed, then pour over the artichokes.

SERVES 4

RED BEANS AND RICE

1 pound kidney beans
¼ pound sliced salt pork (parboiled for 3 minutes) *or* a ham bone with some meat on it *or* about ¼ pound diced raw ham; *or* best of all, 2 or 3 ham hocks
Salt and pepper
1 large onion, chopped
3 tablespoons unsalted butter
2 garlic cloves, minced
A large bouquet garni (parsley, thyme, bay leaf, celery stalks, leek greens)
1 small onion, minced
1 cup long-grained rice
Four 4-inch sections of Polish sausage (kielbasa), optional
Minced parsley and butter, for garnish
Large, garlic-rubbed croutons

Rinse the beans and check them over for bits of gravel and foreign matter. Place the beans and pork or ham in a casserole, cover with 6 cups of salted cold water, then bring to a boil. Regulate the heat to a simmer and cover. As soon as the beans are cooking along in sedate fashion, fry the large onion in 2 tablespoons of butter until tender and lightly golden. Stir the onion and minced garlic into the beans and place the bouquet garni in the center of the mixture. The beans will cook for 2½ hours in all. Add a bit of water from time to time to keep the beans just covered with liquid.

A half hour before the beans are finished, fry the small minced onion in 1 tablespoon of butter. As soon as it is wilted and tender, add the rice and stir until it gains an opaque whiteness. Stir in 2 cups of boiling water, then add the rice to the beans and stir them together with a wooden spoon. Cover the pot and continue cooking for about 25 minutes. Add sausage at this point also, if so desired. (This mixture of beans and rice in cooking is a preferential rather than a traditional step so that the rice can absorb additional flavor. Most recipes call for the beans to be served as a topping over the separately cooked rice.) Adjust liquid and seasoning as necessary.

When the beans are tender and the rice cooked, when all is a soothing, creamy mass, remove the bouquet garni (and the ham bone, cutting off and leaving behind any bits of meat). Serve in large soup bowls. Garnish with a lump of butter and chopped parsley. Served with garlic-rubbed croutons, this makes a cheap, filling, and in the Pythagorean sense, spirited meal.

SERVES 6 TO 8

CABBAGE TART ON BREADCRUST

The following tart can either be composed, as described here, on a thin layer of bread and served as a first course, or the cabbage filling, sprinkled with buttery crumbs and minus dough base and sausage, can be baked in an oiled, 8- to 10-inch gratin and served along with pork chops or roasts. The salting and squeezing method here outlined to remove moisture from cabbage allows that rough vegetable to condense and refine itself into a tasty and benign creature.

FOR THE FILLING:

1½ pounds cabbage
⅓ cup salt
1 large onion, sliced thin
2 tablespoons unsalted butter
2 eggs
1 cup heavy cream
½ cup grated Gruyère cheese
Pepper
Nutmeg
12 thin slices Polish sausage (kielbasa) *or* summer sausage

Once-risen pain au levain (based on 1 cup water) see page 18

Remove any wilted outer leaves from the cabbage, cut the head into quarters, and slice out the core. Shred the cabbage into thin chiffonade and place the cuttings in a large bowl. Sprinkle the salt over the cabbage, turning the shreds with the hands so that the salt disperses throughout the mass. Leave overnight. The following day, over a large sieve to catch any dropped pieces, give the cabbage at least two good squeezings (say, one in the morning and another in the afternoon before the pie is baked). Aim to leave the mass as limp and dry as possible.

Slowly cook the onion in 1 tablespoon butter over low heat. Do not allow it to brown. Mix onion and cabbage together.

Roll out the bread dough into a large thin circle. Lightly oil a 12-inch pizza pan and place the dough on it. Make a small rolled-up border around the edge. Scatter the cabbage evenly over the crust. Beat eggs, cream, cheese, and seasoning together and pour over tart. Place in a 350° oven for 15 minutes.

Remove the pie from the oven only long enough to slant the sausage slices (at about a 30° angle) into the filling in a circle 2 inches from the edge. Spear the remaining table-spoon of butter onto a fork and glide it over the surface. Re-place tart in the oven for another 15 to 20 minutes, or until the top is nicely golden.

Cut into pie wedges with a bread knife.

MAKES 12 SERVINGS

GRATIN OF CARDOONS WITH MARROW SAUCE

Cardoons, found frequently at market in the winter months, look like imposing, overgrown, silver-green bunches of celery. They are, however, members of the thistle family, as are artichokes. To further confuse matters, they are treated during growth like bulb fennel (i.e., their bases are protected with a banking of earth so that they blanch and the interior hearts become tender and white). Cardoons, like artichokes, will blacken when cut and cooked unless care is taken to acidulate and protect them.

    3 tablespoons flour
    Salt and pepper
    Juice of ½ lemon
    3 ounces suet, chopped
    1½ to 2 pounds cardoons
    ½ lemon
    4 tablespoons unsalted butter
    1 generous cup marrow (from beef shank bones)
    1 cup fresh bread crumbs
    ⅓ cup grated Parmesan cheese
    ⅓ cup dried bread crumbs

Prepare a white stock (*blanc*) in which to cook the cardoons. Stir a small ladleful of cold water into the flour and make a smooth paste. Gradually whisk in another 2 cups of water, then strain the liquid into a large pot. Add water until the pot is almost half full, then add a tablespoon of salt, the juice of ½ lemon, and the chopped suet. Bring the *blanc* to a boil and maintain. (This stock will keep the cardoons white as they cook; the beef suet in particular will melt and act as a defensive layer of fat to protect the cardoons from a discoloring meeting with air.)

Prepare the cardoons. Using a stainless knife, remove any wilted or discolored outer stems and cut the tender interior lengths into 2-inch pieces. Rub them over with a cut lemon half. Trim the heart and slice it across. (String the cardoons exactly like celery wherever needed.) Throw the sections into the boiling *blanc,* cover, and cook until just tender (30 to 40 minutes).

Prepare the marrow sauce. Melt 3 tablespoons butter in a saucepan. Add the marrow and let it melt into the butter over low heat. Add the fresh bread crumbs, season, and let the mixture simmer slowly for 30 minutes.

Drain the cardoons. (Check them over and remove any remaining strings.) Butter a gratin dish, add half the cardoons and a good sprinkling of grated Parmesan, then the remaining vegetable. Season well, pour the sauce over the top, and give the dish a shake to mix the ingredients. Stir the dried bread crumbs together with the remaining Parmesan cheese and press the mixture compactly over the surface. Cut the remaining tablespoon of butter into thin shavings and disperse them on top. Place the dish in a 350° oven until a good gratin has formed.

SERVES 4 TO 6

CAULIFLOWER CRUMB TART

6 slices firm bread
6 tablespoons unsalted butter
1 small cauliflower
Lemon juice
2 eggs
½ cup heavy cream
Salt, pepper, nutmeg
⅓ cup grated Parmesan cheese

Reduce the bread to medium-sized crumbs in a food processor or by hand. Melt the butter in a frying pan and stir in the crumbs. Stir and fry them until the bread toasts to a light golden brown. Pat ⅔ of the crumbs over the bottom and sides of a lightly buttered 9-inch pie plate and set aside.

Divide the cauliflower into flowerets and cook in boiling, salted water with a squeeze of lemon juice to acidulate the water and keep the cauliflower white. Strain into a colander when tender, then return the vegetables to the saucepan and shake the pan over heat until all moisture has evaporated. Press the cauliflower through a sieve or purée it in a food processor.

Beat the eggs, cream, seasoning, and cheese together. Stir in the cauliflower and pour the mixture into the baking dish. Scatter the remaining crumbs over the top and put the tart to bake in a 350° oven for 35 to 40 minutes, or until nicely browned. Use on occasion in place of potatoes.

SERVES 4 TO 6

CUCUMBER CUSTARD

>3 large cucumbers
>Salt
>2 tablespoons fine-minced parsley
>1 egg yolk
>½ cup heavy cream
>⅓ cup grated Gruyère cheese
>Pepper
>2 tablespoons butter

Peel the cucumbers and cut them into lengthwise quarters. Slice out the seeds from each piece and cut the strips into ½-inch cubes. Sprinkle the cubes with a teaspoon of salt and let them sit for 15 minutes. Take them up by the handfuls and squeeze them well over a sieve (this will remove the slightly bitter cucumber edge and reduce the vegetable to its flavorful soul). Mix parsley into the cucumbers.

Stir egg yolk, cream, cheese, and pepper together. Use 1 tablespoon of butter to grease a small baking or gratin dish. Smooth in the cucumbers and pour the cream mixture over them. Dot the top with thin shavings of the remaining butter and put to bake in a preheated 325° oven for 15 to 20 minutes, or until the top is speckled with gold. This dish is a delicious and flattering attendant for fish, fowl, or meat.

SERVES 4

STUFFED FENNEL

>2 large bulb fennel
>Salt
>½ cup grated Parmesan cheese
>Pepper

About ½ cup heavy cream
4 tablespoons unsalted butter
Fine dry bread crumbs

Cut off the bulbs at the base of the leaf stalk and trim the root end. Remove the first outer leaves and any others that might be bruised or wilted. The bulb leaves contain strings exactly like celery. Try to "string" the exterior leaves if possible (some bulbs permit this more than others).

Bring a pot of salted water to the boil and parboil the fennel for 5 minutes. Drain the fennel, slice them in two lengthwise, and press and shake out all water. Combine cheese, pepper, and enough cream to make a mixture of peanut butter consistency. Carefully pry up some leaves on each fennel half and stuff a bit of the cheese under and around them. Smooth some cheese over the top.

Melt 2 tablespoons butter in a small casserole, place in the fennel cut side up (all 4 tops pointing toward the center), and add ½ cup of water. Cover the pan and simmer gently for 30 minutes. At the end of this time, the fennel should be starting to cook only in fat and their undersides should be beginning to brown. Pat some crumbs over the surface of the bulbs, cut the remaining 2 tablespoons of butter into thin shavings, and dot the crumbs with the butter. Transfer the dish to a 350° oven, add a bit more water, and let the fennel continue cooking until completely tender. (Ascertain this by pushing a knife through the center and testing a thick underleaf with a fork.) Transfer to the broiler briefly to brown the crumbs.

SERVES 4

PURÉE OF FENNEL WITH ANISE SEED

2 large bulb fennel
6 tablespoons butter
Salt and pepper
1 teaspoon anise seed

Trim and string the fennel as in the preceding recipe. Slice
the fennel into large dice and put it to boil in salted water
until very tender. Strain out the fennel, then put it back in the
same pan and shake over heat briefly, until all moisture has
evaporated. Purée the fennel in a food processor or, bit by bit
and with an added moistening of water, in a blender. In
either case, press it through a sieve with a pestle to remove
any small strings. The resulting purée will be quite loose
and watery. To condense the vegetable, place some heavy
paper toweling on its surface. Keep lifting off the water-laden
towel and replacing with dry toweling until the fennel is
thick and relatively dry.

Put the purée back over the heat and whisk in butter,
seasoning, and anise seed. Add butter until the purée reaches
a nice balance that allows the anise flavor just to dominate the
essence of butter. A purée like this is meant to be served in
very small portions—an elegant vegetal dab upon the plate—
and to be thought of almost as a condiment to season and set
in relief the more important serving of fish or meat. Excellent
with poached, baked, or grilled fish, or with lamb.
SERVES 4 TO 6

LEEK HASH

6 large leeks
4 tablespoons unsalted butter
½ teaspoon flour

Salt, pepper, nutmeg
⅔ cup heavy cream
2 slices white bread, crusts removed
2 egg yolks
Lemon juice
Minced parsley, for garnish

Trim the root ends of the leeks and cut off the tops leaving an inch of green. Remove the outer layer of leaf, slit the leeks through lengthwise almost to the end and, spreading the leaves apart, wash them in cool running water.

Cook the leeks until tender in boiling salted water. Drain and refresh under cold water. Press the leeks gently to expel water, then chop them fine.

Put the leeks and 2 tablespoons of butter in a small saucepan over medium heat. When the butter is melted and the leeks have begun to fry, sprinkle them with flour and season to taste. Add the cream, stir well, and leave to simmer over low heat for 10 minutes.

Cut the bread in two diagonally. Melt the remaining butter in a frying pan and slowly fry the bread on both sides until golden.

Remove leeks from heat, let cool a moment, then stir in the egg yolks. Place pan over heat briefly, stirring all the while, until the mixture thickens somewhat. Add a small squeeze of lemon juice. Mound the leeks into a heated serving dish and place the croutons around the base of the vegetable. Sprinkle with parsley and serve.

SERVES 4

Note: be sure to retain and dry the greens of leeks for use in bouquet garnis and to flavor stocks.

LENTILS AND GREENS IN
THE ITALIAN MANNER

The following leguminous composition can be served as a side dish or as a humble but wholly delicious full meal.

2 cups (1 pound) lentils
A pinch of baking soda
A generous bouquet garni (parsley, bay leaf,
  celery stalk)
1 tablespoon of mixed fresh oregano, rosemary, basil,
  or a small dried portion of each
12 to 15 peeled garlic cloves
10 ounces canned tomatoes, totally drained
Salt
About 1 cup olive oil
2 tablespoons red wine vinegar *or* lemon juice
10 ounces of either collards *or* spinach,
  washed and dried

Pick over the lentils, removing any bits of foreign matter, and rinse them well in cold water. Place in a medium-large saucepan and just cover them with boiling water. Let the lentils soak for 1 hour.

Add to the pot a pinch of baking soda, the bouquet garni, herbs, garlic cloves, tomatoes, and 1 teaspoon salt. Add 1½ cups of boiling water and ½ cup of olive oil. Cover the pot and simmer for about 1 hour or until the lentils are tender. (There should be little water left at this point—just a layer of oil in the pan's bottom.)

While the lentils are cooking, prepare the greens. Stem the greens. If using spinach, let the leaves remain whole; if using collards (whose roughness will be more closely akin to the wild *borragine* used in this dish in Italy but unavailable here), cut them into thick strips.

Cook the greens in a pot of boiling, salted water until just tender. Drain and refresh them under cold water, then squeeze them as dry as possible. Heat 2 tablespoons of oil in a sauté pan and fry the greens for 1 minute while they absorb the oil. Stir in the vinegar or lemon juice.

Mix the greens into the cooked lentils, let the stew simmer for 5 minutes, then ladle out portions in large soup plates. Place on table a small pitcher of olive oil and a pepper mill that gives a coarse grind. Each person anoints his lentils with oil and grinds on pepper to taste. If this dish forms the entirety of the meal, serve some thick garlic-rubbed croutons along with it.

SERVES 4 to 6

MAIZE CUSTARDS WITH MUSHROOM PURÉE

A gentle dish to serve alongside grilled liver or lamb chops or a roasted chicken, and a sophisticated presentation for cornmeal that could easily fit into the most elegant of meals. Because the proportion of meal used in these custards is much less than that used in traditional pones and polentas, the batter bakes into a light biscuit/cake topped with a frosting of soft egg custard.

FOR THE CUSTARDS:

⅓ cup fine-ground yellow cornmeal
¼ teaspoon salt
Pepper
2 eggs, beaten together
¾ cup heavy cream
Butter for mold

FOR THE MUSHROOM PURÉE:

> 4 ounces mushrooms
> 2 tablespoons unsalted butter
> Salt and pepper
> About ¼ cup heavy cream
> Lemon juice

Mix the cornmeal, salt, and pepper in a bowl. Make a well in the middle and slowly stir in the eggs and then the cream. Let the mixture sit for 10 minutes, covered with a kitchen towel. Preheat the oven to 325°.

This recipe will make 8 custards. Butter a muffin tin or 8 small soufflé cups. Give the batter a good stir, then divide it equally among the molds. Place a baking tin holding 1 inch of hot water in the oven and set the molds in the water. Bake for 30 minutes, checking once to make sure that the water is not boiling around the custards. Turn the heat down if necessary.

For the mushroom purée, clean the mushrooms (rub with a dampened, salted cloth) and trim off any tough portions from the stems. Chop them to a fine watery purée in blender or food processor. Melt the butter in a saucepan over fairly high heat, add mushrooms and seasoning, and cook briefly until the mushrooms have given off all their water and appear quite liquefied. Pour cream into the purée until there appears to be a smooth "sauce" of medium consistency. Remove pan from heat and add a small squeeze of lemon juice. Taste again for seasoning. Reheat the sauce right before serving, if necessary.

Gently pry the maize custards from their cups with a fork and place them, two to a serving and shiny side up, on each diner's plate. Spoon mushroom purée over the custards.
SERVES 4

MUSHROOMS COOKED AS SNAILS

This dish is designed to provide a very small side serving of mushrooms. I present the mushrooms, six to a portion, in those round ceramic butter containers that resemble overgrown snail pots. A pot is placed directly on each dinner plate and might accompany duck and wild rice or might simply appear as one of two vegetables in a starchless meal.

    24 firm white mushrooms, about 1½ inches in diameter, wiped clean
    ¼ cup dry white wine
    1½ tablespoons red wine vinegar
    3 tablespoons unsalted butter, softened
    1 tablespoon minced shallot
    1 garlic clove, minced
    1 tablespoon fine-chopped parsley
Salt and pepper
Small pinch cayenne pepper
    2 tablespoons fine, dry bread crumbs

Twist or cut off the mushroom stems at the cap. Fold a mushroom into two layers of paper toweling and place a thumb in the stem indention. Holding the towel-covered mushroom in the other hand, firmly press and squeeze the cap. The towels will absorb a certain amount of moisture and the mushroom will shrivel slightly. Repeat with all the caps.

Pour wine and vinegar into a pie tin. Blend butter, shallot, garlic, parsley, and seasonings together and stuff some of the butter into the indented bottom of each cap. Spoon bread crumbs over the butter and place the mushrooms, filled side up, in the pie tin. Bake in a 350° oven for 10 minutes.

SERVES 4

FRICASSEE OF MUSHROOMS

½ pound firm white mushrooms
2 tablespoons unsalted butter
Salt and pepper
⅔ cup heavy cream
2 egg yolks
½ teaspoon red wine vinegar
Chopped parsley, for garnish

Trim off the stems level with the caps and wipe mushrooms clean. (Reserve stems for the likes of duxelles.)

Melt the butter in a frying pan and sauté the mushrooms over fairly high heat until they are lightly browned. Remove pan from heat and reduce the fire to medium low. Season mushrooms generously with salt and pepper.

Stir together the cream, egg yolks, and vinegar. Place the pan back over heat and pour in the cream mixture. Shake the pan until the cream warms and thickens into a smooth coating sauce. Do not allow to approach the boil. Place the creamed mushrooms in a heated serving dish and garnish with chopped parsley.

SERVES 4 TO 6

MUSHROOM PANCAKES

A nice idea for a lightly farinaceous side dish, these small pancakes are, in spirit, similar to the thin, crisp potato *crêpes vonnasienne* at La Mere Blanc in Vonnas which are served either with the meal or as a separate course. These flavorful crêpes are companionable with red meats—particularly, I see a slice of rare lamb, some mushroom pancakes, and an amiable purée of green beans.

FOR THE DUXELLES:

2 tablespoons unsalted butter
1 medium onion, chopped fine
1 garlic clove, minced
3 cups mushrooms (about 4 to 5 ounces), caps and
   stems, cleaned, trimmed, and chopped fine
Salt, pepper, a scraping of nutmeg
1 teaspoon parsley, chopped
¼ teaspoon mixed dried herbs (oregano, thyme, etc.)

1 large, heaped tablespoon flour
Pinch of salt
1 large egg
½ cup milk
Butter for frying

Melt the butter in a frying pan and stew onion and garlic over low heat until tender but not browned. Raise the heat to medium high and add mushrooms, seasoning, and herbs. Cook briskly until, first, the mushrooms render their water, and then the water reabsorbs and evaporates. (The mixture should be very dry.) Set aside.

Place the flour and salt in a small mixing bowl. Whisk in the egg and then the milk until the crêpe batter is smooth. Stir in the duxelles. Melt 1 tablespoon of butter in a frying pan and add in the batter by the tablespoon. Fry the delicate pancakes on both sides until the outer rims are crisp and brown, then transfer them to a plate and hold in a warming oven. Add a bit more butter to the pan and continue cooking until all are fried. Makes about 20 pancakes 2½ inches in diameter.

SERVES 4 TO 6

PUFFED ONIONS

2 tablespoons raisins
3 medium-large onions, sliced or chopped
3 tablespoons melted unsalted butter
3 tablespoons flour
½ cup heavy cream
Salt, pepper, nutmeg
2 eggs, separated, plus 1 egg white
1 tablespoon minced parsley
1 scallion, sliced thin
Butter for the gratin dish

Place the raisins in a small pan and cover them with water. Bring to a boil, then remove from the heat and let them sit and plump until needed.

Cook the onions in the melted butter over low heat for 30 minutes, stirring frequently, until they turn a mellow gold. Sprinkle the flour over the top and continue cooking and stirring for another 3 minutes. Pour in the cream and season the onions. Cook for another 5 minutes over medium-low heat so that the cream can thicken. Purée the onions in a food processor or press them through a sieve with a pestle. Stir 2 egg yolks, minced parsley, scallions, and raisins (blotted dry) into the onions.

Butter an 8-inch gratin dish. Whisk the 3 egg whites until they form stiff, firm peaks. Stir ⅓ of the whites into the onions, then fold in the rest of the whites and pour the batter into the buttered dish. Bake the onions in a 350° oven for 20 to 25 minutes. Do not let them overbrown. Delicious with veal or pork, which will be nicely complemented and balanced by the onions' sweetness.

POTATO CAKE WITH MUSHROOM STUFFING

4 or 5 large all-purpose potatoes
6 tablespoons unsalted butter
⅓ cup thin-sliced shallots
1 large garlic clove, minced
1 tablespoon minced parsley
Salt, pepper, nutmeg
4 ounces mushrooms, trimmed, cleaned, and chopped
¼ cup chopped black olives
Parsley, for garnish

Peel the potatoes and cut them into ⅛-inch-thick slices (a *mandoline*/slaw slicer is the quickest cutting tool). Put the slices to soak in a large bowl of cold water for 30 minutes.

Melt 1 tablespoon of butter in a small frying pan and cook the shallots over low heat until limp. Add garlic, parsley, seasoning, and then the mushrooms and olives. Turn up the heat and cook the mushrooms until they have released their moisture and then the liquid evaporates. Remove from heat and set aside.

Drain the potato slices and layer them out on a kitchen towel. Place another towel on top and blot each slice immaculately dry—a tedious bit of work but necessary if the potato cake is to crisp and hold its shape. Melt 3 tablespoons of butter in a 9-inch frying pan. Arrange a neat, overlapping layer of potatoes in the bottom, then continue building the cake until half the slices are used. Spread the mushroom hash over the potatoes, leaving an inch of potato clear at the border. Put the remaining slices on top, salt and pepper the cake, then cover the pan and leave to cook for 15 minutes over medium-low heat.

Press the potatoes down firmly and neaten the cake with the back of a fork. Let it continue cooking until the bottom and sides are brown, the cake slips easily in the pan, and the surface potatoes are limp. Place a plate over the top of the pan and reverse the cake onto it. Melt the 2 remaining tablespoons of butter in the pan, then slip and nudge the cake back in to finish browning on the other side. Season the top and cook, uncovered, until the bottom is crisply browned. Turn out on a platter and garnish with parsley.

SERVES 6

(This cake may be made thicker or thinner, according to need, by simply adjusting the quantity of potatoes.)

POTATO "QUICHE"

Potato "quiche" bears little resemblance, other than a vague physical one, to a true quiche. The potatoes act as both crust and filling, though the light top layering of cream and cheese makes it appear that the "quiche" is filled with other ingredients. This dish is, then, potatoes, and meant to complement meat. A small scattering of crisp, crumbled bacon could be added if the accompanying meat course so allows.

> 3 medium-large all-purpose potatoes,
>   boiled in their skins, cooled
> ½ cup flour
> 3 tablespoons unsalted butter, softened
> Salt and pepper
> 4 strips crisp bacon, crumbled (optional)
> ½ cup heavy cream
> ¼ cup grated Parmesan or Gruyère cheese

Peel the potatoes and put them through a ricer or push them firmly through a sieve with a large pestle. There should be about 2 cups of riced potatoes. Sprinkle the flour over the potatoes, add butter and salt, and mix the ingredients rapidly with the fingers as if one were working pie crust. Incorporate flour and butter into the potatoes until just blended, but do not overwork so that the mass becomes glutinous. Pat the potatoes into a compact ball of dough and roll the dough out on a lightly floured surface to a 12-inch-diameter circle. Transfer the dough to a pizza pan, press any small breaks back together, and crimp an edging design around the border, as for a pie.

Preheat oven to 350°. If using bacon, sprinkle it on, then drizzle cream over the surface and top with the grated cheese. Place "quiche" in the oven for 25 to 30 minutes or until the surface is browned and the potatoes golden at the edge. Transfer to a large heated serving platter or simply keep the "quiche" in the cooking dish and beautify the border with parsley sprigs. Cut sections with a knife; serve with a spatula. This recipe may easily be halved.

SERVES 8

LULU PEYRAUD'S POTATO BOUILLABAISSE WITH SAUCE ROUILLE

Serve this potato stew plain or with a simple poached, baked, or broiled fish. For an even more pronounced "bouillabaisse" flavor, substitute fish stock for the water. The recipe can be easily adapted to larger or smaller numbers of diners.

2 large onions, sliced thin
4 garlic cloves, peeled and flattened with a knife blade
2 large leeks, the white parts sliced thin
6 canned or home-preserved tomatoes, cut in quarters
⅓ cup olive oil
A large bouquet garni (parsley, thyme, bay leaf,
    a 2-inch strip of orange peel)
1 teaspoon dried fennel weed (or a large sprig of fresh)
½ teaspoon powdered saffron
8 to 10 large all-purpose potatoes, peeled and cut
    in ¼-inch-thick slices
3 tablespoons Pernod
1 dozen mussels (optional)

FOR THE ROUILLE:

6 garlic cloves, peeled
Cayenne pepper to taste
About 1 cup fresh bread crumbs
Olive oil

Place onions, garlic cloves, leeks, and tomatoes in a large, rustic casserole (an old black iron dutch oven is handsome). Add olive oil, bouquet garni, fennel, and saffron and fry the melange briskly until everything is tender. Lift out the bouquet garni and a large part of the vegetables.

Place half the potato slices in the dish and lay the bouquet garni in the center. Strew some of the vegetables around, cover with the remaining potato slices, and top with more vegetables. Pour water (or fish stock) over the potatoes until it almost covers the top layer. Add the Pernod and mix everything well. Cover and cook slowly on top of the stove or in a moderate oven. Check the progress with a fork, and when the potatoes are almost done, encircle the edge of the dish with the mussels and let them steam open in the covered pot for 10 to 12 minutes. Carry the pot to table and ladle out both potatoes and juices into large soup bowls. Serve a large slice of fish on top and pass the *rouille* separately.

For the *rouille:* pound or purée the garlic cloves and cayenne to a paste. Moisten some bread crumbs in water, then squeeze them dry. Start alternating additions of crumbs and olive oil to the garlic and build the sauce to the thickness of a mayonnaise. (The *rouille* should be sharp, hot, flavorful—a small dab sufficing as a powerful heightener. Don't stint on cayenne.)

SERVES 10 TO 12

COLCANNON

An Irish dish traditionally eaten on All Saints' Day (Halloween eve), colcannon provides, in addition to a delicious mash-up of potatoes and kale, a chance to participate in a small ritual akin to the hiding of the bean in Provençal twelfth-night pastry. Hidden within the potato mound can be a ring (denoting marriage), and a toy jewel (denoting wealth). To whomever falls the prize is guaranteed marriage and/or money. It is only fair to warn people when you play this game, so that no guest breaks a tooth on any foreign object.

About 5 ounces kale
4 or 5 medium-large all-purpose potatoes,
    cooked and mashed
1 tablespoon grated onion
Salt and pepper
3 or 4 tablespoons heavy cream
4 tablespoons melted unsalted butter or more, to taste
1 ounce sliced almonds, lightly toasted
A toy ring and/or coin (optional)

Remove the thick stems from the kale by bending them backward and stripping them off on the back side of the leaf. Wash the leaves well, then cook them in plentiful boiling, salted water. To keep the leaf as green as possible, taste a small piece from time to time and when the kale is just tender, drain at once into a colander and refresh with cold water. Squeeze all water from the leaves and purée them in a food processor or blender. (The mass should be very dry. If at all moist, place it over heat briefly and steam off any liquid.) Mix potatoes, kale, grated onion, seasoning, and cream. Heat until very hot, then mound the colcannon into a small heated serving bowl. (Hide the ring if you are using one.) With the back of a fork, fluff and mound the mixture to a rugged, peaked mountain. Lightly flour the end of a wooden spoon and use it to make a large hole down through the mountain's center. Pour the melted butter into the hole, filling it and then some, so that the butter cascades down the sides. Sprinkle the almonds over the mountain and serve in any situation calling for flavorful mashed potatoes.

SERVES 4 TO 5

BAKED POTATOES WITH
EGGS AND ANCHOVIES

    4 large baking potatoes
    2 hard-boiled eggs, diced
    4 anchovy filets, blotted of any oil and chopped fine
    3 tablespoons fine-minced shallots
    3 tablespoons mixed minced parsley and chives
    Salt and pepper
    4 tablespoons unsalted butter
    Heavy cream
    2 tablespoons grated Parmesan cheese

Bake the potatoes. Cut a lid from the top of each potato and scoop out the soft interiors. Mash the potatoes with a fork (they should be somewhat lumpy, not purée smooth) and combine with eggs, anchovies, shallots, herbs, seasoning, and butter. Add enough cream to make the potatoes pleasingly emulsive, then stuff the mixture back into the baked cases and sprinkle on the cheese. Place under a broiler briefly to brown the cheese.

SERVES 4

OMELET WITHOUT EGGS

The following recipe, recounted by Madame Alice Lallement and translated from *L'Art du bien Manger* (Paris, 1910), presents a clever way to make an "omelet" when there are no eggs in the house. The delicious method is discovered when a basket holding eggs for an important luncheon is upset and all its contents broken. Madame Lallement's ingenious *cordon bleu* Jeanne comes to the rescue:

Very delicately she peels the potatoes cooked in their skins and then cuts them into small morsels. Next to her, on the fire, waits a *poêle* with a good layer of sweet butter which sputters and melts like a dream. . . .

The butter crackles and sings. Just at the moment it starts to brown, Jeanne, with a light hand, puts in the potatoes, which she turns and crushes carefully as if she wished to make a golden dough.

On this compact and gilded bed, she sprinkles pepper and salt, some garlic and parsley chopped very fine, and over the surface she sprinkles a few discreet drops of virgin oil from Aix.

Then, knocking the handle of the *poêle* with a sharp, authoritarian blow, Jeanne quickly turns the crusted golden omelet which slides from the smoking *poêle* into a well heated, white porcelain plate: a charm for the nose, a pleasure for the eye, a feast for the mouth, a triumph for *le grand art culinaire*.

2 large all-purpose potatoes, cooked in their jackets, then peeled
3 tablespoons unsalted butter
Salt and pepper
1 garlic clove, minced
1 tablespoon minced parsley
1 tablespoon olive oil

Cut the potatoes into exceedingly small dice. Melt the butter in a 10-inch frying pan and add potatoes. Crush them gently with a fork (it should be a rough mash, not purée smooth) and press and round the potatoes into a neat circle. Season, sprinkle the surface with minced garlic and parsley, and dribble on the olive oil. Let the cake brown uncovered and over medium heat for about 12 to 15 minutes. (The bottom should be quite brown, not just golden.)

Slide the potatoes into the curve of the pan, and quickly reverse/turn the cake onto a heated dish so that it folds double into a half circle. Rub the top of the "omelet" with a lump of butter to make it glossy and eat at once.

SERVES 2

POTATO ROSETTES

A thin, single-layer "doily" of potatoes to serve centered on each individual's dinner plate and topped with a brochette, a small roasted bird, or a chop.

TO MAKE ONE ROSETTE:

1 large all-purpose potato
3 tablespoons softened unsalted butter
Salt and pepper

Peel and round the potato and cut it into 15 or 16 slices about ⅛ inch thick. (For visual effect I sometimes trim each slice into a perfect circle with a 2-inch cookie cutter, but as long as the slices are basically round, this is not necessary.) Put the potatoes to soak for 30 minutes in cool water, then blot them impeccably dry on clean toweling.

Melt 2 tablespoons butter in a 9- or 10-inch frying pan. Arrange 9 of the potato slices in an overlapping circle that is

7 inches in diameter. Continuing in a flower petal pattern, arrange another 5 or 6 slices in a smaller layer on top and center the last slice in the middle so that the entire circle is compactly covered.

Use the remaining tablespoon of butter to grease the *bottom* (the *outside*) of a small, 7-inch saucepan. Fill the pan with 2 inches of water and set it carefully on top of the potatoes to act as a compressing weight. Cook the rosette over a leisurely, medium-low heat for about 10 minutes. Lift off the saucepan and check to see if the potatoes have formed a single, cohering whole. It will be readily apparent when all the "petals" have joined into the rosette, for the small cake will shake loose in one piece and the crusted bottom will hold all together. When this point is reached, turn the cake over with a large spatula, and replace the pan on top for another 5 minutes. After this time, remove the pan, season the potato, and let it cook and crisp another 5 minutes, or until nicely browned on the bottom. This rosette may be held in a warming oven while others are cooked. Wipe the pans clean between each frying. I would use two sets of pans to speed this process, but 4 is the number of rosettes I would stop at. A larger number of diners could have their potato needs filled more easily by one of the following three recipes.

POTATO SPIRALS

A pretty tendril/garnish to surround a small roast. A potato may be wasted when one first tries this technique, but it is not a difficult trick to master.

   4 medium-large, evenly shaped, all-purpose potatoes
   1 quart peanut oil for frying
   Flaked sea salt or kosher salt

Peel the potatoes, smoothing and rounding each in the process. Using either an apple corer or a swivel-bladed vegetable peeler, plunge through the lengthwise center of a potato, and dig out a neat round core. If a vegetable peeler is used, first slip it through the potato, twist the blade in a full circle to remove a slender, central cavity, then enlarge the hole to ¾ inch in diameter.

With a small, sharp knife, start turning the potato. The tip of the knife should protrude into the hollow but no further. Cut continuously round and around, always spiraling down and aiming for a consistently even slice about ¼ inch thick. (The outline of the knife should be barely visible under the slice—a thinner cut will tear the potato, a thicker one will result in an inflexible layer that can break when spread apart.) When you have achieved five or six good spirals, cut off the length and start a second coiled section. Drop the spirals into a bowl of cold water and let them soak for 30 minutes, then dry them with paper towels.

Pour 3 inches of oil into a deep-fryer or heavy saucepan and heat the oil. When a thin slice of potato dropped into the pot sizzles immediately and bounces to the surface, the oil is hot enough. Pick up the end of one potato spiral with tongs, hold the other end with a fork, and stretch it carefully apart like an accordion. Lower the spiral into the fat and hold it there for a few seconds until it hardens in its outstretched shape. Then leave it to deep-fry and repeat the process with more spirals. Remove each spiral when it has fried to a crisp, golden whorl. Drain on paper towels, sprinkle with salt, and place in a warming oven until all are finished. As this is, of necessity, a last-minute dish, it would be difficult to attempt a large quantity without assistance.

MAKES 12 SPIRALS

TURNIP AND POTATO PANCAKE

About ¾ pound turnips
1 large all-purpose potato
¼ cup grated Gruyère cheese
1 tablespoon cognac (optional)
1 tablespoon flour
Salt and pepper
4 tablespoons unsalted butter

Cut a good thick peel from the turnips. Slice them into large chunks and grate them through the medium blade of a Mouli-julienne or, by hand, through the large hole of a hand grater. Pick up the turnips by handfuls and squeeze until the mass is relatively dry.

Peel and grate the potato, add it to the turnips, and stir in cheese, cognac, flour, and seasoning.

Melt 3 tablespoons of butter in a 10-inch frying pan. When the butter foams, add the potato mixture, using a fork to firm and shape the gratings into a neat circle. Cook over medium-low heat for about 15 minutes. When the pancake is good and brown on the bottom, hold a dinner plate on top of it and turn the frying pan over, reversing the patty onto the plate. Melt the remaining tablespoon of butter in the pan and slip the pancake back. In another 10 to 15 minutes, the cake should be browned on the other side, but the heat could also be regulated down so that the pancake remains on hold, browning gently over a good half hour's time and adapting itself with some flexibility to waiting until needed. Each diner should butter his slice.

SERVES 4 OR 5

GRATED POTATO GRATIN

This recipe will be presented mainly as a formula, for it can be made as a single serving (use 1 potato), or six servings (use 4 to 5 potatoes and an 8-inch gratin dish), or 12 servings (use 8 or 9 potatoes and a paella pan).

Unsalted butter
All-purpose potatoes
Gruyère cheese, grated
Salt
Milk
Heavy cream
Pepper

Lightly butter a gratin dish. Grate the potatoes, preferably through the medium blade of a Mouli-julienne. Place a thin but dense layer of potatoes in the dish, then scatter on a handful of cheese. Salt and add another layer of potatoes and then more cheese. Heat some milk to steaming and pour it over the potatoes until they are almost covered. Bake in a 350° oven for about 40 minutes, then drizzle a thin coat of cream over the surface. Replace in oven for another 5 to 10 minutes or until golden on top, and serve.

This dish is particularly attractive when made in a large round pan which can also serve at table so that small grilled birds or chops or sausages can be placed regularly and directly on its browned surface and interspersed with small bunches of watercress. A pretty picture.

POTATOES À LA BARIGOULE

16 small all-purpose or new potatoes
1½ cups veal or soup stock or bouillon and water
3 tablespoons olive oil

1   teaspoon red wine vinegar
1   small onion, cut in half
2   garlic cloves, peeled
Salt
A bouquet garni (parsley, bay leaf, thyme)
A small handful of fresh bread crumbs
Pepper
A handful of parsley minced together with 1 garlic clove
Olive oil for sauce

Peel the potatoes. Place them in a frying pan with the stock, 2 tablespoons of oil, vinegar, onion, garlic, salt, and a bouquet garni. Cover pan and let the potatoes cook over fairly brisk heat for 10 minutes. Remove the cover and continue letting the potatoes cook while the stock reduces. Give the pan a shake from time to time and when the liquid thickens, fish out the onion, garlic, and bouquet garni. Finally the stock will disappear, leaving only a film of oil in the pan. Add another tablespoon of olive oil, then let the potatoes start browning over the same brisk heat. Shake the pan occasionally to turn the potatoes. When they are a lovely crusted gold on all sides, add the bread crumbs. As soon as they have absorbed the oil and toasted lightly, season the potatoes with pepper and throw in the parsley/garlic. Give the pan a final swirl to coat the potatoes with green, then place them in a heated serving bowl. The total cooking time should be 30 to 35 minutes in all. A small pitcher of olive oil should accompany this dish. As each diner cuts and slightly mashes his aromatic potatoes at table, he should drizzle them with oil in lieu of butter.

SERVES 4

CREAMED RADISHES

2 bunches of large, round red radishes
1 cup heavy cream
2 tablespoons unsalted butter
Salt, pepper
Fine-chopped parsley

Cut a careful, thin peel from the radishes so that no red remains on them. Allow the radishes to cook in boiling salted water until nearly tender. Drain them and, placing them in a small saucepan, put them briefly back over heat until thoroughly dry.

Pour the cream over the radishes, bring to a simmer, and cook until the cream thickens to the point of appearing a thin cream sauce. Stir in butter, seasonings, and herbs. People will assume the dish is creamed onions, so the slightly piquant, rooty quality of the radishes will offer an interesting mealtime diversion.

SERVES 4

SOUBISE GRATIN

In a traditional soubise, equal volumes of onions and rice are simmered together until tender, then sieved and thinned with butter and cream to either a thick purée consistency or a slightly more attenuated sauce. For this gratin, the onion side of the marriage is intensified by stewing in butter until lightly golden, which perforce adds a certain sweetness to the dish. Serve it, therefore, in lieu of mashed potatoes, with simple meats—pork, lamb, veal, and beef roasts, or chops.

The Basmati rice called for is a generic name for a type of

grain rather than a brand name. Basmati rice makes the perfect, firm-grained pilaf and, of course, it is untreated in any way. Buy it at specialty food shops where it is most often to be found in sections devoted to Middle Eastern and Indian foods.

> 3 large onions (not Spanish red)
> 4 tablespoons unsalted butter
> ⅔ cup long-grained rice (preferably Basmati)
> 1⅓ cups boiling chicken stock
> Salt and pepper
> About ¼ cup heavy cream
> ¼ cup grated Parmesan cheese
> ½ cup dry bread crumbs (coarse or fine)

Slice the onions thin and put them to sweat with 2 tablespoons of butter in a small, covered sauté pan over very low heat. Give the onions an occasional stir, and in about 45 minutes they should begin to turn a pale straw gold.

Place the rice in a saucepan and pour over it the boiling stock. Bring the rice to a boil, then regulate the heat to a low simmer and cook until the grains are tender and the stock has just evaporated (about 24 minutes). Purée the rice by pressing it through a sieve with a heavy spoon or pestle. (Do not use a food processor for this step—it would turn the rice to a glutinous lump.) Purée the onions (this *can* be done in the processor or, again, through the sieve) and mix onions, rice, seasoning, and enough heavy cream to turn the mixture to a thin mashed-potato consistency.

Butter a gratin dish and spoon in the soubise. Mix cheese and bread crumbs together. Melt the 2 remaining tablespoons of butter and stir into bread crumbs, mixing lightly with the fingers until the crumbs are uniformly buttery. Pack crumbs over the surface of the soubise, place the dish in a 350° oven, and in 20 to 25 minutes, a golden gratin will have formed.

SERVES 4 TO 6

SPINACH COOKED IN CREAM

10 ounces fresh spinach
½ cup heavy cream
Salt, pepper, nutmeg
Lemon juice

Wash and stem the spinach. The spinach must be very dry, so shake it in a salad basket, blot it with paper towels, whatever it takes to do the job. Heat the cream in a medium-sized saucepan. Crowd in the spinach and let it cook over a medium-high flame. Stir the mass over as the bottom leaves wilt. When all the spinach has reduced, season it and leave to simmer briefly, just until the cream thickens somewhat. Stir in a small squeeze of lemon juice and place the spinach in a heated serving bowl.

SERVES 4

SPINACH AND TOMATO TIAN

10 ounces fresh spinach
2 medium-large onions, sliced thin
4 tablespoons unsalted butter
One 28-ounce can tomatoes, drained
1 teaspoon sugar
1 teaspoon mixed dried herbs (oregano, marjoram, thyme)
Salt and pepper
1 garlic clove, minced
¼ cup pine nuts
A large handful of fresh bread crumbs
4 or 5 slices firm bread, crusts removed
Olive oil

Wash and stem the spinach. Place it in an uncovered pan and cook it in just the water clinging to its leaves. When tender, drain the spinach in a colander and refresh under cold water. Squeeze the mass until dry, then chop it fine.

Cook the onions in the butter over medium-low heat until they are limp and just beginning to color. Add the tomatoes, sugar, herbs, seasoning, garlic, nuts, and spinach to the onions and combine well, dividing the tomatoes, in the process, into small pieces. Let the tomatoes simmer briefly, then add enough bread crumbs to absorb excessively watery juices (the mixture should remain moist and somewhat soupy, however). Spread the mixture in a small, oiled gratin dish.

Soak the whole bread slices briefly in water, then press each slice between the palms of your hands. Place these moist and compact slices on top of the *tian* (trim them to a totally covering fit) and crisscross drizzles of oil over the top. Put to bake in a 350° oven for 25 to 30 minutes, or until the top is crisp and brown.

SERVES 4 TO 6

SQUASH CHARLOTTE

Here is a vegetable charlotte rethought in terms of the classic dessert apple charlotte. That sweet is composed in a bread-lined mold filled with a purée of apples so thick as to be almost a marmalade, while this derivative version substitutes an egg-bound mass of curry, onions, and squash. Other renditions are possible as long as it is kept in mind that the purée/filling must be strong enough (meaning dry enough) to support the encasing bread walls. A mass of desiccated tomatoes (peeled, seeded, squeezed until very dry) expanded with herbs, onions, and moist bread, is an attractive filling. And standard poultry stuffings or more refined mixtures of spinach, ricotta, Parmesan, and eggs could also find their way into the charlotte guise for presentation's sake. Apple charlotte needs its moistening cream . . . vegetable charlottes will also need anointing juices, be they from meat, a thin sauce, or just melted butter.

1 stick unsalted butter, softened
7 or 8 slices firm white home-style bread
About 4 pounds of dark orange winter squash
   (such as Butternut or Hubbard)
2 medium onions, chopped
½ teaspoon curry powder
¼ teaspoon sugar
Salt, pepper, nutmeg
3 egg yolks

Use 2 tablespoons of butter to generously grease a standard 3-pint charlotte mold. Completely line the bottom and sides with bread slices trimmed of their crusts. The traditional lining procedure is to cut five slightly heart-shaped pieces which overlap on the bottom. (For the best cutting guide use a 3½-inch, heart-shaped cookie cutter and push up its top indention.) Remove some of the excess bread at the center. Cut the remaining slices lengthwise and overlap them around the sides of the mold.

Cut the squash in pieces, remove seeds, and cover lightly with aluminum foil. Bake at 350° to 375° for about 45 minutes or until soft. Stew the onions in 2 tablespoons butter over low heat until purée soft, but do not let them brown. Mash the squash, add onions, curry powder, sugar, and seasoning. When the mixture has cooled a bit, stir in the egg yolks and fill the charlotte mold. Cover the top with a slice of buttered bread. Bake at 350° for 40 minutes. Remove from oven and let rest and settle for 5 minutes before unmolding. Melt the remaining butter and let it turn a light nut-brown. Serve in a small pitcher.

SERVES 6 TO 8

SAUTÉ OF GRATED ACORN SQUASH

1 large acorn squash
4 tablespoons olive oil
1 garlic clove, minced fine
Salt, pepper, nutmeg

Peel, seed, and grate the squash, preferably through the largest julienne blade of a Mouli-julienne. Place the squash in a large bowl and cover with cold, salted water. The water will immediately cloud over with exuded feculent starch. Drain the squash and cover again with cold water. Leave the squash to soak about 45 minutes, changing the water once more during this time.

Drain the squash well and pat it dry with paper towels. Heat the olive oil in a large sauté pan. Add the garlic and squash and cook over medium-high heat for no more than a minute or two. Keep the squash moving by shaking and flipping the pan. Taste frequently to test the texture. (What one is aiming for is an interestingly different textural consistency— not the usual mush/squash.) When the squash is just cooked but still pleasantly firm, season with salt, pepper, and nutmeg, then serve.

SERVES 4

TOMATO MARMALADE TART

Three 28-ounce cans of tomatoes, well drained *or*
  4 cups drained, home-preserved tomatoes
Salt
Pinch of sugar
  1 small garlic clove, pressed
  1 teaspoon minced parsley
  ½ teaspoon mixed dried thyme and oregano
A bay leaf
Pepper
Puff pastry or rich plain pastry
Parsley sprigs (preferably Italian parsley), for garnish

Drain the tomatoes very well. Press them gently to expel even more juice, then place the tomatoes in a saucepan with salt, sugar, garlic, and herbs. Mash the tomatoes to a pulp with a fork and let them stew for 35 minutes. Stir them several times during this period and continually spoon off accumulated juices. The result should be a thick and dry crush of tomatoes. Remove the bay leaf and season with pepper.

Roll out the pastry very thin and either line the outside of an upside down 8- or 9-inch tart tin (leaving 1-inch hanging down) or make 4 to 6 individual tarts by cutting circles 4 inches in diameter, moistening their perimeters lightly with water, and then laying on a ½-inch-wide strip of dough as a border. Leave the pastry to rest for 30 minutes before baking (so it will not oven-shrink), then bake in a 350° oven for about 12 minutes or until it has expanded fully but has not begun to brown. If you have made one large shell, remove the tin after baking.

Spoon in the tomatoes. Press a pretty sprig of parsley in the center and place the tart back in the oven for 35 to 40 minutes. The pastry should turn dark brown, the tomatoes should dry further and even brown in a spot or two. Serve as a lone accompaniment to red meat: the crust provides the farinaceous touch, the tomatoes are the vegetable, and nothing else is needed.

SERVES 4 TO 6

ZUCCHINI PATTY

2 large firm zucchini
½ teaspoon salt
1 small garlic clove, minced
3 tablespoons olive oil
1 egg
Pinch of marjoram
Salt and pepper
Chopped parsley, for garnish

Grate the zucchini through the medium blade of a Mouli-julienne or through the large holes of a hand grater. Sprinkle the shreds with salt and leave to drain for ½ hour. Squeeze the zucchini by handfuls (over a large sieve placed in the sink) until it is very dry. Sauté the zucchini and garlic in 1 tablespoon of oil for a brief time—just until it turns a vivid green. Let the vegetable cool slightly, then stir in the egg, marjoram, pepper, and remembering the previous salting, a discreet amount of salt.

Preheat the broiler. Heat 2 tablespoons of oil in a 9-inch frying pan. When hot, pour in the zucchini and let the patty cook on top of the stove until the bottom is nicely browned (about 6 minutes). Put the pan under the broiler just long enough for the top to set, then flip the cake over onto a pre-heated dinner plate. Sprinkle with parsley and serve.

SERVES 3 OR 4

VEGETABLE CLAFOUTI

A pudding that is usually a cherry-filled dessert, the *clafouti* is here rethought in terms of vegetables. Some variation is permissible—instead of mushrooms or peas, try asparagus, zucchini, green beans—but retain the onions and tomatoes in any case. I like to serve this creation with a roasted chicken and simply put the dish to bake in the chicken's last half hour of roasting time. In this case, one can spoon a tablespoon of the bird's basting fat over the pudding, exactly as if the *clafouti* were a Yorkshire pudding baking under a spitted roast of beef and receiving its anointing juices.

⅔ cup peeled pearl (silver-skin) onions
⅔ cup green peas, preferably fresh
3 tablespoons unsalted butter
⅔ cup small cleaned mushrooms
1 can (28-ounce) tomatoes, well drained,
   chopped coarse
1 teaspoon mixed dried herbs
1 teaspoon chopped parsley
⅓ cup floor
¼ teaspoon salt
2 large eggs, beaten
¾ cup warm milk
Pepper
2 garlic cloves
Pinch of cayenne

Parboil the onions in boiling salted water until almost tender. Lift out the onions with a slotted spoon and parboil the peas in the same water, again stopping short of fully cooked.

Melt 2 tablespoons of butter in a sauté pan. Toss the onions, peas, mushrooms, half the tomatoes, and the herbs in the butter and let the mixture stew briefly until no moisture remains.

Butter a small gratin or pie plate with the remaining table-spoon of butter. Mix the flour and salt in a bowl. Make a well in the center, add the eggs and then the milk, gradually incorporating the liquids into the flour. Add pepper and mince 1 garlic clove through a press into the batter.

Turn the vegetables into the buttered dish and pour the batter over them. Put to bake in a 375° to 400° oven for about 25 minutes, or until the pudding is puffed and golden.

Put the remaining half can of tomatoes in a small pan. Add a minced clove of garlic, salt, pepper, and cayenne to taste, and let stew for 10 minutes. Rub the tomatoes through a sieve and serve this very small sauce along with the *clafouti*.

SERVES 4 TO 6

SAUTÉ OR SALAD OF BRIGHT WINTER VEGETABLE FLOWERS

An attractive all-purpose mix of crisp, cheerful vegetables that can be served hot or, when cooled to room temperature and intensified with seasoning, as a garnish/salad.

> 1 cup small pearl onions, peeled
> 1 large carrot, scraped
> 2 celery stalks
> 1 large sweet red pepper
> 1 medium zucchini
> 1 garlic clove
> 3 tablespoons olive oil
> 1 tablespoon minced parsley
> ½ teaspoon fine-grated zest of lemon
> 1 tablespoon lemon juice
> Salt and pepper

Parboil the onions in boiling, salted water. With a vegetable stripper or a small knife, make five or six evenly spaced grooves down the length of the carrot. Cut the carrot across in ¼-inch-thick slices which will resemble small flowers. When the onions are just tender, add the carrots and continue to boil for 2 minutes, then drain the vegetables into a colander.

String the celery stalks and cut them into thin, 2-inch-long strips.

Halve the red pepper, seed it, and cut the pepper into vague tulip flower shapes, each about an inch square.

Cut the peel off the zucchini in thick, wide lengths. Cut these strips into squares, then round the corners so each square becomes a circle. (All of these vegetable preparations can be done ahead of time and kept wrapped tightly with plastic wrap and refrigerated until needed. Use the zucchini interior in another vegetable dish.)

Peel the garlic and press down on it with the side of a knife blade to flatten the clove. Heat the oil and garlic together briefly, then let the oil steep (off the heat) for 10 minutes. Remove the garlic. Reheat the oil and when it is hot, add the vegetables. Sauté them over high heat, shaking the pan all the while and letting the vegetables turn and mix in the oil. When the vegetables are hot—the zucchini a vivid green and the celery just at a tender crunch—add the parsley, lemon zest and juice, and seasoning. Give the pan a final shake and dish the vegetables into a small heated serving bowl.

SERVES 4 TO 6

To make the dish into a salad, let the vegetables cool to room temperature or colder. Intensify the acidity by adding vinegar to taste, and moisten with more oil.

THE HAPPY SURPRISE OF WINTER SALADS

The preceding recipe, both vegetable and salad, leads to a few general words on winter salads, for it is challenging to think, during the dark months in off-season ways for a change, to rethink the fresh produce of winter in salad terms, and to imagine full salad meals of cooked then cooled vegetables, seafood, and meat attractively arranged on plates.

Two possible methods come to mind. The first is a rapid stir-fry or steamed-wilt of winter greens, as in the wilted watercress, kale, and green bean salads described below. These vegetables, left to cool after cooking, are so much more interesting than just another lettuce salad, and yet they are only a little more bother to prepare. The slight bitterness of watercress, the deep-bodied kale, the odd-textured green bean can all stand in their simplicity as direct complements to the most involved of preparations.

The second method involves cooking vegetables, then allowing them to marinate and cool in acidified juices or sauce, as in the following salads of stuffed Brussels sprouts, spiced onions, and sunchokes—all of which would make good lukewarm or cool accompaniments to meats of various kinds. Rethink corned beef and cabbage as a salad plate with a handsome slice of meat surrounded by bright, semi-pickled Brussels sprouts with rose pink centers. Think of cold sunchoke salad and its garlic-laden sauce accompanying a hot grilled sausage.

A particularly glamorous salad is the following Farmer's Pot, which best typifies the full salad meal. (It, like the Winter Vegetable Flowers, can also be a hot dish.) The presentation, directly in its cooking utensil, will certainly surprise and please guests, and it is possible to expand this dish in quantity until it fills a spectacular paella pan and serves 10 to 12 people. Notice the salad's wilted lettuce addition and think of using this technique in other settings. Lightly steam-wilt some leaves of escarole or purple leaf lettuce (they will look like seaweed) and place the leaves under a mixed array of seafood: stuffed mussels, oysters on the half shell, large shrimp cooked in the shell in their own sauce of white wine, oil, and herbs. Or wilt some spinach leaves, season them, then place a slice of cold or hot terrine on top.

FARMER'S POT—VEGETABLE OR SALAD

½ cup olive oil (for the Salad Pot)
or
6 tablespoons unsalted butter (for the Vegetable Pot)
1 garlic clove, pressed
2 medium-large artichokes
2 lemons
1½ cups pearl onions, peeled and scored with an X
on the stem end
8 small new potatoes, peeled and rounded
4 leeks, trimmed, washed, cut to 4-inch lengths
Salt and pepper
2 small zucchini, trimmed and sliced thin
½ cup green peas (fresh or frozen), parboiled
for 2 minutes
1 tablespoon minced parsley
1 large scallion, sliced thin
Boston or Bibb lettuce (for the Salad Pot)
Vinaigrette dressing (for the Salad Pot)

Heat the oil or butter with the pressed garlic and then set it aside to steep until needed.

Break off the stems from the artichokes. Even off the stem end with a stainless steel knife, then cut off the upper inch of the vegetable. Trim off the sharp points from the leaves with scissors, then cut the artichoke lengthwise through the middle. Run the knife around and under the fuzzy choke and lift it out (along with the small purple interior leaves), so that there is a neat, pear-shaped cavity in the center. Immediately squeeze lemon juice over and into the cut portions to prevent discoloration. Have a large pot of salted water at the boil. Squeeze in the juice of half a lemon and put the artichokes to cook, cut side down, in the water. When a knife point just pierces the heart (after 10 to 15 minutes), strain out the artichokes and leave them to drain upside down.

Remove the garlic clove and put 3 tablespoons of cooled fat in a 9- or 10-inch frying pan and add the onions, potatoes, leeks, and ⅓ cup of water. Season, then cover the pan and let the vegetables cook over medium heat. When the leeks are close to tender, remove them. Continue cooking the onions and potatoes, uncovered, until the potatoes are almost done. (It may be necessary to add more water to the pan.) Notice the liquid in the pan. When water and oil are mixed, the liquid appears creamy. It bubbles and the cooking sound is soft. When the water disappears, the clear fat will remain and the cooking sound will be a sharp, staccato fry. (Note this distinction—it will be important later.)

When the potatoes begin to be tender, arrange the artichokes in the pan, stems toward the center, leaves pointing toward the edge. The center should be empty and the onions and potatoes should be divided in the spaces between the leaf points. Fill the artichoke hollows with green peas. Radiate the leeks, one section between each pair of artichokes, from the center. Arrange the zucchini slices around the edge of the pan. Sprinkle the parsley and scallion over the vegetables and season well. Pour in a bit more water and drizzle the remaining fat over the vegetables, then cover the pan and continue cooking until the peas are tender.

To make a Vegetable Pot, uncover the pan and listen for the cooking sound. Turn the heat to medium high and let all water evaporate. Let the vegetables fry for 10 to 12 minutes in pure fat. Place 4 lemon wedges in the center hole and serve. The green vegetables should be just tender crisp; the white vegetables will be gilded brown from their fry. Squeeze the juice of half a lemon over the dish and carry to table. Serve with large garlic-rubbed croutons.

To make a Salad Pot, uncover the pan and rim the edge with small lettuce leaves. Take the pan off the heat, place the cover back on briefly, and let the lettuce half wilt to a bright green. Remove the cover and let the dish cool to room temperature or colder. Place 4 lemon wedges in the center hole. Sprinkle the vegetables lightly with lemon juice and make a small amount of highly acid vinaigrette dressing to serve on the side. Place the pan on table and serve forth.

SERVES 2 FOR A FULL MEAL, 4 AS A SIDE VEGETABLE OR SALAD

Note: the springtime freshness of this dish will depend on its careful timing. Do not overcook anything. Keep all vegetables *al dente* and remember that a combined cooking time follows the individual first cooking. For convenience, do all the peeling and trimming of vegetables ahead and cook the artichokes before also.

LA SALADE JAPONAISE

One of the most famous and hearty of salads is *salade Francillon* or *salade japonaise* as it is sometimes known. The following quotation, translated from the play *Francillon* by Alexandre Dumas, fils, appears in the first act, and the salad, even down to its truffled cap, was very chic in the late nineteenth century.

Cook some potatoes in bouillon, cut them in slices as for an ordinary salad and, while they are still warm, season with salt, pepper, a very good and fruity olive oil and vinegar—preferably Orléans vinegar, but it is not very important; what *is* important is a half-glass of white wine —Château Yquem if possible; also a generous amount of *fines herbes* chopped fine, fine. Cook, at the same time, some large mussels in a court bouillon with a stalk of celery; drain and add the seasoned potatoes; turn gently (fewer mussels than potatoes—the mussels should not dominate). When the salad is finished and has been turned (gently), cover it with a sort of skull-cap made with sliced truffles (which, of course, have been stewed in Champagne).

The salad should be prepared two hours before serving so that it will be well chilled at time of eating.

ALEXANDRE DUMAS, FILS

(*Francillon,* Act I, Scene 2, Annette's recipe)

To restate the recipe in more specific and realistic terms, prepare a dressing. Put in a bowl some salt, some fresh-ground pepper, and 2 tablespoons of white wine vinegar. When the salt is dissolved, stir in ⅓ cup quality olive oil and ⅓ cup quality sweet white wine (Château Yquem is a grand gesture but not necessary. Try instead a less expensive Sauternes. Château Filhot always seems a particularly good buy; or a Barsac, or a Vouvray.) Add 1 tablespoon each of minced parsley and either chives or tender scallion greens.

Prepare a court bouillon. Simmer a chopped onion, a sliced carrot, a celery stalk, a bay leaf, some parsley, and seasoning in a mixture of 2 cups white wine and 2 cups water for 30 minutes. Scrub and debeard 1½ pounds of mussels and put them to cook in the broth just after the potatoes begin to cook. When the mussels have opened, drain them from the stock.

Cook 2 pounds of unpeeled new potatoes in salted water. When they are tender-firm (as opposed to tender-mushy), drain the potatoes, then peel them and cut them across in ¼-inch-thick slices. Remove the mussels from their shells and add mussels and dressing to the warm potatoes. Turn and mix everything carefully. The salad can be cooled and eaten as is (taste carefully for seasoning); *or* a few mushrooms can be sautéed in oil and scattered over the top; *or* one can order fresh truffles (from Paul Urbani, 130 Graf Avenue, P.O. 2054, Trenton, N.J. 08607, in the winter months), slice them thin, warm them in Champagne, and flaunt them over the top.

SERVES 4 TO 6

WILTED WATERCRESS SALAD

2 large garlic cloves
3 tablespoons warm olive oil
2 large bunches watercress
Salt and pepper

Peel the garlic cloves and squeeze them through a garlic press into a small cup holding the warm olive oil. Let the oil steep for 15 minutes, then strain it through a fine sieve into a medium-sized saucepan.

Wash the watercress and break off the truly thick portions of stem. Dry the cress immaculately in paper toweling. Heat the oil and, when it is quite hot, add the watercress, stirring it rapidly with a spoon until it wilts, dramatically reduces in bulk, and turns a vivid green (about 1 minute in all). Season with salt and pepper and place in a small bowl to cool. Serve just cool or at room temperature. The crunchy stems and the slightly acrid astringency of the leaves make this salad a bright and pleasing on-plate accompaniment to all manner of mildly bland meats and fish.

SERVES 4

WILTED KALE SALAD WITH BACON DRESSING

1 pound kale
1 teaspoon sugar
Salt and pepper
4 strips of bacon
2 tablespoons red wine vinegar
2 hard-boiled eggs, sliced
4 lemon wedges

Stem the kale and wash it carefully. Discard any yellowed leaf portions. Bring a large pot of salted water to the boil. Add the teaspoon of sugar and throw in the kale. Cook, uncovered, until the kale is *just* tender (keep testing a leaf), then strain into a colander and refresh under cold water. Press the greens gently and dry them as much as possible. Place them in a small, round dish, and fluff up and arrange the leaves prettily. Season well.

Dice the bacon and put it into a frying pan over low heat. Let the fat render out, then pour it over the kale. Quickly pour the vinegar into the hot pan, swirl it about over heat, then pour it onto the salad. Garnish the edges of the dish with egg slices and lemon wedges.

SERVES 4

WILTED GREEN BEAN SALAD

A basic method for treating green beans in Chinese cooking is to fry them in hot oil until shriveled, then combine them with a sweet, gingered mince of pork and scallions. This adapted version, mixed with a Provençal sensibility, makes a tasty dish out of technically fresh but over-large, off season winter beans. Choose the beans as small and tender as possible, however.

> 1 pound fresh green beans
> 1½ cups olive oil
> 2 garlic cloves, minced
> 6 scallions, whites and tender greens, sliced thin
> 4 anchovy filets, dried and minced
> 6 canned or home-preserved tomatoes, squeezed dry
> 2 tablespoons chopped parsley
> ½ teaspoon mixed dried herbs (thyme, oregano)
> Salt, pepper, cayenne
> Zest and juice of ½ lemon

Rinse, stem, and string the beans, then dry them well. Heat the olive oil in a wok or a medium-sized saucepan. Drop in some of the green beans (they will be cooked in 3 or 4 batches) and let them fry until puckered and wilted. Lift out the beans with a strainer and continue with another batch until all are fried. (Let the beans drain on several thicknesses of paper toweling to absorb excess oil.)

In a small frying pan, place 3 tablespoons of the cooking oil, the garlic, and the scallions. Let the scallions cook and soften briefly, then add anchovies, tomatoes, parsley, herbs, and seasoning. Let the mixture stew over low heat for 10 minutes. Add the lemon zest and juice to the tomatoes, then stir sauce into the beans. Let the salad cool to at least room temperature or colder before serving. Check the seasoning carefully and add salt, pepper, or more lemon as needed.

SERVES 4 TO 6

STUFFED BRUSSELS SPROUT SALAD

½ cup white wine vinegar
1 teaspoon salt
½ teaspoon whole peppercorns
A bay leaf
About 2 pounds large Brussels sprouts
Olive oil
¾ cup diced hard sausage of choice *or* an equal amount
   of cooked, leftover meat
½ slice fresh bread, crumbled
1 teaspoon grated onion
1 small garlic clove, pressed
Salt, pepper, nutmeg, allspice
1 teaspoon coriander seeds
1 tablespoon minced parsley

Combine vinegar, seasoning, bay leaf, and 3 cups of water in a covered frying pan and let the mixture simmer for 10 minutes.

Trim and wash the Brussels sprouts, removing any wilted outer leaves. Let the sprouts sit in cold water for 20 minutes, then drain them well. With a small, sharp knife, dig out ½-inch cores from the top center of each sprout, but leave the bottom stem intact.

Add the sprouts to the vinegar brine. Cover the pan, turn the heat to low, and let the sprouts steam. (There should be little agitation in the cooking water.) When they are tender but still crisp, strain them out and leave to drain and cool.

Heat a tablespoon of oil and sauté the sausage, bread, onion, and garlic together briefly. Drain off any oil, then purée the mixture to a paste in a food processor or blender. Season with salt, pepper, a touch of nutmeg and allspice.

Press a bit of the mixture into each Brussels sprout indention. Arrange the sprouts in a single, close layer in a dish that will just hold them. Drizzle oil over the top, scatter on the coriander seeds and parsley, then cover with plastic wrap and put to marinate in the refrigerator overnight. Serve slightly chilled.

SERVES 4 TO 6

JERUSALEM ARTICHOKE SALAD WITH GARLIC CLOVES AND CREAM

2 pounds Jerusalem artichokes
⅓ cup olive oil
30 large garlic cloves
2 tablespoons red wine vinegar
1 cup heavy cream
Salt and pepper
¼ cup Niçoise olives and minced parsley, for garnish

Bring a saucepan of water to the boil. Clean the Jerusalem artichokes by rubbing them over lightly with a kitchen brush under cool running water, then drop the vegetables into the water and let them parboil for 5 minutes. Drain well.

Heat the olive oil in a sauté pan. Add the unpeeled garlic cloves and ⅓ cup water. Cover the pan and let the garlic stew over medium heat while you peel the chokes. When the chokes are peeled, add them to the pan and re-cover. Let the vegetables and garlic cook until both are tender and pierceable with a fork, but do not let them brown. Shake the contents of the pan frequently as the end of cooking approaches, and add a bit more water if necessary. When the chokes are tender, they should just begin frying in pure oil.

Pour the contents of the pan into a bowl. Add the vinegar to the pan and let it cook off and evaporate over low heat. Stir in the cream and season well. Raise heat and give the cream a brief simmer until it turns to a thick sauce. Replace the chokes and garlic in the pan and shake the pan well so the vegetables become coated with the sauce, then pour into a serving dish. Sprinkle the minced parsley over the top and garnish with olives. Cool to room temperature (or slightly cooler, but not chilled), before serving.

SERVES 4 TO 6

CHICKPEA SALAD

    4 cups dried chickpeas
    ½ teaspoon bicarbonate of soda
    2 large onions, sliced thin
    2 garlic cloves, minced
    A bouquet garni (bay leaf, parsley, thyme, celery,
        a 2-inch piece of orange peel)
    Salt, pepper
    ¼ teaspoon sugar
    6 canned or home-preserved tomatoes, squeezed free
        of juices and chopped
    2 tablespoons minced parsley

Cayenne, to taste
¾ cup olive oil
Juice of 1 lemon
Grated zest of 1 small lemon, for garnish

Look over the chickpeas carefully for any foreign matter. Wash them under cool water, then put them in a pan, add the bicarbonate of soda, and cover generously with water. Let stand overnight.

Rinse the chickpeas well and at length, then place them back in a pot. Add the sliced onions, garlic, bouquet garni, and salt, and cover with 2 quarts of water. Bring to a boil, skim off any frothy scum, then regulate the heat to a bare simmer and cover the pot. Cook for 2 hours or until the chickpeas are just edibly tender.

Drain the chickpeas, remove the bouquet garni, then place peas back in the pot. Resalt, add pepper, sugar, tomato pulp, minced parsley, cayenne, and olive oil. Squeeze in the lemon juice, then pour in ⅔ cup hot water and let the peas stew, uncovered, until the water reduces and the oil, onions, and tomatoes melt into a tasty liaison. Pour into a serving dish, scatter the lemon zest over the top, and put to cool. Retaste for seasoning (which should be sprightly) before serving.

SERVES 4 TO 8

SPICED ONION SALAD

 2 pounds pearl onions
 ½ cup olive oil
 ½ teaspoon sugar
 ¼ cup red wine vinegar
 1 cup white wine
One 28-ounce can tomatoes, very well drained,
    then chopped to a pulp
 6 cloves
 ¼ teaspoon cinnamon
A bay leaf
 2 tablespoons raisins
 1 tablespoon minced parsley
 1 medium-sized sweet red pepper, seeded and cut into
    short, thin strips
Salt and pepper
 ⅓ cup of slivered almonds or pine nuts, lightly toasted
Minced parsley, for garnish

Keep the onions in a bowl of cold water to facilitate peeling.
Peel them with a stainless steel knife and notch a small X in
the stem end of each onion.

Heat the olive oil in a sauté pan. Add the onions, along
with a pinch of sugar, and let them turn a pale gold over
medium heat. Shake the pan frequently to roll the onions and
gild all surfaces. Add the vinegar and let it cook and fume
briefly, then add wine, tomatoes, cloves, cinnamon, bay leaf,
raisins, parsley, and red pepper strips. Season generously and
give the pan a good shake to mix the elements evenly. Cover
the pan and simmer very slowly for about 50 minutes. The
onions should be tender, the remaining ingredients a rich,
blended, stew-like sauce with a visible oiled-dressing appearance. Add a bit more oil if necessary. Stir in the nuts, then
spoon the onions into a rustic serving dish and scatter parsley
over the top. This salad is best after it has been refrigerated

for 24 hours and then brought back to room temperature. Make sure that it is seasoned adequately by tasting the dish after refrigeration and adding more salt or pepper if need be. SERVES 4 TO 6

EGGPLANT AND APPLE CHUTNEY SALAD

And finally a salad of such ambrosial richness that it can only lead in to dessert. Serve this one with roasted or grilled lamb, cumined rice, and Indian bread for a meal of instant exotica.

FOR THE SAUCE:

½ cup raisins, preferably Malaga (plumped in hot water for 20 minutes, then drained)
½ cup mango chutney
1 garlic clove, sliced
2 large shallots, sliced
1 teaspoon Dijon-style mustard
3 tablespoons red wine vinegar
Large pinch of cinnamon
¼ teaspoon powdered ginger
¼ teaspoon salt
Pepper
Olive oil

1 eggplant (about 1¼ pounds)
1 medium onion, sliced thin
2 tablespoons olive oil
1½ pounds apples, peeled, cored, cut into 8 sections
(firm, crisp eating apples will hold their shape best)
Juice of 1 lemon
Grated zest from 1 lemon and minced parsley,
for garnish

Combine raisins, chutney, garlic, shallots, mustard, vinegar, cinnamon, ginger, and seasoning in a blender or food processor bowl. Purée together, adding in the process 2 or 3 tablespoons of olive oil to turn the mixture in a sauce-like direction. Set aside.

Cut the eggplant into 1-inch-thick slices and cut these slices into 1-inch cubes. Salt the cubes lightly and leave them to drain for 30 minutes.

Fry the onion in 2 tablespoons of oil over low heat. When it is just starting to turn pale gold, add the apple slices, cover, and let them sauté until tender. Spoon the apples and onions into a bowl and wipe the frying pan clean.

Squeeze the eggplant cubes gently, to help them expel their water. Sauté the cubes in sufficient olive oil until cooked. Draw the eggplant to the side of the pan with a slotted spoon. Press on the mass to allow any cooking juices to run off, remove and discard the oily juices, then add apples to eggplant. Pour on the reserved sauce and mix everything together by carefully folding the elements over and over each other until the sauce is well distributed. Simmer the entire salad for 5 minutes, adding a bit of oil if necessary to moisten the sauce. Put the salad to chill overnight. Taste for seasoning the next day, then spoon the salad into a rustic dish and garnish with grated lemon zest and minced parsley.

SERVES 6

Desserts

He was three years old when he took his earliest step in education; a lesson of color. The second followed soon; a lesson of taste. On December 3, 1841, he developed scarlet fever. For several days he was as good as dead, reviving only under the careful nursing of his family. When he began to recover strength, about January 1, 1842, his hunger must have been stronger than any other pleasure or pain, for while in after life he retained not the faintest recollection of his illness, he remembered quite clearly his aunt entering the sick-room bearing in her hand a saucer with a baked apple.

HENRY ADAMS *The Education of Henry Adams*

BAKED STUFFED APPLES ON CROUTONS

FOR EACH SERVING:

>   1 large cooking apple
>   4 tablespoons unsalted butter
>   1½ tablespoons brown sugar
>   ½ teaspoon cognac
>   Cinnamon
>   1 tablespoon raisins (plumped in warm water)
>   Red currant jelly, melted
>   1 slice firm white bread, trimmed into a round

Cut a 1-inch plug from the bottom of the apple. Core out the apple (use either an apple corer or a small knife), leaving a neat, inch-wide cavity. Place the bottom plug back in the apple and cut a slight incision in the skin around the apple's girth to prevent it from bursting during its bake.

Put 2 tablespoons of butter, the sugar, cognac, and cinnamon in a small bowl and knead them together to a smooth paste. Mix in the raisins and stuff the apple. Place the apple in a small, buttered baking tin. Add a few tablespoons of water to the dish and generously brush the top and sides of the apple with melted jelly. Put to bake in a 350° oven for about 30 minutes, or until tender.

Fry the bread round in 2 tablespoons of butter until nicely browned on both sides. When the apple has baked, place it on the crouton in a bowl. Add a tablespoon of water and one of jelly to the juices in the pan and pour over the apple. (Some cream might be appreciated here, also.)

It would be particularly romantic to bake the apples first in the oven, then transfer them to an iron skillet and allow them to spend their last few cooking minutes on a hot fireplace hearth:

. . . And, for the winter fireside meet,
Between the andiron's straddling feet,
The mug of cider simmered slow,
The apples sputtered in a row. . . .
JOHN GREENLEAF WHITTIER, "Snowbound"

CARAMELIZED APPLE PANCAKE

3 firm, medium-large eating apples
6 tablespoons unsalted butter
1 tablespoon cognac
5 tablespoons sugar
¼ teaspoon cinnamon
¼ cup flour
Pinch of salt
2 eggs, lightly beaten
½ cup heavy cream
½ cup milk
Chilled, heavy cream

Prepare the apples. Have 2 tablespoons of butter melted in a frying pan. Peel, core, and cut the apples into dice, adding them immediately to the butter so they do not discolor. Sprinkle them with cognac, 2 tablespoons of sugar, and the cinnamon, then cover and, shaking the pan frequently, let the apples stew over medium-high heat until all liquids evaporate and the apples are tender but have not disintegrated.

Mix flour and salt in a bowl. Make a well in the middle and stir in the eggs, cream, and milk. Stir the apples into the batter.

Melt 1½ tablespoons of butter in a 9-inch frying pan and when the butter is very hot, pour in the apple batter. Let the pancake cook, covered and over medium heat, for a good 10 to 12 minutes. (The bottom of the pancake should be thoroughly brown; the cake itself should slide easily in the pan; and the top of the pancake should be almost firm.) Tilt the pan up and slide the pancake out carefully onto a dinner plate. Melt another 1½ tablespoons of butter in the frying pan. Holding the plate and the frying pan at angles to each other, quickly reverse the pancake, unbrowned side down, into the frying utensil. Let the pancake cook for another 10 minutes uncovered, so that the bottom has a chance to crust and brown. (This cooking time can be drawn out if need be by turning the heat to low.)

In a small saucepan, melt the remaining tablespoon of butter. Stir in 3 tablespoons of sugar and let the mixture cook, unstirred, over low heat until the sugar melts and turns a medium caramel color. Immediately drizzle and swirl the caramel over the gilded top of the pancake.

When the cake has finished browning, slide it out onto a round, heated serving platter. Serve at once onto dessert plates and pour a thin stream of cold, heavy cream over the portions so that its chill can harden the still warm caramel into a thin, crisp brittle.

SERVES 5 OR 6

APPLE FRITTER RINGS

FOR THE BATTER:

⅔ cup sifted flour
Pinch of salt
1 tablespoon sugar
1½ tablespoons unsalted butter, melted
1 tablespoon cognac
2 egg whites at room temperature

Juice of 1 lemon
3 tablespoons Calvados *or* cognac
4 or 5 crisp eating apples
1 quart frying oil (peanut or safflower)
Cinnamon sugar

Combine the flour, salt, and sugar in a mixing bowl and make a well in the center. Stir in the butter, cognac, and ⅔ cup lukewarm water, mixing just until the ingredients seem smooth. Cover the bowl with a kitchen towel and let the batter rest for 1 hour. Immediately before its use, beat the egg whites to firm peaks and fold them into the batter.

Place the lemon juice and Calvados in a bowl. Peel the apples whole, cutting the peel off in a long rounding spiral. Core the apples with an apple corer or a small knife. Slice the apples across into rings about ¼ inch thick and dip the rings immediately in the lemon juice to discourage discoloration.

When the apples are finished, begin making the fritters. Heat the oil in a large sauté pan. (Test the heat by dropping in a small piece of batter: when it sizzles immediately, sinking then bobbing back to the surface, the oil is ready.) Blot the apple rings dry and dip them, a few at a time, into the batter. Fry the rings to an inviting brown. Strain the fritters out and let them blot briefly on a platter lined with several thicknesses of paper toweling, then roll the rings in abundant cinnamon sugar. Hold the finished fritters in a warming oven until all are done. These look particularly nice served in a basket lined with a red or blue checked napkin.

SERVES 6

TARTE TATIN

There are many versions of and methods for that most famous of French winter apple desserts, *tarte Tatin*. This one was told me by Madame Claude Peyrot of the restaurant Vivarois, and I always appreciate its plump, whole apple look. The ideal dish in which to make it is a round, straight-sided copper pan such as that used for *pommes Anna*. But students say they make it successfully in black iron skillets, Corning ware, and even tall aluminum cake pans if they watch the initial caramelizing carefully. The pan should be 2 to 3 inches tall, straight-sided, and able to be used both over a burner and then again in the oven. The listed apple amount will fill a 10-inch pan, but the tart can be made thicker, thinner, smaller or larger. One should also have a bulb baster handy.

4 to 5 tablespoons softened unsalted butter
Sugar
A good 5 pounds crisp apples, such as Winesaps,
   Cortlands or, failing all else, Yellow Delicious
Cinnamon
Pie pastry (plain or puff, leftover scrap is fine)

Spread a thick layer of butter onto the sides and over the bottom of the cooking dish. Sprinkle the pan's bottom with a layer of sugar. Give the pan a small shake to even the granules and measure the depth with a finger. The layer should be about ¼ inch thick. Place the pan over a medium-low fire and allow the sugar to caramelize. Resist the urge to stir but watch as the butter and sugar melt and small spots of deep caramel gold appear. Move the pan around on the burner and with a wooden spoon draw out the brown in careful swirls, mixing it into the as yet uncaramelized sugar until the whole pan bottom is a rich, fairly dark amber. Again, do not stir at any point and risk turning the mixture to a sugared, fudge-like grain. Remove pan from the heat.

Preheat the oven to 350°. Cut the apples in two lengthwise, peel them, and dig out the cores. Cover and crowd the pan surface with the most perfect halves, full rounded side down. Slice the remaining apples over the top, heaping them slightly in the middle and sprinkling on cinnamon from time to time and to taste. Roll out some pastry and cover the pan. Leave a generous border around the top and tuck the dough into the pan and securely down around the apples on the sides. Put to bake for about 1 hour.

At the end of this time, remove from oven, tip the pan slightly, and using a bulb baster, draw off any and all juices into a small saucepan. Reduce these juices over a good flame. Reverse the tart onto a serving platter. The apples may be pushed into better cosmetic shape with a spoon if necessary, and I sometimes score each apple's surface gently with the tines of a fork for small, decorative effect.

When the juices have become a jelly glaze, brush it over the tart for finishing gloss.

SERVES 8

APPLE AND ALMOND GRATIN

    2 slices firm white bread
    ½ cup sliced almonds
    ½ cup sugar
    3 tablespoons melted unsalted butter
    Juice of ½ lemon
    7 or 8 firm eating apples (Winesaps, Cortlands, etc.)
    1 egg plus 1 egg yolk
    1 cup heavy cream
    ½ teaspoon cinnamon

Place bread, almonds, half the sugar, and the butter in a blender or food processor and chop to a relatively fine grind. Set aside.

Place the lemon juice in a large mixing bowl.

Peel, core, and quarter the apples. Grate them through the large hole of a hand grater or through the medium blade of a Mouli-julienne. Place a sieve over a bowl and as handfuls of apple are finished, squeeze the gratings over the sieve, then drop the apples into the bowl containing the lemon juice and give them a quick turn.

Preheat the oven to 350°. Beat the eggs, cream, and cinnamon together and stir into the apples. Butter a gratin or quiche dish and pour in the apples, smoothing the top of the mixture as even as possible. Cover the surface with the bread/ nut topping and sprinkle the remaining sugar over the top. Put to bake for 25 to 30 minutes, or until the crust resembles a nicely browned gratin. This relatively dry and only mildly sweet dessert may be accompanied with cream, ice cream, or Sauternes.

SERVES 6

APPLE AND ALMOND OMELET

FOR THE APPLE FILLING:

     5 firm eating apples such as Winesaps
     3 tablespoons unsalted butter
     2 tablespoons sugar
     Cinnamon to taste
     ⅓ cup heavy cream
     2 tablespoons Calvados (optional)

FOR THE FLAT OMELETS:

     6 eggs
     2 ounces toasted, ground almonds
     1 tablespoon sugar
     2 tablespoons heavy cream
     4 tablespoons unsalted butter

FOR THE TOPPING:

     2 eggs, separated
     Sugar
     ¼ teaspoon cinnamon
     A handful of lightly toasted, sliced almonds

Both the apple filling and the flat omelets can be compiled ahead. At assembly time, heat the apples while the topping is being made.

For the apple filling, peel, core, and cut the apples into thick slices. Melt the butter in a frying pan and add apples, sugar, cinnamon, and cream. Let the apples stew until just cooked, but do not let them dissolve into a soft mush. Shake the pan frequently rather than stirring the contents so as not to break the tender fruit. Add the Calvados toward the end of cooking time. The final filling should be quite thick. Set aside.

To make the flat omelets, mix the eggs, almonds, sugar, and cream until well blended. Melt 2 tablespoons of the butter in a 9-inch omelet or frying pan and when the butter has foamed then subsided, pour half the eggs into the pan and let the omelet cook until set through and firm on the top. (Smooth uncooked egg to the edge of the pan and shake the omelet gently throughout cooking.) Slide the finished egg out flat onto a dinner plate. Melt another 2 tablespoons of butter and make another omelet in the same manner.

To compose the dessert, preheat the broiler. Place one flat omelet in a lightly buttered, round gratin or quiche dish. Spoon on the hot apples and cover with the second omelet.

Make a topping by beating the two egg whites with an electric mixer until firm. Place the egg yolks, 3 tablespoons of sugar, and cinnamon in another bowl and, continuing with the same unwashed beaters, blend the yolks and sugar until thick and lemon colored. Fold yolks and whites together and frost and swirl them over the top of the omelet cake. (Pipe the mixture from a pastry bag for a more decorative effect.) Scatter the almonds and then a handful of sugar over the surface and put the omelet under the hot broiler until the "frosting" is lightly tipped with brown.

SERVES 6

BROWN SUGAR OMELET

¼ cup granulated sugar
5 eggs, at room temperature
3 tablespoons unsalted butter
3 ounces cream cheese, softened and mashed to a paste
   with 2 tablespoons brown sugar
Heavy cream

Put the granulated sugar and ¼ cup water in a small sauce-pan. Bring slowly to a boil, then simmer for 5 minutes.

Separate 3 eggs, place the whites in a bowl, and beat them with an electric mixer until stiff. Pour the syrup over the whites in a thin stream and allow the mixer, on medium speed, to combine the two. (This loose, marshmallow-like substance, called Italian Meringue, is more stable than plain beaten egg whites, hence its use where "body" is required and when items are to be "flashed" or quickly browned in the oven.)

Place the remaining 2 whole eggs and 3 egg yolks in a bowl. Without cleaning the beaters, mix these eggs until thick and foamy.

Preheat the broiler; melt the butter in a 9-inch omelet or frying pan. Fold together the egg yolks and the meringue and, when the butter in the pan has foamed and subsided, pour the eggs into the pan. Turn the heat to medium low. Shake the pan gently, smoothing the uncooked egg to the edges as the center sets, and let the omelet cook and set slowly. When the bottom has firmed (though the top will still be liquid), disperse the mashed brown sugar and cheese over a 5-inch circle in the omelet's center.

Place the omelet pan under an intense broiler until the cream cheese melts, the sugar bubbles, and the eggs are puffed. Slide the omelet out onto a heated serving platter,

folding it over double in the process. Pour a small moistening
of unsweetened heavy cream over each portion.

SERVES 4

BREADED OMELET WITH STRAWBERRY SAUCE

> 2 tablespoons raisins
> 2 slices fresh white bread, crusts removed
> ⅓ cup heavy cream
> 2 tablespoons sugar
> 3 eggs
> 3 tablespoons unsalted butter
> 1 cup strawberries and juice (home-preserved *or*
> thawed frozen berries) mashed to a chunky sauce
> and sweetened to taste

Put the raisins in a small saucepan with 2 cups of water. Heat
them to a boil, then remove pan from heat and let the raisins
steep for 20 minutes until nicely plump. Drain well.

Cut the bread into ½-inch cubes. Sprinkle the cubes with
the cream and let them absorb for 10 minutes.

Beat the sugar and eggs together until thick and pale
lemon colored (use an electric mixer for fastest results). Stir
in the raisins and bread.

Melt the butter in a 9-inch frying pan, and when it has
melted, foamed, and just begun to brown, pour in the eggs.
Let them cook over medium heat until the bottom is set.
(Shake the pan gently and draw the uncooked egg to the
edges of the omelet.) When the omelet is set (though the top
should be fluffy and moist), slide the omelet to the edge of
the pan and double it out onto a round, heated serving platter
so that it folds neatly in two. Spoon the strawberry sauce
over the top.

SERVES 2

BREAD AND BUTTER PUDDING

Unless, as a child, one was overfed that most famous of English nursery foods, bread and butter pudding (in which case, like Ambrose Bierce, one might imagine all custard to be "a detestable substance produced by a malevolent conspiracy of the hen, the cow and the cook"), the mild sweet simplicity of that dish can still be found charming and a great comfort in later years. The pudding must be gently cooked, however, so that its delicate baked egg custard does not shrivel and toughen from too intense heat.

> 4 slices firm white bread, crusts removed
> Softened unsalted butter
> ¼ cup sultana raisins
> 3 eggs
> ¼ cup sugar
> 1 teaspoon vanilla
> 2¼ cups warm milk
> Nutmeg
> 2 tablespoons sugar for surface

Spread a thin coat of butter on both sides of the bread and cut slices diagonally into two triangles. Lightly butter an 8-inch gratin dish and overlap the slices down its center. Scatter the raisins over the surface.

Whisk the eggs, sugar, and vanilla together until well blended. Slowly whisk in the just warmed milk, then pour the custard through a sieve into a clean bowl. Pour half of the mixture over the bread and let stand for 45 minutes. (This step is necessary, for it allows the bread to become heavy with moisture and thus ensures that it remains an integral element within the pudding rather than just a floated-to-the-surface bit of dry bread on top.)

When the bread is soaked, preheat the oven to 325°, whisk

the remaining custard lightly and pour it over the top of the pudding. Dust the surface with a fine grating of nutmeg and then 2 tablespoons of sugar.

Set a baking tin half filled with hot tap water in the oven. Place the custard in this *bain-marie* and let it cook for about 45 to 50 minutes. The pudding should just set and its surface become lightly golden. At no time should the water around the pan approach a boil or the eggs will curdle, a condition made manifest by a series of small holes appearing throughout the custard and a surface that is puckered and skinned. Turn down the heat if necessary.

When the pudding is cooked, remove from oven. Clean any specks of crusted brown from around its rim with damp toweling and serve immediately.

SERVES 4

NUTMEG TART

An almost embarrassingly quick and easy dish, this mild, sweet cheesecake/tart looks the essence of a country farmhouse dessert. Bake and serve it in a rustic ceramic dish.

> 1 **pound cottage cheese**
> 3 **eggs**
> ½ **teaspoon vanilla**
> ⅓ **cup sugar**
> 2 **tablespoons unsalted butter, softened**
> 3 **tablespoons flour**
> 2 **tablespoons golden raisins**
> **Nutmeg**
> **Butter and sugar for dish**

Place cottage cheese, eggs, vanilla, sugar, butter, and flour in the bowl of a food processor and blend until smooth. (Or stir all the ingredients together in a bowl, then press the cottage cheese through a sieve so that it is perfectly smooth.) Stir in the raisins.

Preheat the oven to 350°. Lightly butter a 10-inch pie tin or rustic flan dish. Pour the cheese into the dish, smooth the top, and grate nutmeg over the surface. (The nutmeg will provide the main flavoring essence, but don't overdo it, all the same.) Sprinkle the top with 2 tablespoons of sugar and put the tart to bake for 25 to 30 minutes. Let the tart cool to room temperature and then refrigerate briefly before serving. Can be accompanied by home-preserved fruit.

SERVES 6 TO 8

FIGGY PUDDING

¾ cup sugar
3 cups dried figs, stemmed and cut into small pieces
4 tablespoons unsalted butter, melted
2 eggs slightly beaten
⅓ cup milk
1⅔ cups sifted flour
Large pinch of salt
¼ teaspoon cinnamon
1 teaspoon baking soda
Butter for mold

Stir ¾ cup sugar together with ¾ cup water in a saucepan. Bring to a boil over medium heat, then add the figs. Cook at a simmer until the figs are tender and jam-like. Let cool, then add butter, eggs, and milk. Mix the flour, salt, cinnamon, and soda together and stir the dry ingredients into the figs.

Generously butter a mold. (As the pudding is to be steamed, use a traditional pudding mold and steamer if you possess one. Or use a charlotte mold or a fancy mold with a central tube. In any case, the batter should fill it by two thirds.) Spoon the pudding mixture into the mold, then cut a piece of kitchen parchment or waxed paper into a large circle and fit it over the top of the mold. Use kitchen string to tie the paper on in a neat cap. (This will prevent water that accumulates on the steamer's lid from dripping into the pudding.)

Heat the water in the steamer and place the pudding on the cooking rack. (Or place a cake rack on the bottom of a large pot so that the mold does not rest directly on the bottom. Add enough water to reach three quarters of the way up the side of the mold. Bring the water to a steam and set in the pudding. The steam should be just short of a simmer and should not involve noisy rattlings of the mold or small boiling bubbles.) Cover the pan tightly and steam for 2 hours. It may be necessary to add water at some point to maintain its level.

Remove the pudding and let it sit for 5 minutes. Untie the paper, run a knife around the edge, and turn the pudding out onto a serving dish. The pudding, served hot or warm, can be accompanied with pouring cream, a dessert sauce of your choice, or:

VANILLA HARD SAUCE

Cream 4 tablespoons of butter, then add ½ cup of granulated sugar, ⅓ cup of brown sugar, and ½ teaspoon vanilla. Beat for a good 5 minutes (let a machine do the work), until the sauce is very smooth and fluffy. Chill. Place a cold lump of this hard sauce on each serving and let it melt over the pudding.

MAKES 8 PORTIONS

ALI-BAB'S DATE PUDDING WITH ALMOND CREAM

The neat engineering of this date pudding, adapted from Ali-Bab's *Gastronomie pratique*, is a marvel. Consider the economy of effort, the efficiency, of the following: a mold is filled with layerings of dried ingredients; an almond cream is prepared, part of which is poured into the mold; the mold is then baked while the remaining cream is thickened just slightly to the consistency of a sauce—and there you have a pudding and a topping from a single stroke. The original recipe calls for *biscuits à la cuiller* (sponge finger biscuits), but a variety of other elements will work, including that old standby, bread.

> 10 to 12 homemade ladyfinger biscuits
> *or*
> several thin slices of *génoise* cake
> *or*
> 5 or 6 slices crustless white bread
> 1 pound pitted dates
> 1 cup raisins
> About ¼ cup sugar

FOR THE ALMOND CREAM:

> 5 eggs
> ⅔ cup sugar
> 1 stick unsalted butter, melted
> 1 teaspoon vanilla
> ⅔ cup heavy cream
> 1½ cups blanched almonds, ground
> Butter and sugar for mold

Generously butter and sugar a 2½-quart soufflé or charlotte mold. Cut the cake or bread into thin, inch-wide strips and arrange them over the bottom of the mold and then neatly around the sides. Put the mold to chill. (Some cake should remain to cover the top.)

Chop the dates to a near purée (a two-cleaver alternating mince is the most rapid method). Layer some dates into the mold, then some raisins, and then a thin powdering of sugar. Place biscuit strips on top, then continue layering in this fashion and end with strips of biscuit.

Preheat the oven to 350°. Prepare the almond cream. Beat the eggs and sugar together with an electric mixer until pale and foamy. Stir in the butter, vanilla, cream, and almonds. Pour a scant ¾ of this mixture into the mold and give the dish a good tap on a countertop to settle it. Cover the mold with aluminum foil, place the dish in a *bain-marie*, and put to bake for 50 minutes to 1 hour.

Just as the pudding finishes its bake, place the remaining cream mixture in a small saucepan and whisk it over low heat until it thickens slightly. Remove the pudding from the oven, let it sit for 5 minutes, then run a knife around its edge and carefully unmold it onto a platter. Present the almond cream on the side.

SERVES 8

ROLY-POLY PUDDING

FOR THE SUET CRUST:

3 ounces suet
6 tablespoons unsalted butter, cut in small dice
3 cups flour
¼ teaspoon salt

A berry jam of choice

Make sure that what is sold to you as suet is truly such. The fat should be a glossy, waxy white, and it should be dry enough to crumble easily between the fingers. It should come from the area directly surrounding the cow's kidney (indeed, one can often see that smooth indention wherein the kidney has lain curled). I mention this because sometimes what is sold as suet meanders away into pure fat and that is not what is wanted.

Crumble the suet into a bowl, removing in the process any paper-thin membranes or red veinings. Add the butter and work the two fats together with the fingertips until smooth.

Combine the flour and salt, then start working in the fat. Rub the elements together between the fingers until the fat is well incorporated into the flour and the flour appears flaky. Add enough ice water to bind the flour and pack the dough into a neat ball. Wrap in plastic wrap and refrigerate for at least ½ hour.

Roll the dough out on a lightly floured surface to a rectangle at least 8 inches wide and with as much length as possible. Spread a very thick layer of jam over the dough, leaving an inch-wide border jam-free on both short widths and one long length. Roll the dough up lengthwise, starting with the jam-covered length. Moisten the long free border lightly with water and press the edges together.

The pudding can be wrapped in a cloth and boiled, but to my way of thinking, it is much easier to steam it. Lay the pudding on an ovenproof platter. Bring 1½ inches of water to a boil in a roasting pan or dutch oven. Place two soufflé cups upside down on the pan's bottom, and rest the platter on the cups. Regulate the heat so that the water is at the barest simmer, cover the pan, and steam the pudding for about 1 hour. The next step is nontraditional. Remove the platter and place it in a preheated 350° oven for 15 to 20 minutes so that the top crust can brown and crisp. Serve the pudding, cut in slices, with preserved fruit, a Melba sauce (sweetened

raspberry purée), or just whipped cream flavored with a bit of jam.
SERVES 6 TO 8

VANILLA RICE PUDDING/SOUFFLÉ

I am not greatly fond of rice puddings, but this minimally riced dessert is both simple and pleasant. It can be served hot from its baking dish as a soufflé, or it can be unmolded and left to chill—in which case it prefers to be thought of as a pudding. In the latter case, garnish it with crystallized mint leaves and pour a decorative stream of Melba sauce (sweetened raspberry purée) over the surface and around the sides.

¼ cup rice
4 cups milk
4 to 5 tablespoons sugar
1 teaspoon vanilla
3 eggs, separated
Large pinch of salt

Bring a small pan of salted water to a boil. Add the rice, stirring in the process, and then let the rice cook for 5 minutes. Drain well.

Heat the milk in a saucepan and add the rice. Simmer over very low heat, stirring frequently, until the rice cooks over a period of time to the consistency of an oatmeal gruel. Mix in sugar (taste and sweeten, to your own pleasure), then add vanilla. When the rice has cooled, stir in the 3 egg yolks and salt.

Preheat the oven to 350°. Beat the egg whites to stiff peaks and fold them into the rice. Pour the mixture into a buttered soufflé dish and place the dish in a *bain-marie* (a larger pan

containing 1 or 2 inches of water). Bake for 25 to 30 minutes.
Serve hot or cold.
SERVES 6 TO 8

CHOCOLATE SOUFFLÉ SAXON

A dessert that falls halfway between a pudding and a soufflé,
this custard will rise upon baking, sink upon unmolding, and
thus live up to its nominally designated "Saxon" character by
being heavier in spirit than its "soufflé" suggests. The complementary amalgam of chocolate and cinnamon provides its
always happy marriage, and the soufflé, though best warm, is
also good cold.

Butter and sugar for mold

1 stick unsalted butter
½ cup sugar
⅔ cup flour, sifted before measuring
Generous ¼ teaspoon cinnamon
⅔ cup milk
4 ounces semisweet chocolate
6 eggs, separated

1½ cups heavy cream
Vanilla, sugar, cinnamon

Butter a 2-quart soufflé dish, sprinkle in a scoop of sugar, and
turn the dish until a goodly amount of sugar adheres to the
butter. Pour out excess sugar and refrigerate dish until needed.

Cream the butter and sugar together, then stir in the flour
and cinnamon. Place milk and chocolate in a saucepan over
medium heat, stirring frequently to prevent scald. When the
chocolate has melted and the milk is about to lift into a boil,
stir the milk slowly into the butter, beating well until all is
smooth. Pour the mixture back into the saucepan and return

to heat. Beat the soufflé base well and rapidly with a wooden spoon until the mixture has thickened and dried. (It will act much as a *choux* paste in the process but will take longer to leave the sides of the pan.)

Remove the pan from heat. Preheat the oven to 350°. Whisk the egg whites to firm peaks. Stir the yolks into the chocolate and, when well incorporated, stir in a third of the whites to lighten the mass, then fold in the remaining whites. Pour the mixture into the soufflé dish. Sprinkle the top generously with sugar and place the dish in a *bain-marie* (a larger pan holding hot water) in the oven for about 30 to 35 minutes. After the soufflé has come from the oven and stood briefly, run a knife around the edge, invert a platter over the top, and turn out the pudding. Whip some cream lightly, add vanilla and a pinch of cinnamon, and at the last minute, so it retains its granular quality, sweeten to taste with sugar. Put the cream into a pitcher and pour it unabashedly over the soufflé portions.

SERVES 8 OR MORE

CHILLED WHITE CHOCOLATE SOUFFLÉ WITH HOT CHOCOLATE SAUCE

An easy-to-do-ahead soufflé that is again unmolded, but this time it is eaten cold and served with a hot chocolate sauce. The ingredients that compose white chocolate (cocoa butter, milk solids, and sugar) are those which usually compose a sweet soufflé, so few of them need adding in the recipe.

Butter and sugar for mold

½ pound white chocolate
2 tablespoons unsalted butter, chilled
4 eggs, separated
Pinch of salt

Butter a 2-quart soufflé dish or charlotte mold. Sugar the dish generously, turning the mold so that all surfaces are well coated. Put the dish to chill.

Melt the chocolate over gentle heat or in a double boiler. Add the cold butter off the heat and stir until it has melted into the chocolate. When the chocolate is warm (but not hot), add the egg yolks and mix thoroughly.

Preheat the oven to 350°. Add the pinch of salt to the whites and whisk them to firm peaks (preferably in a clean copper bowl). Stir a third of the whites into the chocolate, then fold in the rest. Pour the mixture into the mold and set the mold in a larger pan containing hot water that rises 2 inches up the mold's sides. Sprinkle the top with sugar, then place in oven for about 35 minutes. Test the pudding by thrusting a knife blade down through the center (the soufflé needs to collapse, anyway). If it does not come out clean, bake for another 5 minutes.

Let the soufflé rest for 5 minutes after its removal from the oven, then run a knife around the edge and turn the soufflé out, upside down, onto a fancy serving dish. Let the dessert cool to room temperature, then cover lightly with plastic wrap and put to chill for from 1 to 6 hours. Serve accompanied by a gravy boat of Hot Chocolate Sauce:

HOT CHOCOLATE SAUCE

> 2 tablespoons unsalted butter
> ½ cup sugar
> 4 ounces semisweet chocolate
> 1 tablespoon cognac
> ⅔ cup cream

Melt the butter and sugar together and let them cook over medium heat until the sugar begins to turn a pale caramel.

Add the chocolate and, when it has melted, stir in the cognac and cream. Simmer gently for 2 minutes.

SERVES 8

ALMOND SOUFFLÉ WITH HIDDEN RASPBERRIES

> 10 ounces frozen raspberries (thawed) *or*
> 1½ cups home-preserved raspberries
> Butter and sugar for mold
> ¼ cup flour
> ½ cup plus 2 tablespoons milk
> Small pinch of salt
> ¼ cup sugar
> 2 tablespoons unsalted butter
> 3 eggs, separated, plus 2 egg whites
> ⅓ cup sliced almonds, lightly toasted, then ground
> 2 tablespoons almond liqueur (optional)
> ¼ teaspoon almond extract
> A small handful of almond slices, for garnish

Strain the raspberries through a sieve. Press lightly on the berries and reserve the juice. (Hold berries and juice in separate stainless steel or china bowls.)

Butter a 1½-quart soufflé dish, sprinkle the interior with sugar, and turn the bowl until its entire surface is thickly coated. Tap the bowl and turn out any excess sugar. Fold a piece of aluminum foil in two lengthwise and encircle the dish so that the foil stands in a 2½-inch collar above the rim. Tie the collar on with kitchen string and butter the exposed, inside foil. (This collar will help the soufflé rise straight up.)

Place the flour in a small saucepan and blend it with 2 tablespoons of milk. Heat ½ cup of milk with the salt and sugar, and when the milk is hot and the sugar dissolved, whisk it slowly into the flour. Put the mixture over heat and, whisking all the time, let it come to a slow boil and cook at that pace for 2 minutes. Remove from the heat and cool briefly. Stir in the butter, 3 egg yolks, ground almonds, and almond flavorings.

Preheat the oven to 350°. Whisk the 5 egg whites, preferably by hand, in a clean copper bowl. The correct procedure is as follows: amalgamate the whites by first blending them together. Place the handle of a large balloon whisk between the palms of the hands and rotate it back and forth. When the whites are beginning to foam, switch to a measured, rhythmical beating, and when the whites have finally mounted to stiff peaks, "tighten" the mass with 3 or 4 quick, double-time whips. Whisk a third of the whites into the flour base to lighten it, then gently fold in the rest with a spatula. Spoon half the mixture into the soufflé dish. Nestle the raspberries neatly in the center and top with the remaining mixture. (To help the soufflé lift and rise, run a thumb around the edge, indenting a small moat, as it were, in the batter, then cut a knife blade through the middle of the soufflé and give the mixture a half-moon cut.)

Strew the almond slices over the surface and sprinkle a small amount of sugar over the almonds. Place the soufflé on a baking sheet and put it to bake for about 25 minutes.

Sweeten the raspberry juice to taste and serve it in a small pitcher as sauce to accompany the dessert.

SERVES 6

The happy combination of raspberries and almonds is such an auspicious one that I shall continue with two more recipes featuring it.

FAT JAM PANNEQUETS

FOR THE CRÊPES:

>2 large tablespoons flour
>1 teaspoon sugar
>Small pinch salt
>1 large egg, lightly beaten
>1 tablespoon unsalted butter, melted
>About ⅔ cup lukewarm milk

FOR THE FILLING:

>1 cup raspberry jam
>1 tablespoon Framboise (raspberry liqueur, optional)
>3 whole eggs, separated, plus 2 egg whites,
>   at room temperature
>2 tablespoons confectioner's sugar
>2 tablespoons granulated sugar

>Butter for crêpe pan and baking sheet
>¼ cup sliced almonds, lightly toasted
>Heavy cream

Mix flour, sugar, and salt in a small bowl. Make a well in the center and add the egg, butter, and milk, slowly whisking the liquid ingredients into the dry to a smooth batter. (The batter should be the consistency of heavy whipping cream—add a few drops of water if necessary to bring it to this point.) Heat a crêpe pan or frying pan and rub it with a lump of butter. Add a ladleful of batter, swirl the pan, and pour off any excess running batter. Makes 6 crêpes.

To make the filling, melt the raspberry jam and then strain it to remove seeds. Stir 3 egg yolks into the jam and the optional liqueur. Place the 5 egg whites in a bowl (preferably of clean copper) and beat them to soft peaks. Place the confectioner's sugar in a sieve and sift it over the whites, then continue beating until the whites are firm. Stir a third of the whites thoroughly into the jam, then fold in the remaining whites. Place ½ cup of the mixture in the center of each crêpe and fold the crêpe over. Place the *pannequets* on a buttered baking sheet, sprinkle their tops with granulated sugar, and place them in a 350° oven for about 8 minutes. Transfer the *pannequets* gingerly with a spatula to warmed dessert plates. Sprinkle with toasted almonds and serve, one to a person. Place a pitcher of cream on table for those who might wish it.

SERVES 6

FRANGIPANE TART

FOR THE FRANGIPANE:

- 4 tablespoons unsalted butter
- 4 tablespoons sugar
- 1 egg
- ½ teaspoon vanilla
- 2 ounces ground almonds
- 2 teaspoons flour

Almond Pastry (see following recipe) *or*
    plain or puff pastry
Raspberry jam
1 egg yolk beaten with 1 teaspoon water for glaze

To make the frangipane, cream butter and sugar together. Stir in the egg, vanilla, almonds, and flour.

Roll out the pastry into an 11-inch circle. Place the circle on a damp baking sheet. Spread a thin layer of raspberry jam over the pastry, leaving a ¾-inch-wide border free. Spread the frangipane over the raspberry as smoothly as possible, then top again with a layer of jam.

Preheat oven to 350°. Cut a ¾-inch-wide strip of pastry that is long enough to encircle the rim of the tart. Cut the remaining pastry into 4 strips. Place one across the center, one at right angles to the center, then place the other two at cross angles so that the pie is divided into 8 wedge-shaped pieces. Curl a small piece of pastry into a flower and place it in the center. Moisten the free edge of the tart pastry lightly with water, then press the long strip around the rim so that it covers the ends of the cross-strips neatly. Trim if necessary. Brush the pastry over with egg glaze, then put to bake for 25 to 30 minutes.

SERVES 8

ALMOND PASTRY

1½ teaspoons yeast
2 tablespoons heavy cream
7 tablespoons unsalted butter, softened
2 egg yolks
5 tablespoons sugar
1 tablespoon light rum *or* cognac
⅓ cup ground almonds
1 cup all-purpose flour
½ teaspoon cinnamon

Dissolve the yeast in 2 tablespoons of warm water.

Combine cream and 4 tablespoons of butter in a small sauce-pan and heat until the butter is melted. Let the mixture cool, then add it to the yeast along with the egg yolks, 2 table-spoons of sugar, and the rum or cognac. Mix everything well, then stir in the almonds and flour. When the ingredients are well blended, give the dough a brief knead, pat it into a ball, and place it in a bowl covered with a kitchen towel. Let rest and rise for 1 hour.

On a lightly floured board, roll the pastry out into a rectangle roughly 8 by 12 inches. Try to keep the corners sharp and the edges as straight as possible. Cream together 3 tablespoons softened butter, the cinnamon, and 3 tablespoons sugar. Spread the butter over the pastry with a rubber spatula. (Leave a ½-inch border free.) Fold the pastry as for puff pastry (that is, fold the top down to cover ⅓ of the dough, then fold the bottom third up so that the pastry is triple-folded.) Roll the pastry out again into a rectangle and again fold it into thirds.

Roll the pastry out and shape it as needed for the finished tart. Allow the pastry a 30-minute rest before baking so that it will not oven-shrink unduly. This recipe provides enough pastry for one Frangipane Tart (above) or one Pear and Cranberry Marmalade Tart (see following recipe).

PEAR AND CRANBERRY MARMALADE TART

Here is a recipe for enough marmalade for one tart plus a jam pot extra to spread on breakfast toast or tea biscuits.

FOR THE MARMALADE:

>4 pounds Bosc or Anjou pears
>Juice of ½ lemon
>2 tablespoons unsalted butter
>½ teaspoon cinnamon
>3 cups cranberries
>4 cups sugar

>Almond Pastry (see preceding recipe)
>1 egg yolk beaten with 1 teaspoon water for glaze

Peel, core, and slice the pears. Place the pears in a large, stainless steel pot and add the lemon juice, butter, cinnamon, cranberries, and sugar. Place the pot over medium heat and stir until the pears begin to give off their juices. Cover and cook until the fruit is purée soft. Pass the pears through a sieve or food mill, then return the jam to the pan. Continue cooking for another 30 minutes or until the jam is very thick. Reserve 2 cups for the tart and preserve the rest in a jam pot to use on toast.

Roll out the almond pastry and cut an 11-inch circle. (For an easy guide, place a standard 10-inch dinner plate on the dough and cut an extra inch around it.) Transfer the dough to a pizza pan or baking sheet. Spread the jam over the surface as evenly as possible, but leave an inch-wide border free. Cut the remaining dough into 10 strips and lattice them over the marmalade. Cut the strips off even with the edge of the undercrust. Pinch up the crust into a rustic border and brush the egg yolk glaze over the lattice. Let the tart rest for 30 minutes, then bake it in a 350° oven for about 25 minutes. SERVES 6 TO 8

This tart, as well as the Frangipane, may be composed ahead and kept, refrigerated and covered with plastic wrap, for up to 6 hours before it is baked.

GINGERED PEAR FLAN

A handsome cake built on a thin, shell-like base of *génoise*, Gingered Pear Flan, with its fat pear petals radiating from a dark, caramelized center, has about it a kind of daisy look. This dessert utilizes a sided, 12-inch pan.

> 11 or 12 medium-sized firm Bartlett pears
> Juice of 1 lemon
> 1½ cups sugar
> 1 teaspoon ground ginger

FOR THE GÉNOISE:

    Butter and flour for the baking dish
    ⅔ cup sifted flour
    2 tablespoons melted unsalted butter
    5 eggs
    ½ cup sugar
    1 teaspoon ground ginger
    1 teaspoon fine-grated lemon zest

    Whipped cream, flavored with sugar and ginger

Peel, halve, and core the pears, giving the halves a turn in the lemon juice as soon as they have been trimmed to discourage discoloration. Combine the sugar with 3 cups of water and the ginger in a large saucepan. Bring to a boil and cook for 5 minutes. Regulate the heat to a simmer and poach the pears, in 2 or 3 batches, until they are tender. Lift out the pears with a strainer and retain the syrup.

Make the cake. Generously butter and flour the baking mold. Shake out excess flour. Preheat the oven to 350°. Measure the flour and melt the butter.

Combine eggs, sugar, ginger, and lemon zest in a large metal mixing bowl. Warm the bowl over low heat, all the while stirring with two fingers until the mixture feels warm but not hot to the touch. Remove from heat and beat with an electric mixer for a good 8 or 9 minutes. The eggs will mount to a high, light mass. Lift the beater up and let the batter fall from the end. The batter should form a ribbon-like trail that remains visible on the surface of the mixture. That is your sign that the batter is now thick enough. Sprinkle the flour onto the batter in two portions and rapidly fold the flour in by hand. (The hand can more sensitively feel that moment when the flour is perfectly incorporated than can an insensate spatula.) Fold in the butter, rapidly, gently. Pour the mixture into the baking pan and place immediately in the oven. Bake for about 20 minutes, or until the cake is nicely browned. Remove from the oven and let the cake sit for 4 minutes. Run a flexible spatula under the cake, then turn it out directly onto the platter from which you wish to serve it.

As the cake is baking, place the poaching syrup back over heat. Let it reduce until the sugar starts to caramelize. Let it cook to a pale amber color. With a fork, give the cake a series of light pricks, then drizzle a thin stream of caramel over the hot cake. Immediately place the damp pears on top, starting first with an outer row of halves, stem ends pointing toward the center. Continue with another overlapping row, and then cut a plump round to cover the center. The pears and caramel will combine to form a moist binding layer.

Continue cooking and reducing the caramelized syrup. Bring a small pan of water to a boil and just as the caramel turns a dark amber, add a small ladleful of boiling water. Stir and continue adding water until the syrup is thin and light. Brush the dark caramel over the pears. (Test by brushing a small portion: if the caramel hardens to a sticky toffee, it is still too thick. Add more water. The correct consistency will provide only a light, coloring glaze.)

Serve the tart warm, with the bowl of flavored whipped cream on the side.

SERVES 10 TO 12

WINE GLAZED PEAR TART

Puff pastry or rich pie pastry
1 egg yolk mixed with 1 teaspoon water for glaze

3 cups red wine
Juice of ½ lemon
½ cup sugar
1 cinnamon stick
A 2-inch strip of orange zest
2 cloves
7 or 8 large firm eating pears, peeled, halved, cored

Whipped cream, flavored with vanilla and cinnamon

To make the pie shell, roll out the pastry and cut a 10-inch circle. Transfer the dough to a damp baking sheet and dock it (that is, prick the surface over with a fork). Cut a long inch-wide strip of dough. Moisten one side lightly with water and attach it around the rim of the circle as a border. Using the back of a knife, make a series of indentions (not cuts) around the rim at ½-inch intervals for decorative effect, then brush the border over with egg yolk glaze. Leave the pastry to rest for 15 minutes and then put it to bake in a 350° oven until nicely browned (about 25 minutes). Check 10 minutes into the baking time to make sure that no large bubbles are puffing up the pastry. Prick an air vent with a knife point if necessary.

Place the red wine, lemon juice, sugar, cinnamon stick, orange zest, and cloves in a large non-aluminum pan and bring to a boil. Add the pears, then regulate heat to a bare simmer and allow the pears to poach until they are just tender. Strain them out of the liquid onto a platter covered with several thicknesses of paper toweling. Strain out the cinnamon stick, zest, and cloves with a slotted spoon and continue cooking the wine until it has reduced to a light glaze of syrupy consistency.

Place the pear halves, cored-side down, on a cutting surface. Cut them carefully across into ¼-inch slices, making sure to leave the basic pear shape intact. Sliding a spatula under each half, fan the slices out by flattening them gently with the hand, and place the halves around the edge of the pie crust, their stem ends all pointing toward the center. Overlap the next halves in a smaller circle, then arrange a few slices in a pretty central rosette. Brush the entire wine glaze over the pears until all the fruit is a glinting purple. Serve in wedges with a large dollop of flavored whipped cream.

SERVES 8

FRUITED BRIOCHE TART

Brioche Tart is a great puffy thing created to accommodate preserved or frozen fruit. The base is brioche, baked with its own custard filling. The fruit and its reduced juices are added halfway through baking, and the whole is a plump, handsome feast for mouth and eye. The concept is close enough to bread and jam to pass into the realm of teatime.

FOR THE BRIOCHE:

   1 package yeast (¼ ounce)
   2 tablespoons sugar
   4 tablespoons warm milk
   2 cups all-purpose flour
   1 teaspoon salt
   3 eggs, lightly beaten and at room temperature
   5 tablespoons unsalted butter, softened
   1 egg yolk beaten with 1 teaspoon water for glaze

   1 pound frozen fruit *or* about 3 cups preserved fruit
      plus 2 cups juices (blueberries, raspberries, straw-
      berries, blackberries)
Sugar to taste

FOR THE CUSTARD:

   1 egg plus 1 egg yolk
  ¼ cup sugar
   1 teaspoon vanilla
 1½ cups milk, warmed
   2 tablespoons cornstarch

To make the brioche, dissolve yeast and sugar in the warm milk. Combine flour and salt in a mixing bowl and make a well in the center. Add the yeast and eggs and slowly work the wet ingredients into the dry. Mix and stir the dough until it is very elastic. (Allow a mixer with its flat blade attached to knead the dough for a good 8 minutes, or knead by hand.) When there is a distinct elasticity to the dough, work in the softened butter. Lightly grease a clean mixing bowl and let the dough rise in it, towel-covered and in a warm place, for a good hour.

Place the dough in a buttered and floured 12-inch circular pan. With floured hands, press and pat the dough out from the center to the edge so that the interior is thinner than the rim. Brush the outer 3 inches of the crust with egg yolk glaze. Let the brioche rise for 30 minutes.

Preheat the oven to 375°.

Prepare the fruit. Strain off all juices and put them in a pan. Add sugar as needed, so that the juices are distinctly sweet, then reduce over brisk heat until they thicken. Stir the fruit back in. The ensemble should be thick but slightly looser than jam.

Prepare the custard. Whisk eggs, sugar, and vanilla in a bowl until thick and pale. Whisk 1¼ cups milk into the eggs. Dissolve the cornstarch in the remaining ¼ cup of milk and add it to the eggs. Place the custard over medium heat and whisk until thick. (Do not let the custard approach a boil.)

To compose the tart, put the brioche base to bake for 20 minutes. Lower the heat to 350° and remove the brioche from the oven. Slip a small, serrated knife under the browned upper crust, and cut out and remove and discard a large circle of just the very thin top crust. (Leave a 2½-inch frame of browned crust around the edge.) Immediately smooth the custard over the exposed white center, and spread the fruit over the custard. Place the tart back in the oven and bake for a final 15 minutes. Serve with a pouring of sweetened, lightly whipped cream.

SERVES 8 TO 10

BAKED PRUNE AND SUGAR CUBE "DUMPLINGS"

Here is a small dessert that can be adapted in three different ways. A pitted prune, holding in its center a spiced sugar cube, is wrapped in a pastry coating. If the coat is once-risen brioche or sweet bread dough, the prunes can be placed in a baking tin in the manner of sweet rolls, left to rise, and then baked. Drizzled with icing, they serve as a breakfast pastry. Or try them with a coating of fritter batter (see page 248). Deep-fry them to a crunch and then roll them in sugar. If the coat is plain or puff pastry, the little "dumplings" are put to bake until brown and served with a caramelized cream. And this is a good way to use up pastry scraps. While a large pie bakes, a small pastry with hidden sugar cubes bakes alongside for a child. I shall give a recipe for a single pastry —the concept is obvious and easily multiplied.

> Small sugar cubes
> Butter, melted
> Cognac
> Cinnamon
> Dried prunes (pitted and moist)
> Plain *or* puff pastry scraps
> Egg yolk and water glaze

To make a single pastry, sprinkle 3 sugar cubes with a few drops of melted butter and a few drops of cognac. Powder them lightly with cinnamon. Take 3 large or 2 jumbo prunes, place the cubes in the center, and compress the fruit around the sugar into a neat ball. Roll out the pastry and cut a 4-inch square. Cut a small square from each corner so that the pastry looks like a plump cross. Center a prune on the pastry and wrap the dough neatly up around it, pinching the edges shut in the process. Brush the pastry with egg yolk glaze, prick a small hole on top, and let the pastry rest for 20 minutes. Bake for about 20 minutes at 350°. For a full dessert, serve two or three dumplings per person and top with:

CARAMELIZED CREAM

Combine ½ cup cream and ⅔ cup sugar in a small saucepan. Cook until the mixture thickens and turns a golden brown. Stir in 3 tablespoons melted, nut-brown butter and spoon over the dumplings.

PROVIDES SAUCE FOR 4

Note: if you are making prune fritters, use a single jumbo prune enfolding a single sugar cube.

CINNAMON AND HONEY CAKE

This recipe is for a small cake to serve six. If more servings are desired, double the recipe, bake two layers, and sandwich them together with whipped cream. The dessert is basically a *génoise*, with honey acting as substitute for sugar and nuts enhancing both flavor and the cake's density. The simplest of thin, sugar-crisp toppings is a pleasant change from frostings and butter creams and helps keep this cake in the realm of homely fare.

> Butter and flour for mold
> ½ cup flour
> 3 ounces fine-ground mixed hazelnuts and
>   blanched almonds
> 1 teaspoon cinnamon
> ½ cup honey
> 4 eggs
> 1 tablespoon melted unsalted butter

FOR THE TOPPING:

¼ cup water
¼ cup sugar
½ teaspoon cinnamon mixed with ¼ cup sugar
½ cup heavy cream, whipped and sweetened to taste

Butter and flour a 9-inch cake tin. Preheat the oven to 325°.
Sift the ½ cup flour and mix with ground nuts and cinnamon. Set aside.

The honey and eggs must be gently warmed so that they can expand to the greatest volume while being beaten. Either place them in the metal bowl of a mixer, whisk them over low heat until warm, then let the mixer do the actual beating; or place honey and eggs in a rounded stainless steel bowl over low heat and beat them with a hand-held electric mixer. In either case, beat the eggs for about 8 minutes, in which time the volume will expand fivefold. (If beating over heat, lift the bowl on and off frequently and do not let the bottom become so hot that it cooks any egg.)

I find it easiest at this point to sit on a chair and hold the egg bowl between my unladylike knees. The left hand will sprinkle in the flour/nut mixture while the right hand acts as spatula and folds flour into egg. Work gently and rapidly so as not to lose egg volume. When the flour is incorporated, sprinkle on the melted butter, give a last fold, and pour the batter into the cake pan. Put the pan on a baking sheet and place in the oven for 30 minutes.

Let the cake stand for 5 minutes, then run a knife around its edge and turn the cake out onto a platter. Place plastic wrap over the top (to keep the cake especially moist), and let the cake cool to room temperature.

Place ¼ cup water and ¼ cup sugar in a small saucepan and boil gently for 10 minutes. Brush all the hot sugar syrup over the top and sides of the cake and immediately rub in all the cinnamon sugar. Clean up the platter. Serve with good coffee and large dollops of whipped cream some of which, if so desired, may be stirred into the coffee, some piped over the cake in lazy scallops from a pastry bag for a decorative touch. SERVES 6

ON EATING MAPLE SYRUP
AT A NEW ENGLAND BREAKFAST

In New England, just as winter begins to lift and sap to flow again, you can visit a sugar house and watch the gallons of maple sap condense to maple syrup. An outing to a sugar house for breakfast, particularly on a Sunday morning, is a family ritual, parts of which are not so difficult to recreate anywhere.

In a real sugar house, the scene might progress as follows. Long tables stretch out in a small dining room. They are covered with red and white checked cloths. On the tables are games—checkers, marbles, chess and backgammon boards (old-timers come to "set a spell," even spend the day). In one corner of the room is a stove, a griddle, a waffle maker; facing the other way you see the evaporators, with steam billowing out, working to condense the large amounts of sap (35 gallons boil down to a single gallon of virgin maple syrup). To heat our room, there is an ancient oil drum stove topped by a small electric fan which wafts the heat in our general direction. On the other side, a stone fireplace is alight with fragrant, hickory stoked fire.

A lady comes to take our order. We can have Pancakes and Sausage with Syrup, or Waffles and Bacon with Syrup. We can have Fried Dough with Maple Cream or Homemade Donut Holes to dunk in maple syrup. We can have Hot Apple Pie with Maple Crumb Top or Sugar on Snow. We order one of everything. The small child present must have Sugar on Snow.

Outside there is still clean snow on the ground. The lady goes out, scoops some into a pie tin, and packs the surface down. She heats the syrup, watching all the while a thermometer, until it reaches 240° F. The snow and syrup are carried to table and we watch as she pours out the syrup over the snow where it hardens to a sticky taffy. The child twirls great forks of the substance into his mouth, the sugar whisping and floating in strands about his chin, and then everyone else tries it, too. Served with Sugar on Snow are pickles and saltine crackers to cut the saccharine intensity.

A metal dish, not unlike an old-fashioned ice cream sundae bowl, is set on table. It is heaped with doughnut holes. The lady spills hot syrup over the top and we spear the balls with a fork and pull them out from the mass. Flat crisp pieces of fried dough with whipped maple cream appear. And then come waffles, pancakes, sausage, bacon, more doughnuts, great mugs of coffee, hot chocolate . . . more than we can ever eat, though we will try. We play Chinese checkers until the marbles, grown sticky from our fingers, adhere to the board. The child's hands and chin, his shirt front and his hair shine with syrup . . . which is as it should be. Once in a young lifetime one should be allowed to have as much sweetness as one can possibly want and hold. He even smiles when we wipe him with the warm, soapy cloth which our lady keeps for just such purposes.

Maple syrup is also the sweetening element in Hot Buttered Rum (see page 300). Combine that potent drink with *babas au rhum* and you have:

HOT BUTTERED RUM CAKES

FOR THE DOUGH:

> ½ ounce (2 envelopes) dried yeast
> 3 large eggs, at room temperature
> 1 teaspoon vanilla
> 2 tablespoons sugar
> Pinch of salt
> ⅓ cup raisins or currants
> 1¾ cups flour
> 1 stick unsalted butter, softened

FOR THE SYRUP:

> ¾ cup pure maple syrup
> ¾ cup apple cider or juice
> ¼ cup rum of choice
> Scant ½ teaspoon cinnamon
> 2 tablespoons unsalted butter

> ¼ cup red currant jelly, melted

Dissolve the yeast in ¼ cup of warm water. In a mixing bowl, stir the eggs together until blended. Add the yeast, vanilla, sugar, salt, and raisins, then work in the flour and knead well until a soft but elastic dough results. Either work the dough by hand for about 12 minutes (lightly oil the hands) or let a heavy mixer with a flat blade do the job. When the dough is nicely developed, with a slick, slightly glossed appearance, put it in an oiled bowl, cover with a towel, and let the dough rise in a warm place for 45 minutes.

Punch the dough down and work in the softened butter until it completely integrates. Lightly butter either an 8-cup ring mold or a muffin tin with 8 large or 12 small indentions. Place the dough in the mold (it should fill only half its given space) or muffin tin. Let the dough rise until it comes to the top of the mold, then put it to bake in a hot oven—375° for about 15 minutes for smaller cakes; 400° for 25 minutes for one large cake. Let the cakes sit briefly when they come from the oven, then unmold.

Prepare the hot buttered rum syrup. Combine maple syrup, cider, rum, and cinnamon in a saucepan and bring just to the boil. Off heat, stir in the butter. While the cakes are still warm, place them in the syrup until they have absorbed it all. If you have made one large cake, simply pour the syrup into the cleaned mold and place the cake back in until it has blotted up the liquid. If the cakes are small, dip them into the syrup for a while. For a shiny glaze, melt some red currant jelly and brush it over the top of the cake. Accompany with stiff whipped cream.

SERVES 8

ALMOND GALETTE

This pastry is one of my favorite desserts. It is easy to make and, after being assembled, amenable to sitting and waiting for several hours before it is finally baked. It is exotically "foreign" looking when presented hot, whole, and cinnamon-sugar-slicked at table, and it promotes a pleasant camaraderie as guests reach out and break off flaked portions to eat with their fruit compote, apple sauce, or (as with baklava) yogurt or even plain, unwhipped cream. The dough can either be rolled out by hand or, easier still, worked through a pasta machine.

FOR THE PASTRY:

A generous ¾ cup flour
¼ teaspoon salt
2 tablespoons unsalted butter
Melted butter for the pan

¾ cup sugar
2½ ounces sliced almonds, lightly toasted
2 teaspoons cinnamon
⅓ cup cognac or brandy
6 tablespoons unsalted butter, melted

To make the pastry, mix flour and salt together. Cut the butter into small morsels and work it into the flour until it disappears into infinitesimal particles. Add just enough ice water to bind the flour into a medium-firm dough. Wrap the pastry in plastic and let it rest for ½ hour in the refrigerator.

Coat a 12-inch pizza pan with some melted butter. If using a pasta machine, set the kneading rollers to their widest opening. Divide the dough into three parts and knead each piece through, gradually working down thinner and thinner kneading widths to the next to the last notch. (Coat the pastry with extra flour if it seems at all moist or sticky, and work it patiently through the machine as it is less resilient than pasta.) Place the first strip down the pan's center. Place the other two strips slightly overlapping the center band on either side. The entire pan should be covered and the pastry ends will drape over the edge. If rolling out by hand, divide the dough in two and roll out both halves into thin-as-possible rounds. Place one round on the buttered tin.

Sprinkle half the sugar, almonds, cinnamon, brandy, and finally the melted butter over the dough, then fold the ends over or place the second round on top. Try to cover the entire pastry but avoid letting the dough lump up at any point into more than two layers. (The dough may be cut to size and gently stretched and prodded with the fingers if necessary.)

Now sprinkle the remaining filling ingredients over the top of the dough, ending with a final drizzle of butter. At this point the pastry can be lightly covered with plastic wrap and refrigerated for several hours before baking.

Bake in a preheated, 350° oven for about 15 to 20 minutes. Keep a close eye after 10 minutes for the pastry is fragile. The sugared top should brown and caramelize, but caramel can quickly turn to blackened burn. Remove galette from oven, let cool for a moment, then slide the pastry onto a countertop. Serve within an hour of baking. If I am serving a large party, I place several of these cakes on doily-covered round platters and spread them down the length of the table.

1 CAKE SERVES ABOUT 6

SUGARED LEMON GALETTE

Here is another crisp, wafer-like "cake."

> 1 teaspoon yeast
> 1 stick unsalted butter
> 2 tablespoons sugar
> 1 tablespoon fine-grated zest of lemon
> 1 egg
> 1 tablespoon light rum
> 1⅓ cups all-purpose flour, sifted
> Pinch of salt
> Butter and flour for baking tin
> About ⅔ cup confectioner's sugar

Dissolve the yeast in 2 tablespoons of warm water.

Cream the butter together with the sugar and lemon zest. (It is easiest simply to knead these elements together with a hand.) Add the egg, rum, and then the yeast, and stir with a spoon until the ingredients are as smooth as possible. Sieve the flour over the top, add the salt, and again using the hand, mix the dough into a smooth soft ball. Gently knead the dough for 5 minutes, then put it to rest in a towel-covered bowl for 1½ hours.

Lightly butter and flour a 12-inch pizza pan. Place the dough on the pan and, using a glass tumbler, roll it out to the edges of the dish. Pat and smooth the dough and pinch up a decorative border. Place the confectioner's sugar in a small sieve and sift it over the dough (avoiding the border) in a thick layer. Place the cake in a 375° oven for 10 to 12 minutes or until the border has browned. For the most attractive presentation, slide the galette onto a wooden cutting board or a large round brie basket/grid.

The next decorative step is not necessary but it adds a certain foreign and rustic charm to the dessert. Take an unpainted metal coat hanger, hold the edge with a potholder, and rest the long, straight length directly on a very hot burner or over a flame. Let the metal heat, then place the edge down the center of the cake. The metal will sear a dark, caramelized line into the sugar. Quickly move over 1½ inches and sear another line. Wipe the hanger clean with paper towels, reheat it, then continue the pattern. There should be 5 parallel lines going one way and another 5 lines crisscrossing them in diamond pattern another way. (This technique for forming a dark grid pattern is used in many large professional kitchens in a wicked way. Order grilled fish and chances are a chef will simply fry the fish in butter, then grab a thin, red-hot poker and criss criss criss cross cross cross a "grill" pattern onto the fish's side. They save the *real* grill for meat.)

Serve this delicious cake warm, with either fruit (fresh or in compote) or ice cream. Or, have it for tea.

SERVES 6

FLORENTINE TART

An opulent teatime sweet, this tart is actually a huge Florentine cookie built upon a *pâté sucre* base. The fruited filling caramelizes over the pastry and the traditional chocolate then embellishes the top (rather than the bottom) of the fruit. This is a very rich tart which keeps for 3 or 4 refrigerated days.

FOR THE CRUST:

> 4 ounces unsalted butter
> 2 tablespoons sugar
> 1 egg
> ½ teaspoon vanilla
> 1½ cups flour

FOR THE FILLING:

> 1¼ sticks unsalted butter
> ½ cup sugar
> 4 tablespoons heavy cream
> Grated zest of 1 lemon and 1 orange
> ¾ cup mixed candied red and green cherry halves
> ½ cup mixed dark and gold raisins
> ½ cup slivered or sliced almonds

FOR THE TOPPING:

> 4 ounces semisweet chocolate

To make the crust, cream together the butter and sugar. Stir in the egg and vanilla, then add the flour and work it in lightly with the fingertips. When the ingredients are smooth enough to pack into a ball, gather the pastry together, wrap it in plastic wrap, and refrigerate for at least 30 minutes.

Take the pastry from the refrigerator and let it sit at room temperature for a few minutes to facilitate rolling. Lightly flour a counter surface and roll out the pastry to a 12-inch circle. Transfer the dough to a pizza pan or baking sheet. (Never mind if the dough cracks a bit. Simply pinch it together and piece the edge if necessary.) Refrigerate the tart base for 15 minutes, then bake for 10 minutes at 350°.

Cut three 3-inch-wide strips of aluminum foil. Tuck them snugly under and around the pastry base to act as protective barriers when the filling is poured into the crust.

To make the filling, heat the butter and sugar in a small saucepan over medium heat. When the sugar has dissolved and the mixture is at a rolling boil, add the remaining ingredients all at once. Stir briefly, then remove from heat. Pour the filling over the crust and try to leave a small border free as the filling will expand outward as it heats. Distribute the fruit evenly. Bake at 350° for about 20 minutes. Watch carefully toward the end of cooking time. The filling will first bubble up and look as if it has sugared, then it will dissolve into a smooth caramel which will grow darker as it bakes. The tart should be removed when it turns a pleasant gold. Let the tart cool to room temperature (the caramel will solidify in the process) and transfer it to a serving platter. Melt the chocolate and when it is cool enough to handle, drizzle some free form over the top and spoon the rest into a pastry bag with a small star tube. Border the edge of the tart with a chocolate scallop. Refrigerate. Serve cut into pie wedges.

SERVES 10 TO 12

"SAUSAGE" AND "CHEESE"

It always amuses me to serve the following two recipes together. The sausage is composed of a thick chocolate, nut, and raisin mixture which, when cut, looks amazingly like a slice of *saucisson* studded with bits of nut *lardons* and black raisin "truffles." The "cheese," a simple round of shortbread sprinkled with confectioner's sugar, resembles a brie. The two sweets are placed on a wooden cheese board for service (along with a cheese knife) and a few slices of "sausage" are cut and laid out in display. The two make a nice accompaniment for a simple fruit dessert or a whimsical conceit to grace a tea table.

"SAUSAGE"

⅓ cup shelled, natural pistachio nuts
10 ounces ground, blanched almonds
6 ounces grated bittersweet chocolate
Large pinch of cinnamon
½ cup dark seedless raisins
1 egg
½ cup sugar
1 tablespoon unsalted butter, melted
Granulated sugar, confectioner's sugar, cocoa

Prepare the pistachio nuts by placing them, for 1 minute, in a small pot of boiling water. Drain the nuts and rub them with a kitchen towel. The skins will remove themselves and the bright green nutmeats will stand alone.

Mix pistachios, almonds, grated chocolate, cinnamon, and raisins in a bowl.

Beat the egg with ½ cup granulated sugar until it is thick and pale. Add egg and melted butter to the dry mixture and combine all ingredients with the hands. Knead and compress the mass, then, still using the hands, place it in a saucepan over very low heat. Continue stirring and turning until the chocolate becomes slightly warm (there should be no *melted* chocolate). Remove the chocolate from the pan and divide it in two. Sprinkle a mix of granulated sugar, confectioner's sugar, and cocoa on a work surface and firmly roll each half into compact sausage shape. (The sugar-cocoa mixture will provide the effect of a striated outer "casing.") Let the sausages cool, then wrap them in aluminum foil and refrigerate. A small netting of string tied around each sausage and looped at the end will further enhance their *trompe l'oeil* duplicity.

"CHEESE" (PITCAITHLEY BANNOCK)

A word should be said about shortbread, for this Scottish staple, in form at least, sprung from ancient and mystical tradition (the spiraling sun ray border carved into the common wooden shortbread mold was once a symbol of sun worship), is still a part of ritual life in rural Scotland. The buttery cake is eaten at Christmas, and on New Year's Eve it is offered to the "first footers" who walk from home to home (much like Halloween trick-or-treaters) offering good wishes for the coming year in return for a treat. The humble shortbread sometimes serves as a poor "bride's cake," when an intricately decorated round of it is broken over the head of a newly married girl as she enters her first home. The fragmented portions are then presented to her bridesmaids to place under their pillows and dream on.

The finest shortbread should be composed from the freshest of ingredients and rapidly assembled. Always use superfine sugar and unsalted butter if available, and keep all the ingredients as cold as possible. The following rich variety, called Pitcaithley Bannock, contains chewy bits of citron peel and ground almonds.

> 4 tablespoons superfine granulated sugar
> 1 stick unsalted butter
> ¼ cup rice flour

1½ cups all-purpose flour
1 ounce fine-ground almonds
2 ounces chopped citron peel
Sugar for mold
Confectioner's sugar

Cream the sugar and butter. Sieve the rice flour and the all-purpose flour together. Add flour, nuts, and citron to the creamed butter. Using the thumbs and the tips of the fingers held together, rapidly work the dry ingredients into the butter. Mix *very* lightly. The ingredients should remain flaky. (It is possible to work them into a compact dough but this is *not* what should happen.) There will not be a perfect amalgamation of butter and flour, and some slicks of each will probably be apparent in the bowl.

Select a shortbread mold or an 8-inch pie dish and sugar it generously. Pack in the dough, pressing it down well with the flat of the hand, then turn the mold sharply over onto a baking tray. Remove mold. Bake at 350° for about 25 minutes or until the shortbread turns a pale biscuit color. To simulate a "brie cheese," sieve some confectioner's sugar over the smoother side when the cake has cooled.

Teas, Toddies, Analeptics

"Stay me with flagons . . ."

TEAS

A very cold day. Indeed, I might have remarked the beginning of winter. No leaves to speak of left on the trees now; a sharp chill in the air. One's room after tea most emphatically a little centre of light in the midst of profound darkness. . . .

VIRGINIA WOOLF, from her *Diary*

That the ritual of tea is no longer with us in America is a great pity. It was, at one time, almost as prevalent a social custom as it is in England, though here today the taking of tea (and I am interested in the broadest, ceremonial sense of that expression) seems left to be the province of small girl children and elderly ladies. Again, more is the pity.

There is a sort of timeless appeal in tea, tea rituals, and equipage, for the taking of tea has long denoted the civilized man and nation. Each civilization that has embraced the beverage has added to its lore and mystique by bending and refining the ritual to suit the ideals and needs of its society. In the beginning (and in a nutshell) was China. When the rare and cherished leaves passed from that country to the Japanese, their very rarity necessitated the formation of specialized and particular ways to honor tea consumption. The nobility and the monks (the only ones who could afford the substance) dictated the formalities and refined the occasion until tea, intermingling with Zen aesthetics, became, in fifteenth-century Japan, a full-blown cult:

Teaism is a cult founded on the adoration of the beautiful among the sordid facts of everyday existence. It inculcates purity and harmony, the mystery of mutual charity, the romanticism of the social order. It is essentially a worship of the Imperfect, as it is a tender attempt to accomplish something possible in this impossible thing we know as life.

. . . it is hygiene, for it enforces cleanliness; it is economics, for it shows comfort in simplicity rather than in the complex and costly; it is moral geometry, inasmuch as it defines our sense of proportion to the universe.

—OKAKURA KAKUZO, *The Book of Tea*

And so, in his humbler teas at home, the Japanese tea drinker offers the bowl first to his ancestors and then to his honorable parents. When invited as a guest to partake in the formal ceremony of tea, he dresses in muted clothing. He purifies himself symbolically at his host's outside water basin, then admires the still moss, the reflective garden pool, the juxtaposition of stones and willows in the garden, turning his thoughts all the while from the world, until his host calls him to the tea room. He removes his shoes, stoops low to enter the doorway (humbling himself in the process), silently enters the almost barren room, and kneels. While the host boils the water, everyone listens to the swaying of the pines in the kettle's song. The bright green tea is whisked to a froth and passed to the guest of honor. He sips, gives the bowl a quarter turn, then passes it on. When the tea is gone, the guests inspect the ceramic drinking bowl, amazed at and admiring of its form and surface, its long familial history. Sometimes there is a simple meal. And when the interlude, in its time, is over, the guest dons his shoes again and thus the world, and returns refreshed into the outer universe.

When tea passed to England in the early seventeenth century (and thence on to the rest of Europe and to America) it lost much of its aesthetic but not its social significance. Again it was a rarity and again it first provided a diversion for the nobility. The equipage this time was of finest wrought silver. When tea became more accessible, and when it came to America in the late seventeenth century, polite society strove to emulate its betters. Each family purchased the finest equipment possible. Hopefully there would be real china teacups; a teapot, tongs, and strainer from the best silversmith; a marvel of a caddy. Everything would be left out in the parlor to be seen, admired, and ready in prescribed position at the correctly appointed hour. And again the equipage would become a part of familial history with many a will reading: "To my eldest son I leave the house and all my lands; to my eldest daughter, the silver tea service."

So tea moves from the religion, philosophy, art of the East, toward the art, craft, and purely social etiquette of the West. And so the tea-drinking guest of eighteenth-century America enters the house of his host in his most lavish finery, is ushered into the best parlor to be comfortably seated until all guests arrive. He admires, perhaps covets, the fine appointments of the room and of the tea table. The tea pourer, either the mistress of the house or a pretty, marriageable daughter, sits at the tea table and measures leaves into the pot. The boiling water, carried in by a maid, is poured over the leaves and left to steep. There are plates of sweetmeats, tarts, jams, breads. The hostess pours the tea, mixing it to taste with sugar and cream, then, with a graceful turn of the hand, the lace falling briefly from the milk-white inner arm, she extends the cup to the honored or oldest guest. The conversation all about is bright and witty and tends toward the feminine. Gossips, flirtations occur; perhaps music and song, but always good talk around the fire and more tea until the guest signals that he can drink no more by reversing his cup on the saucer and laying his spoon on top. He leaves refreshed, titillated, full of tea and society.

In our time, the ceremony of tea has suffered both in Japan (where it frequently becomes a quaint touristic display) and in America (where we have not world enough or time). To sense the timelessness of tea we must go elsewhere . . . to an Arab country for tea thick with sugar and mint, served on a brass tray and poured by the man of the house; to Russia for tea brewed up in a great and antique samovar, then served in glass tumblers with lemon slices and jam as a sweetener; to England for high teas. And as it was to England that we looked in the past for our ceremonial inspiration, so might we still look today.

There are, of course, a variety of tea styles in all levels of English society, from the trolley with its tired sweets and canteen tea wheeled through factories in the afternoons, to the garish plastic and chrome tea shops of the large cities that offer tea and those peculiar English teatime dishes, beans or canned spaghetti on toast, to dowdy matrons. There are grand high teas in fine old comfortable hotels, with reserved, formally attired waiters maneuvering carts of sweets, carts of savories among the white tables where sit fragile, gloved, and hatted ladies.

But the very best teas are away from London in small villages and in private homes, when an industrious lady turns her front room into a tea parlor—the kind of place where a pretty girl in ruffled apron, perhaps a daughter, offers home-made crumpets and scones, thick homemade preserves, Devon cream; where there are two homemade cakes to choose be-tween, a platter of sandwiches, and hot, hot tea. I am not suggesting that we could have the same daily ritual in our lives as the English—that would involve an entire rescheduling of time and national priorities—yet could we but will our-selves a bit of ease, surely once a week or month, on a long winter's Sunday, that gentle ceremony, with friends, relatives, children attending, might be reinstated.

The iron kettle would be singing as it hung from its hook over the kitchen fire, the clock ticking on the wall, a white cloth spread on the table for our tea, a loaf from our weekly batch, butter from one or other of the neigh-bouring farms marked in the pretty lozenge-shaped pat-tern traditional in the neighbourhood, our own raspberry jam, in a ruby glass jam-dish; my glass of milk set aside from the morning on the cold slab of the larder, its cream a band at the top, narrower or wider as the cow was newly calved or going dry.

KATHLEEN RAINE, *Farewell Happy Fields*

TO MAKE A TEA

There will be a string quartet playing on the phonograph, preferably Mozart or Schubert.

A teapot; a kettle; a pitcher of hot milk (for those who would take tea in the French manner); a pitcher of cold milk or cream (for those who follow the English school); an empty bowl or pitcher (called a slop bowl) to receive the rinsing water; cups, saucers, small plates, forks, spoons, and napkins should all be assembled. A truly grand tea will also offer coffee and hot chocolate.

In four matching bowls, if possible, place four different sugars: granulated white and Demerara sugars; and lumps, both white and brown . . . the lumps particularly for children so that they may dip them in hot drinks like the *petites canards* (little ducks) much loved by infant French.

The table will have on it a white cloth, showing the folds where it has been ironed.

There will be a platter of sandwiches, cut into shapes and trimmed of crust (bread spread with softened butter, mayonnaise, then watercress or thin-cut radishes or translucent cucumber slices).

There will be a glass bowl containing celery sticks.

There will be two, perhaps three homemade small cakes or pastries.

There will be hot buttered scones or crumpets or toast, and numerous jams.

The hostess will boil water in the kettle. When the water is hot, she will pour some into the teapot to warm its interior, then pour the water out again into the slop bowl. Into the pot goes a teaspoon of tea for each cup needed plus extra for the pot. When the kettle sings and whistles at full, rushing boil, she will pour the water over the leaves and steep them for 5 minutes. The tea will then be poured into cups, creamed or sweetened, and offered first to the most distinguished guest.

TODDIES

If teas are the aesthetic, the artful, the feminine, then toddies might be called the masculine antithesis. Steaming hot, rough with spices, spiked with potent spirits, toddies conjure a world of Victorian gentlemen travelers seeking warmth at wayside inns ("A Posset, my good man," he bellowed, jumping from the hansom, "and be quick about it"); and of rugged, he-men explorers:

Cap seized a bucket and went to work. In it he put two cups of maple sugar, added an inch of hot water and stirred until the sugar was dissolved. He poured in two quarts of rum, added a lump of butter the size of his fist, threw in a handful of powdered cinnamon; then filled the bucket to the brim with steaming hot water. So briskly did he stir the mixture that it splashed his shirt. . . .

"This here," he said, "aint the proper way to make it. I put hot water in this here, but what you ought to have is hot cider. You take three or four drinks of this, made the right way, and you don't worry about what kind of food you're eating, or about anything else, either . . . you take enough hot buttered rum and it'll last you pretty near as long as a coonskin cap."

—KENNETH ROBERTS, *Northwest Passage*

I use the term toddies generically and loosely for a spate of hot, old-fashioned drinks that originated mainly in northern European countries and that were created to provide immediate, stroking warmth and to offset sore throats and chilblains. True toddies and grogs (rum or brandy, hot water, and sugar) were fit for the male and for loving cups. Caudles, gruels, and possets (infusions of groats and spices, boiled up then strained, with added sugar and spirits) might also do for a woman on occasion, if she were feeling poorly. When the alcoholic addition was only wine, as in Bishops, the drink could serve any polite society for dances and for wassail.

It is in the ritual ceremonies of the wassail bowl and the loving cup that I am particularly interested, for they are pretty customs, both. The holiday wassail is composed as follows: take a scant ½ teaspoon of grated nutmeg, some cloves, 1 teaspoon each of powdered ginger and allspice, some mace, and 1 tablespoon of cinnamon. Place these in a cup of water and bring to the boil. Cool and bring to the boil again. Select four bottles of good claret wine. Heat the wine and spices together and dissolve in the wine 2 cups of sugar or honey to taste. Beat a dozen egg whites together until they firm and peak. Beat the yolks separately and then fold the two together. Pour over them the hot wine, slowly beating all the while, then heat until the brew is frothy. Pour the drink into a heated punch bowl and float some apples (roasted and hot) on the top. The fifteen or so partakers of the drink cheer and toast each other with raised cups. *"Wæs hæil,"* they say, those medieval words meaning "Be thou well."

If a nonalcoholic drink is wanted, it is easy enough to fill the bowl with mulled cider: tie a quantity of cloves, nutmegs, allspice berries, and cinnamon sticks into a bag. Heat some good cider, along with the spice bag and brown sugar to taste. Boil for 10 minutes. Remove the spice bag and pour the cider into a heated punch bowl. Float on top some apples stuck with cloves and cinnamon sticks.

The loving cup might contain any drink, warm or cold, though historically it was filled with sack (sherry). The double-handled cup was passed, like the chalice at the sacrament, from man to man, each taking a communal sip. The origin of the loving cup is again an ancient one, sprung from the guildhalls and masculine societies of the Middle Ages, and it was traditionally offered, according to the *Encyclopaedia of Practical Cookery,* to strangers:

Immediately after the dinner and grace, the masters and wardens of the company drink to their visitors a hearty welcome; the cup is then passed round the table, and each guest, after he has drunk, applies his napkin to the mouth of the cup before he passes it to his neighbor. The more formal practice is for the person who pledges with the Loving-cup to stand up and bow to his neighbor,

who, also standing, removes the cover with his right
hand, and holds it while the other drinks; a custom said
to have originated in the precaution to keep the right, or
"dagger hand" employed, that the person who drinks may
be assured of no treachery. . . .

As in the Eucharist, once again mutual forbearance is held
within a cup.

ANALEPTICS

Analeptics include all those foods or substances which are
considered to be restoratives, strength promoters, comforting
builders of health in times of convalescence, whether from a
serious illness, a simple cold, indigestion, or a hangover. The
art and preparation of the analeptic cure is one not much
practiced in these days of quick chemical reparation, but not
so long ago, cookbooks were filled with sections on Invalid
Cookery (often subtitled "Food for the Poor"). Indeed, had
this book been written fifty years ago, a lengthy chapter on
the subject would here ensue.

There are, it seems, almost as many schools of thought con-
cerning culinary cure-alls as there are foodstuffs:

I place the greatest importance on *toushi*, pickled black
beans, one of the greatest creations of Chinese cuisine. It
helps digestion to the extent that it takes away all feeling
of heaviness after a sumptuous dinner. Given a bit of this
crushed black bean, the stomach has a feeling of positive
happiness in doing its duties.

LIN YUTANG, *The Pleasures of a Nonconformist*

Listen, then: let any man who shall have drunk too deeply of the cup of pleasure, or given to work too many of the hours which should belong to sleep; who shall find the accustomed polish of his wit turned to dullness, feel damp oppression in the air and time hanging heavily, or be tortured by a fixed idea which robs him of all liberty of thought; let all such, we say, administer to themselves a good pint of ambered chocolate . . . and they will see marvels.

BRILLAT-SAVARIN

———

. . . garlic, the smell of which is so dreaded by our little mistresses, is perhaps the most powerful remedy in existence against the vapours and nervous maladies to which they are subject.

BERNARDIN DE SAINT-PIERRE

———

. . . and the list goes on and on. There is, for instance, that homeopathic element within the French suggesting that all ailments can be cured by the specific ingestion of healthy portions of that organ which is diseased in man. Thus, a Frenchman, apprehensive for his liver after too much drink, doses himself with a quantity of good calves liver (perhaps grilled and with a vinegared sauce); or another fearful for his kidneys feeds upon the healthy organ of a lamb (sautéed with mushrooms).

It is almost universally accepted, however, that the most powerfully healing of analeptics are those which are based on decocted broth, the stock drawn from animal carcass, as if the essential energy of a dead unselfish beast could be condensed to vital spiritus.

———

What comforted me? That is easy. It was a strong cold chicken jelly so very, very thick. My Mother's Chinese cook would fix it. He would cook it and cook it down, condense it—this broth with all sorts of feet in it, then it would gell into sheer bliss. It kept me alive once for three weeks when I was ill as a child. And I've always craved it since.

JAMES BEARD

Though I must remark that James Beard was the only one among all the people I asked to name their most comforting food who admitted to cold comfort (and perhaps this is only indicative of his youthfully advanced gastronomic sensibilities), still the substance he found so healing, the proverbial "chicken soup" proffered by a worried mother, was one of the two most sustaining substances that came to mind among all people, all nationalities. It is, of course, of the same family as the English beef tea (beef defatted, covered with water, skimmed, and boiled for an hour). Both are old-fashioned remedies and both are to be found, along with others of their ilk, in forgotten recipe books. There were crayfish broths for purifying the blood; mucilaginous bouillons built upon seaweed and chicken feet for inveterate coughs, and a host of other decoctions, some of which border on the arcane: "Take two dozen garden snails, add to these the hind quarters only of two dozen stream frogs, previously skinned; bruise them together in a mortar; cover with saffroned spring water and bring to the boil. . . ."

Other substances, steeped in water, were also found to be health giving. Oatmeal or bread, toasted until hard and brown, with boiling water poured over, was considered "very useful in stopping sickness." The Provençal (as do I) swear by the garlic broth aïgo bouïdo to settle a stomach or sooth a sore throat. (Take 10 or 12 peeled garlic cloves and boil them for 20 minutes in a quart of salted water, along with two sage leaves, an optional bouquet garni, and a spoon of olive oil. Strain, puréeing the garlic through, if you like, and drink.)

And finally, there seems to be one analeptic, easeful drink recognized by all. Sometimes people know its name, but more often it is just a substance that they remember, comforting but without nominative identity, as sweetened milk, or eggs with milk. In Israel it is *goggly mogly:* egg yolk, a touch of vanilla, some sugar in warm milk. In Greece, it is *krókos,* hot milk with egg yolk and sugar. In France it is *lait de poule* (chicken's milk) or *groggi* with a spoon of gallic cognac added for a cold. In America it's simple eggnog. Poland, where it has no name I could discern, serves hot milk and egg with honey. In Russia, a pinch of baking soda is added for sore throats. In England they might boil the milk first with enriching groats, then strain it before adding egg and sugar. In Italy, grown men drink it to enhance virility . . . that rich yellow milk, warm and sweet, that has no name.

Appendix A

ON MENU PLANNING

I AM MOVED to write a short piece on menu planning to end this book for several reasons, the first being that the theme and subject of the recipes in *Comforting Food* seem to necessitate such an undertaking. The very cooking that we do in winter and for comfort is perforce more complex and at the same time more limited than what we do in summer. There are more sauces, more starches, fewer fresh ingredients to choose among. How do we best cope with this wintery fact of culinary life?

The second motivation concerns a common plea for help that, as a cooking teacher, I often receive from nervous students (and after years of cooking I still sometimes find myself thinking hard about the same problem), and that is what, precisely, am I going to serve for that important dinner party on Saturday night? Even people who are serious cooks, who have a whole spate of dishes in their repertoire from which to choose, find that placing those individual dishes in imaginative order, plotting a logical and climactic set of courses, and fitting those component parts into a meaningful pattern can be difficult.

The following thoughts are an attempt to do something practical about these concerns, to suggest that there are certain steps and rules to the creation of a successful menu that can be prethought, and to suggest a small science of menu planning. Even then, in the long run, menu planning will probably be learned by hit and miss, chance and error, the immediate on-the-occasion-experience teaching far more than any set of rules can ever hope to. But learning at the expense of favored guests is not the most satisfying way, and we all undoubtedly remember meals early and even late in our experience as cooks when the "balance" of the evening was off somehow. Usually these meals were the result of either a showy straining beyond our capabilities or a nervous fear that there would not be enough to eat, so that we threw an extra component into the meal that weighted it incorrectly and sated the guests—and we learned.

Let me start, then, with some general (albeit personal) rules—rules that are most likely in the heads of most good cooks and entertainers, put there by both instinct and experience. We will proceed to a menu planning checklist, then to some very specific suggestions on planning menus, their psychology and their drama.

SOME KNOWN GENERALITIES

1. First, consider the time that can be devoted to a given occasion. If you have the night before and the whole day of the dinner free, the preparation can be more elaborate than if you have to think in smaller blocks of time in which to cook. Don't, in other words, load yourself with a quantity of dishes requiring your ministrations all in the hour before sitting at table. A first course or dessert could have been chilling two days earlier, a soup made the night before and reheated, etc.

2. Consider your stove space to avoid last-minute confusion. Will you have room to heat and bake everything? Will you find that you need places for three pans but have only two burners?

Consider your serving utensils. Will you, at the last minute, discover two dishes requiring round platters and have only one? Will there be space for everything on the buffet? Are you going to pass dishes at table, and will the dishes be awkward for the guests to serve themselves from? Would it be easier for you yourself to serve in the French style? The more logistically one thinks ahead, the smoother things will go.

3. It is best not to have a meal based entirely on dishes with which you are unfamiliar. No more than one should be new and that one firmly fixed in your head as to procedure, and even this is not to be advised unless you are an experienced cook. Push yourself as far always as you can go with ease, but no farther.

4. Prethink the garnish of dishes. What will the final presentations look like? Have the garnish prepared and waiting. This should prevent a repetitive use of the same garnishing elements in a meal, or a last-minute scattering of broadside parsley over everything.

5. It is usually foolish to fear not having enough food, particularly enough variety. This needless phobia used to upset

my early menus . . . it was almost as if I had had a deprived and famished childhood, so worried was I that there would not be enough to eat. Yet, like the loaves and fishes, I've seen meals planned for four stretch and miraculously feed eight with no one the worse for it. And particularly with our current social trend to eating fewer and smaller portions, even if there *is* too little you can rationalize it in the name of chic.

6. Your guests should be carefully considered. Are they old or young, both in body and spirit? Would they enjoy a new eating experience or should you think more traditionally? (There are even *young* dogs to whom you can't teach new tricks.)

Hopefully, guests will have the courtesy to notify you of any dietary restrictions, and you will have the courtesy to remember them. (There is nothing you can't get around if you know about it in advance—from a salt-free menu to a fat-free menu to a lean portion for a sincerely dieting guest.) If a guest waits until dinnertime to announce that he can't eat salt, that is his problem and you should not be sent into a panic about it. And there is another class of people who will loudly inform you that they don't like "fish" or they don't like "lamb" or some other perverse generality. They *should* be fed fish or lamb if you must have them to table.

7. Whether friends are old or new may determine the degree of a meal's formality, both in terms of food and spirit. Old friends can be treated as such. If you indulge them in garlic they won't mind; if the meal is one hearty peasant *en famille* dish, they will be delighted. New people pose a different problem, and you must consider what you hope the end result of the meal to be. If it is merely a social duty at which to impress, by all means pull out heavy, formal guns. If you desire continued friendship, or if, for some reason, you fear that a mixture of people who don't know each other could lead to awkwardness, a good way to start the meal (and end it, too) is with a participation dish where everyone's hands are actually in the food, where people have to dip or gnaw

or tear apart—or a good old-fashioned Rabelaisian juices-dripping-down-the-chin kind of dish.

8. When serving out portions, try not to put too much food on people's plates. Older people in particular frequently eat smaller amounts. It is more encouraging to eat if you know you will make it through your serving, and most people like to compliment a host by going back for seconds if they possibly can.

9. If you are putting on an extravaganza, be courteous enough to inform guests of the fact beforehand. This can save consternation on the part of the guests. A vague invitation, particularly for "cocktails" or "a cocktail/buffet," can lead people to wonder whether they should have a bite to eat before they arrive. If I entertained in such a cocktail manner I would go ahead and *feed* people and let them know this. Forced and social half-meals at mealtime put hungry men into sullen humors.

And in the same vein, it is also considerate to let people know the extent of a meal at table. Again, if you are staging an extravaganza, and people think the first two courses are *it* when in fact there are four more to come, a meal can become most awkward. Write the menu out bistro-style and hang it on the wall, or place a small elegant, handwritten copy by each guest's dinner plate.

10. If you care for your own cooking, and you intend your guests too also, limit pre-dinner drinks and snacks. Thirty to forty-five minutes of black olives and a pleasant white wine, which is then carried to table to accompany the first course, should be sufficient. (I personally would not, say, set out a *pâté* or terrine and let people pick away at it. It is better if a slice of terrine is a controlled portion of the meal and, if you spend time to make a good one, it will be more appreciatively received at table.)

11. If something goes desperately wrong with a dish, either fake it with style or carry it off with a laugh. Don't apologize for the meal or critically pick it to pieces in front of guests.

Remember that long hours over the stove can confuse or negate one's own abilities to taste. You may wish things to have gone better, but nice guests are easily pleased with even small efforts and rarely are as critical as we would fear. Un-nice guests don't matter.

(After rereading these generalities, I am struck by what may seem to some a sort of flipness. It is less that than an endeavor to keep a necessary sense of humor about food, cooking, menus—to keep a sense of enjoyment behind one's entertaining endeavors. Too much seriousness and dinner parties can turn into grueling defensive/aggressive indoor sports, fraught with culinary "macho" and tense with epicurean one-upmanship.)

COMBINING DISHES INTO MENUS

A well-planned menu should tease the imagination. It should offer constant surprise and pleasure and, at the same time, it must build to or aim at a directed goal. The more one becomes experienced at entertaining, the more enjoyment one can have with these very goals. You can set frameworks for truly memorable meals; you can shock, amuse, jolt your guests in the most pleasant ways; you can think in psychological terms, artistic terms, dramatic terms, and when you feel free enough to consider the total and overall aura of an occasion, composing a menu can be most pleasurable. But to return to our first concern. What dishes will you choose for that important dinner party on Saturday night?

Let us imagine a situation so that we can talk in specifics. A sit-down dinner is planned for eight on Saturday night and you determine the menu is to be semi-formal. You will entertain in a coursed, French style, and you have all of Saturday to work. A certain flow starts in your mind—kinds and types of foods that you prepare best. You settle on a tentative list. Write the dishes down (it helps to see this when you first start—later it will run through your head) and pass them through the following checklist. Think of the predominant characteristics of the dishes, in terms of their impact on the senses.

Is the dish hot/lukewarm/cold?
Is the texture smooth/rough/crisp?
Is the dish frivolous/serious in intent?
Is it delicate/moderate/robust in flavor?
Is it elegant/rustic in presentation?
Is it colorful/dull/monochromatic in appearance?
Is it sauced/unsauced? Dry/juicy?
Does it contain an overpowering element (garlic, spices, cayenne, etc.)?
Is it predominately sour/acid/sweet?

Consider these characteristics in the light of your prospective dishes. If your list reads . . .

First course—lukewarm, rustic, moderate flavor, moist
Second course—hot, elegant, neutral, smooth, serious, sauced
Third course—hot, colorful, robust, juicy
Salad—frivolous, cold, rustic, acid
Dessert—neutral, crunchy, dry

. . . then you know you have at least a sensorially interesting meal, though other factors need to be considered, of course. If, on the other hand, your list tends to mostly elegants, mostly neutrals, mostly sauced, mostly anything, you should rethink it. Distrust a white meal. There will be too much sauce, starch, visual blandness to be of interest.

Other factors to be considered:
1. Once introduced to a pungent dish, the palate cannot

return to something bland with any joy. Decide whether a dish will "kill" anything that follows due to its spice or garlic content. If so, this dish should probably be the climax of the meal. (If a cleansing salad is to follow, place a touch of the spice or garlic in the dressing so the salad does not taste flat.)

2. There are certain dishes known to kill accompanying wines, and vice versa. A strong cheese like Roquefort will kill a good red wine. Wines don't really go well with eggs. The acidity of a vinaigrette salad dressing can spoil a wine. A dessert should not overpower a sweet wine in sugar content. A Sauternes is best served with a mellow, slightly warm fruit composition. Chocolate and ices will kill a Sauternes. (These are not just arbitrary rules. Test them out for yourself and let your palate experience them.)

3. If a dish is sauced and complex, it should be placed early in a menu before the palate becomes jaded in any way. It should be followed by something unsauced and simple. Sauces are rich. Consider carefully if you think to serve more than one.

4. Consider whether juices will mingle on a plate satisfactorily. Should one dish stand on its own? Does one dish need to meet an absorbent, bland, farinaceous dish or bread to allow its juices to be fully savored?

5. Control the amount of bread passed and therefore the amount of bread eaten during the meal, particularly if you make tasty, homemade loaves, or guests will tend to fill up on it.

6. If you are planning several courses, allow time between them. Sitting at table should be a pleasant experience and a small wait can only encourage expectations. (These time lapses can occur for longer periods later in the meal when the guests have grown expansive and convivial.)

7. Help guests appreciate the move from one course to the next by allowing them to cleanse their palates. A few lettuce leaves in an agreeably acid dressing can only refresh the outlook. (In a French menu, of course, this cleansing occurs after the climactic main course and before the cheese—the salad

obliterating any traces of lingering sauce and preparing the mouth for cheese or, for what can be even more important, a major wine that accompanies the cheese.) In multi-coursed and elegant French meals, if there are to be more than two courses before the main course, a menu will sometimes include a sorbet to encourage flagging appetites. The sorbet should be bland rather than sweet and it could be composed of a simple iced cantaloupe purée, a Champagne ice, a mellow lemon or grapefruit ice, etc. There is no doubt that the ice jolts the system, and I've known one or two dinner parties to be quite literally saved (the pace quickens, the conversation revives) by a sorbet's intervention at the precise moment when guests began to feel lethargic. A third method exists to cleanse the palate, though it is not so genteel. A bite of bread is pushed around the surfaces of the mouth by the tongue, and in so doing, it acts as a swab. Teaching that to guests and letting them try it tends to liven up a party.

8. Be particularly mindful of the temperature of the dining room. If it is pleasantly warm at the beginning of a meal, the room can rapidly turn too hot midway through dinner. Drop the temperature below normal . . . let it be a bit brisk even, so that guests remain lively during the heated exertion of eating.

9. Light meals can end in heavy desserts; beware a heavy meal ending in a heavy dessert. A great glutted feeling can steal over guests when faced with such prospects.

10. As the component dishes of any meal should mesh, expand, and build, so should the accompanying selection of wine have its plan and logic. A dry white wine gives way to a rich, deeper white gives way to a pleasant young red wine gives way to a complex, fully mature older wine, etc. It isn't necessary to move through wines from the least to the most expensive though sometimes it turns out that way. Your best red wine will probably be shown to fullest advantage over the right cheese.

MENU PATTERNS

To this point, most of our thinking has been concerned with traditional menus, traditional sit-down situations where a composed series of dishes are offered that form themselves into a total menu. Let us look more closely at some menu patterns, both traditional and nontraditional.

THE FORMAL, ELEGANT FRENCH MENU OF THE OLD SCHOOL

Hors d'oeuvres (pâté, terrine, small things eaten at table)
Soup
Fish course
Sorbet
Meat or fowl (accompanied by something farinaceous and a
   vegetable)
Salad
Cheese
Dessert
Coffee, Liqueurs, etc.

This menu, prepared in the home, is obviously the most complex endeavor possible. It is a full evening's entertainment —the entire thrust of the evening being the meal. I myself, and without help, will undertake it once, twice in a year at the most (though I used to feel the need to show off more often). This is the kind of menu that is nice to do on Christmas Day or New Year's Eve. It is best done indoors in winter, and in an elegant dining room. It is an occasion for which to dress. It is a menu that can go wrong easily by sliding into faulty timing and overabundance, but when done to perfection, it can provide the cook with a true sense of culinary accomplishment and the guests with a most memorable evening. This menu will be most successful:

—if you are a cook secure in your own abilities.

—if you retain an almost Japanese sense of portion control. (Serve the thinnest slice of terrine, a cup of soup, the smallest portion of fish. Let there be a break in time with only the sorbet to eat. Again, a thin slice of meat, a symbolic dab of potato and vegetable; two or three salad leaves; cheese to take or leave as people please; a dessert that is either very small or very airy.)

—if you have a sure sense of orchestrating both people and mood. (You must know when to prod people on, slow them down, lift them up; yet at the same time you should not convey any hint of planning or manipulation behind the meal. All must seem effortless.)

The pattern of this meal can be diagramed, and though I have likened a formal meal to a short story before, the analogy bears repeating. Here is the strategy and the desired emotive response.

There is first a steadying introduction, one that sets the tone of the meal. ("This slice of terrine is most elegant. It is layered and truffled and built with skillful artistry. What a sumptuous meal this is going to be.")

The soup comes next. ("We are taking off now, getting serious. What is this essence? How smooth this is, how rich.")

The fish course. ("Such complexity . . . I am lifted further. The sauce is richer, finer than the soup. I am floating upward. Will I make it through the meal—can there be anything greater after this?")

The jolt of sorbet. ("What is this? Lemon? Grapefruit? It hits my head—I feel alert, ready for anything. Something must be coming. The company around me is uplifted. Listen to the hum and pitch of us.")

Into the room comes the main course in spectacular presentation. ("Ah, a slice of perfect, rare lamb. Strange, but I do need this, even after all the rest. Here is reality . . . the lamb in my mouth, the small golden potato, the purée of green beans intermingling and then the heavenly Burgundy. Oh, the beauty of it all . . . I am replete.")

The acid leaf of lettuce. ("I eat my greens . . . how virtuous I am. My mouth feels clean. What a nice meal that was. Listen to the hum now . . . gentle, subdued, greatly content.")

Cheese. ("Just a bit of Gruyère. Nutty, dry. The last bite of bread. The meal is over. Time . . . mellow time passing. What fine friends we all are.")

Dessert. ("Sweet, light, a party favor of a small meringue, a spoon of raspberry ice. It makes me happy.")

Coffee. ("I'm on an even keel again. I've come full circle. I will sleep well tonight. What an extraordinary evening.")

The meal charts thusly:

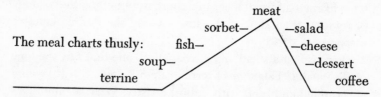

What is important here is the continuous upward drive, the maintenance of forward pitch, the steady building to the collective and climactic apogee that everyone should reach simultaneously, with mood, ambiance, menu all combining, each reinforcing the other. To break the pattern breaks the evening. And it must all be spontaneous, appear effortless.

THE INFORMAL FRENCH MEAL

Here the pattern simplifies. It continues in a traditionally coursed manner but simply omits items. This is the kind of meal you would be apt to receive in a middle-class French home. (The French would take you to a restaurant for the formal experience.)

Hors d'oeuvres or fish course
Meat and vegetable *or* farinaceous dish
Salad
Cheese
Fruit or Dessert

Even this kind of simplification can, obviously, lead to a very elegant meal. The number of dishes that the cook is responsible for is fewer and therefore more easily done in a home kitchen. And until one gains a secure kitchen assurance (or unless one has kitchen help) this simplification is greatly to be desired. Even here one of the first two courses can be cut, and again I say, unless you have the self-assured ability to carry off two complex and elegant courses—if there are any doubts at all—cut something. Don't complicate your life by worrying that you won't have enough to eat or that your meal won't be impressive enough and therefore strain to add another dish. People can always fill up on cheese. Make extra dessert and offer second helpings, whatever. It is better simply to make more of one thing and have leftovers if need be, than to attempt two dishes if it makes you nervous.

SIMPLE MEALS

Here we have a series of further simplified menus, each containing three elements, that relate more seriously to the ways we eat in daily life, but they should also relate to how we can entertain. When one stops to consider, one realizes that most mistakes made in menu planning occur before company, and those mistakes have less to do with individual dishes failing than with a collective disaster of mood and food that seems to strike the entire evening. In our everyday family meals, on the other hand, we may have an occasional experimental dish that fails, but we can rummage around and come up with something so that the whole evening is not lost. There is a lesson to be learned here. How much more comfortable everyone would be if we could think in more familial ways before guests. What do we honestly like to eat ourselves? (If the bloody old Beef Wellington we feed our guests is truly all that wonderful, why don't we have it for our beloved family's Sunday dinner instead of plain roast beef? The answer is that plain roast beef is better but "too easy" for guests.)

Simple Menu Patterns

Soup or Stew	Pâté	Salad	Tart	Vegetable
Salad	Vegetable	Fish	Soup	Eggs
Dessert	Cheese	Fruit	Dessert	Fruit, etc.

The magic number is three. I am more and more convinced that the tripartite meal is the perfect one for, as Aristotle says, ". . . the whole world and all things in it are summed up in the number three. . . ." A thoughtfully constructed menu, with beginning, middle, and end, provides the force and scope necessary for any tonal or dramatic possibilities that one could possibly wish to incorporate within a given meal.

ON THE DRAMA OF MENUS

People most enjoy planning menus when they feel free enough to relax and stop worrying about whether they are being "French" or not. (Not that one won't continue to think in continental ways, but that one won't be *obsessed* by continental ways.) What concerns and interests me as I plan menus are the dramatic possibilities of any given occasion. Certainly the formal, elegant French meal is rife with dramatic possibilities, but the drama of that situation is based on fulfilling a pre-existing and pre-established pattern, and most sophisticated diners probably will have partaken of this ritual before. (I receive more satisfaction from introducing novitiates to this elegant way of dining than from reproducing an occasion yet again as a piece of culinary one-upmanship for knowing guests.)

A more interesting drama is one that is produced by doing something unexpected—by breaking routine and shuffling set patterns. This drama depends less on individual dishes (those *trompe l'oeil* items that look like a mushroom but turn out to be mashed potatoes) than on how one plays the cards of the entire menu. For instance,

—Assuming there is to be a "climax" in the meal, for imagination's sake, try to get out of the meat rut. Consider a marvelous all-vegetable potée as the main course and see how that would shake and loosen up the rest of the menu. Would you need salad after? No.

Learn from the masters of *nouvelle cuisine*. What if the first course is an elegant arranged salad with something meaty in it . . . how does that affect what follows? Everything lightens down the line, a richly sauced fish mousse turns out to be the "climax."

—Can you lead people to expect one kind of a meal then abruptly switch to something different? Why not. Play with tonality. Try a move from the sublime to the ridiculous and see what happens. Or a move from low life to high life . . . a nourishing peasant stew (the low life) to cheese (the bridging middle) to a divinely rich, ethereal dessert.

—Offer people choices—a particularly good scheme for feeding a crowd. Think in restaurant terms. The first course is a cart or small buffet table filled with a marvelous display of made-ahead *hors d'oeuvres variées* (terrines, composite salads, tarts, antipastos). Let people jump up and down from table and go back as much as they wish. Then follow with a clear or creamed hot soup (a small, set portion) and dessert (again, a small, set portion). Or reverse the procedure. Offer a wholesome first course, a small green salad, then wheel out a dessert cart. Let the preceding food instill such a sense of virtue that guests will feel themselves positively entitled to all the dessert they want.

Think thematically. Do a rustic Brueghel feast. Research a setting and meal in the manner of Matisse. Plan an Orientally inspired dinner but rethink the food in Occidental terms. Serve a full-meal high English tea. Or try another English culinary pattern. Serve a small main course, then a dessert. Move into the living room and, after a break, serve traditional English savories (like bacon wrapped around grilled scallops, Welsh rarebit, and the like) with port. If the dessert is wholesome and only moderately sweet, and if you let people know in advance what is happening, this can be an amusing occasion.

ON WINTER MENU PLANNING

And finally to end with menu planning as it relates to this book. The recipes herein adapt themselves most readily to informal and simple menus. There is a series of thin, first-course tarts in the hors d'oeuvres chapter that would be nice to set out hot and whole (each labeled with its name as if it were in a fancy food shop) for guests to sample as a first course. Likewise, a series of thin, crisp tarts and galettes that would make a good ending to supper.

I have already dwelt on the ritual meal, and in the following appendix there is a list of those dishes that involve some ritualistic or participatory element. There comes then the fact that winter food tends to look the same—that is, its colors are white, gold, speckled brown, stew brown, bread brown. As long as we think in simple menu terms this is no problem. One dish, two dishes with this look (as long as they are diverse in nature) bind the meal into a rustic whole. The psyche *needs* this look in winter. Heat the body with a golden gratin, then tease the mind with a cool composed winter salad. Warm guests with hearty soups and stews and bready eggs and cheese. Give them oxtail and chicken wings to gnaw on. Revert them to childhood with a simple dessert. Comfort their souls in humble ways and forget about social pretenses and culinary complexities. It is the soul that matters.

Appendix B

CULINARY CATEGORIES

1. Participation dishes, wherein people have to suck bones, pour on seasonings, press garlic cloves, probe eggs, break off portions, etc.:

> Poppy Seed Grids
> Kneppes
> Flamiche in the Ancient Manner
> Gougère
> Soft-Boiled Eggs Eaten from the Shell
> Four and Twenty Meatballs Baked in a Pie
> Grandmother Olney's Noodle Soup
> Blò Blò

Leg of Lamb with Garlic Cloves and Bread Sauce
Grilled Oxtail with Mustard Sauce
Beef Ribs with Mustard and Onions
Artichokes Barigoule
Lentils and Greens in the Italian Manner
Turnip and Potato Pancake
Potatoes à la Barigoule
Almond Galette

2. Ritual dishes, dishes of such character that they can dominate meals, providing their focus and, when often repeated, their emotive recall:

Oxtail Daube
Master Plan for a Stuffed Bird
Garbure
Pot-au-feu
Pasta il Forno
New England Boiled Dinner with Beef Suet Dumplings
Colcannon
Baeckaoffa
Red Beans and Rice
Périgord Soup
Grandmother Olney's Noodle Soup
Mother's Navy Bean Soup

3. Children's dishes, that they will like and wish to help prepare:

Soft Pretzels
Flannel Crumpets
Cheese Toasts
Fried Bread Fritters
Filigreed Crêpes (with jam)
Soft-Boiled Eggs Eaten from the Shell
Chicken Lollipops
Potato Spirals
Caramelized Apple Pancake

Apple Fritter Rings
Baked Prune and Sugar Cube "Dumplings"
Almond Galette
"Sausage"

4. *Abat-faims,* filling, inexpensive, substantive dishes:

Miques
Matefaims with Savory Butter
Gaudes
Oat Porridge
Kneppes
Potato Gnocchi with Poppy Seed
Noukles
Gougère
Red Beans and Rice
Pasta with Chicken Livers, Onions and Cream

5. Analeptics, reputed to be restorative and strengthgiving:

Aïgo bouïdo
English Milk Soup
Vermicelli Soup
Frittatensuppe
Duck Soup
Congee
Avgholémono with Floating Egg Custards
Bread and Butter Pudding
Nutmeg Tart
Lait de Poule

6. Tea dishes:

Marrow Toast
Frangipane Tart
Fruited Brioche Tart
Cinnamon and Honey Cake
Sugared Lemon Galette
Florentine Tart
"Sausage" and "Cheese"

SEQUENTIAL MEALS

Following is a brief though hardly exhaustive list of dishes that can be composed one day, and then their cooking broths or leftovers used the next day to form another meal. Some possibilities:

Master Plan for Roasting a Bird's leftovers become Duck Soup.

Extra meatballs are made when composing Four and Twenty Meatballs Baked in a Pie—they are turned into a Pasta Snail the next night.

The cooking broth from Oxtail Daube or Grilled Oxtail with Mustard Sauce is used to cook Little Stuffed Lettuces or condensed to make Frittatensuppe.

Extra Saffroned Gratin of Leeks and Scallops can become, the next night, Seafood Cannelloni.

Flank Steak in the Manner of Bordeaux or Leg of Lamb with Garlic Cloves is used up in Ropey Pie.

Cook extra Mushrooms Cooked as Snails—use them to fill Potato Cake with Mushroom Stuffing the next night.

Make extra stuffing when composing Little Stuffed Lettuces. Use it to fill Stuffed Brussels Sprout Salad.

And so on.

SUGGESTED MENUS

Some simple, three-course meals:

Lentils and Greens in the Italian Manner
Spiced Onion Salad
Cheese

A hot, filling participation dish, followed by a cold, sweet salad that no dessert should try to top—instead there is cheese.

Country Terrine with Hazelnuts
Farmer's Pot
Chilled White Chocolate Soufflé with Hot Chocolate Sauce

Two cold, done-ahead dishes, so that one can concentrate on the preparations for and grand presentation of the hot Farmer's Pot.

Scrambled Eggs with Smoked Salmon and Rye Croutons
Spinach and Tomato Tian
"Sausage" and "Cheese" with Fruit

From the sublime to the rustic to the ridiculous joke of "Sausage" and "Cheese."

Soft-Boiled Eggs Eaten from the Shell *or* Artichokes Barigoule
Grilled Oxtail with Mustard Sauce
Almond Galette with Applesauce or Cream

A participatory dish in every course.

Wilted Green Bean Salad
Seafood Cannelloni
Glazed Pear Tart

An interesting mix of sensibilities and cultures.

Cream of Jerusalem Artichoke Soup
Flank Steak in the Manner of Bordeaux
with Grated Potato Gratin
Tarte Tatin

A man's meat-and-potato meal; a traditional offering.

———

Flammenkuchen
A Poached Fish with Potato Bouillabaisse and Sauce Rouille
Caramelized Apple Pancake

The most visually comforting meal I can think of.

TWO MENUS TO FEED A CROWD

MENU 1

First course, a cart or table featuring a selection from the following items, all done ahead as much as possible:

Spiced Onion Salad
Wilted Green Bean Salad
Wilted Watercress Salad
Mushrooms Cooked as Snails (cool and with extra oil)
Crusted Cheese Pie or Turtle Tart
Leek Flamiche (reheated)
Gougère (reheated)
Country Terrine with Hazelnuts
Open Italian Omelet (lukewarm to cool)
Four and Twenty Meatballs Baked in a Pie (reheated)
Artichokes Barigoule (cut in quarters, cool)

Second course, a soup, reheated and hot:
Cream of Mushroom and Hazelnut Soup
or
Cream of Jerusalem Artichoke Soup
Dessert, assembled ahead and put to bake or reheat when
needed. Choose one:

Tarte Tatin or Pear Tarts
Apple and Almond Gratin
Fat Jam Pannequets
Almond Galettes and Fruit

MENU 2

First course, a healthy, rustic full-meal dish. Choose one:

Lamb and Red Peppers with Pulled Bread
Calves Liver with Vinegar and Braised Turnips
A Daube or Garbure

Second course, a rustic, rough green salad
Dessert, a selection of done-ahead riches selected from:

Tarte Tatin
Date or Fig Pudding
Chilled White Chocolate Soufflé
Frangipane Tart
Glazed Pear Tart
Cinnamon and Honey Cake
Sugared Lemon Galette
Almond Galette
and on table also a large bowl of fruit (preserved or in com-
pote) and a large bowl of half-whipped cream with a ladle

Index

Judith Olney has lived and cooked on three continents. She received her professional training as an apprentice at the Westminster Catering School, the Connaught Hotel and the Belgian Pâtisserie in London, and at Avignon. She now conducts regular cooking classes in Durham, North Carolina, where she lives, as well as in various schools and kitchens throughout the country. Mrs. Olney's first book, Summer Food, *was published by Atheneum in 1978, and her articles and recipes have appeared in* Gourmet, Bon Apetit *and* House & Garden *magazines. She is an international consultant to Time-Life Books for* The Good Cook *series.*